THE
FABULOUS PHONOGRAPH
1877–1977

THE
Fabulous Phonograph
1877–1977

SECOND REVISED EDITION

by Roland Gelatt

789.9

MACMILLAN PUBLISHING CO., INC.

NEW YORK

COLLIER MACMILLAN PUBLISHERS

[©1977] LONDON

Macmillan Publishing Co., Inc.
866 Third Avenue, New York, N.Y. 10022
Collier Macmillan Canada, Ltd.

Library of Congress Cataloging in Publication Data

Gelatt, Roland, 1920-
    The fabulous phonograph, 1877-1977.

    1. Phonograph.   2. Phonorecords.   I. Title.
ML1055.G4   1977   789.9'1'09   76-57253
ISBN 0-02-542960-4

Several chapters of this book appeared in 1954 and 1965 as articles in *High Fidelity* Magazine.

First Printing of Second Revised Edition 1977

Printed in the United States of America

TO

ESTHER

CONTENTS

8

ILLUSTRATIONS

9

Following page 288

In text

FOREWORD

A HISTORY OF THE PHONOGRAPH IS AT ONCE THE HISTORY OF an invention, an industry, and a musical instrument. It cannot be otherwise. Science and business and aesthetics are inseparably commingled in the historical progression from Edison's raucous tin-foil apparatus to the high fidelity reproducers and recordings of today. I have attempted to keep these three elements in fairly equal balance. If this balance is occasionally upset in favor of emphasizing the phonograph's musical role, that is as it should be. The inventors and the entrepreneurs played important and fascinating roles, but their work would have little interest for us had it not been allied to the artistry of Caruso and Melba, Beecham and Casals. There are, of course, all kinds of music—and much of it, indeed the bulk of it, purveyed by the phonograph has been of the less enduring variety. The marches and "coon songs" of 1900 were succeeded by the one-steps and the waltzes of World War I, and these in turn were followed by the jazz of the Twenties, the swing of the Thirties, and the mood music of the Fifties. Such forms of musical expression have by no means been neglected here, but they occupy a lesser place in this chronicle compared to the more ambitious and durable musical repertoire that has been entrusted to the phonograph. Again, I think that is as it should be. Those who value Jerome Kern over Mozart or Bix Beiderbecke over Toscanini may disagree.

As this is the first comprehensive history of the phonograph to be undertaken, I should say something about my sources of information. Much of my material has been gathered from periodicals, of which the following proved especially helpful: *The Phonoscope*, published in New York from 1896 to 1900; *Die Phonographische Zeitschrift*, published in Berlin from 1900 to the 1930s; the *Talking Machine News*, published in London from 1903 to the 1930s; the *Talking Machine World*, published in New York from 1905 to the 1930s; *The Sound Wave*, published in London from 1906 to the 1930s; the *Phonograph and Talking Machine Weekly*, published in New York from 1916 to the 1930s; *The Gramophone*, published in London from 1923 to the present; the *Phonograph Monthly Review*, published in Boston from 1926 to 1932; *The American Music Lover* (later *The American Record Guide*) published in New York and Pelham from 1935 to the present; *The Record Collector*, published in Ipswich (England) from 1948 to the present; and various house organs, dating back to 1891, published by the Columbia Phonograph Company, Thomas A. Edison, Inc., the Gramophone Company, the North American Phonograph Company, and the Victor Talking Machine Company. A set of clippings relating to early phonograph history, collected by Stephen Fassett and now belonging to the New York Public Library, cleared up many dubious points.

A few books were of assistance, notably: *The Music Goes Round* by F. W. Gaisberg (New York, 1942), a volume of reminiscences full of absorbing but not always accurate detail; *Edison's Open Door* by Alfred O. Tate (New York, 1938), memoirs by Edison's private secretary during the 1890s; *Emile Berliner* by Frederic William Wile (Indianapolis, 1926), an official biography but useful for all that; *The Romance of the Gramophone* by T. Lindsay Buick (Wellington, New Zealand, 1927), a retelling from secondary sources of the first quarter century of phonograph history; and an unpublished biography of Eldridge R. Johnson, written by Dale Kramer at the behest of the Johnson family and based on documentary material in their possession.

Most valuable of all have been my talks and correspondence with the dramatis personae (or their descendants) of this history. I should like particularly to mention: Edgar M. Berliner, Victor R. Bettini, Walter W. Clark, Josef Hofmann, David Kapp, Joseph P. Maxfield, Joseph Sanders, John D. Smoot, Sir Louis Sterling, Edward Wallerstein, and Wilfrid W. Wetzel. All of them took time and immense trouble to answer my queries and put up good-humoredly with my incessant cross-questioning over small bits of information.

For their suggestions, encouragement, and assistance I am indebted, among many others, to: B. L. Aldridge, R. H. Clarke, John M. Conly, James Dennis, Hans Fantel, Stephen Fassett, Addison Foster, Thomas Heinitz, Irving Kolodin, Norman Speiden, and Ulysses S. Walsh. Bell Laboratories, Columbia Records, the Gramophone Company, and RCA Victor co-operated usefully at all times. Special thanks go to: R. D. Darrell, for entrusting me with his prized collection of phonograph periodicals and for offering much thoughtful advice; John H. Evans, for searching the British Isles until he found the extremely rare English periodicals that I needed; Philip L. Miller and his associates at the New York Public Library, for their unfailing courtesy in putting at my disposal the Library's unique collection of phonograph documents. Finally, a word of appreciation is directed to Lynn Carrick, an understanding and ever-helpful editor.

In the past, writings about the phonograph have often been blemished with serious inaccuracies. Some of these have been willful, the result of *parti pris*. Most of them have been owing simply to carelessness in verifying facts and to the kind of historiography that seizes on one piece of information and constructs a whole hypothetical edifice upon it. I have done my best to sift out the inaccuracies. Wherever possible, I have gone to first-hand sources and checked one against the other. But I cannot hope that my book is entirely free from error. What I can hope is that readers better informed than I about certain phases of this subject will share their knowledge with me.

A NOTE ON THE THIRD EDITION

I began my research for *The Fabulous Phonograph* in 1952, exactly 75 years after Edison's invention. Little did I imagine then that one day I would be preparing a third edition to appear in the phonograph's centenary year. Looking over the acknowledgments in my original Foreword, I realize how lucky I was to have started when I did. In the early 1950s many of the pioneers were still around to provide me with invaluable information and insights. Had I begun my research a decade later, much of the material in the early chapters of this book would never have gone on record.

The original (1955) edition ended with Chapter 22. A second (1965) edition added a brief Postscript. In this third edition, the 1965 Postcript has been eliminated, and in its place are three new chapters that extend the chronicle from 1955 to the present.

It would be impossible for me to acknowledge all the people who have contributed to my knowledge and understanding of the fabulous phonograph as it has developed over the past quarter century. But I should like to seize this occasion to mention a few old friends in the record industry who have been unfailingly helpful over the long years of our association: Robert Altshuler, of Columbia Records; Peter Andry, of EMI Records; John Coveney, of Angel Records; Herb Helman, of RCA Records; and T. A. Mc-Ewen, of Decca-London Records. If this historian has been able to keep at least somewhat *au courant*, it is thanks in great measure to them.

New York, November 1976   R. G.

THE
FABULOUS PHONOGRAPH
1877–1977

1 *TALKING TIN FOIL*

IN HIS LATER YEARS, WHEN EDISON WAS AN OBJECT OF national veneration and his creative spark had cooled, the old man delighted in escorting visitors through his laboratories in West Orange, New Jersey. He would lead them through a series of low red-brick buildings, showing off—as he went along—the scenes of former inventive triumphs. At some point in the tour a visitor was almost certain to quiz him about his *modus operandi.* How did Mr. Edison set about inventing something? Did he deliberately address himself to a specific problem and hatch an invention in abstract from his fertile brain? Or did he just stumble upon his inventions by accident? Edison would reply that his inventions were to be credited neither wholly to luck nor wholly to logic, but to a coalition of the two. "Look," he would say, drawing an imaginary line with his finger, "it's like this. I start here with the intention of reaching here—in an experiment, say, to increase the speed of the Atlantic cable; but when I have arrived part way in my straight line, I meet with a phenomenon and it leads me off in another direction and develops into a phonograph."

The straight line was leading originally to a high-speed telegraph transmitter. For years Edison had labored to increase the efficiency of the telegraph. He had developed the system of quadruplex telegraphy, whereby four separate signals could be sent simultaneously over the same wire, and from the age of eighteen he had tinkered with telegraphic

17

repeaters, which recorded messages at one speed and retransmitted them at a much greater speed. In the summer of 1877 he was working on an instrument that transcribed telegrams by indenting a paper tape with the dots and dashes of the Morse code and later repeated the message any number of times and at any rate of speed required. To keep the tape in proper adjustment he used a steel spring, and he noticed that when the tape raced through his instrument at a high speed, the indented dots and dashes striking the end of the spring gave off a noise which Edison described as a "light musical, rhythmic sound, resembling human talk heard indistinctly."

Edison was not the man to let a phenomenon like this go unpursued. He once laid down a general rule for aspiring inventors: "When you are experimenting and you come across anything you don't thoroughly understand, don't rest until you run it down; it may be the very thing you are looking for or it may be something far more important." In this case the sound "resembling human talk heard indistinctly" was ultimately of far greater consequence than the telegraphic instrument which produced it. For the phenomenon set Edison to thinking that if he could record a telegraph message, he might be able to record a telephone message as well.

The telephone was much in his thoughts those days. That same year, 1877, he had invented a carbon transmitter for Alexander Graham Bell's year-old telephone, the proceeds from which had made Edison at thirty a financially independent man. It was natural that the strange noise emitted by the telegraphic repeater should set the young inventor thinking again about the telephone. The instrument was then a luxury available only to the affluent, and it occurred to Edison that he might bring Bell's invention into more general use by constructing a small, inexpensive machine with which anyone could record a spoken message. That recording could then be taken to a central station where another machine would play back the message and transmit it over the telephone line. It was to be the equivalent of sending a written message by telegraph.

As he was speculating on this possibility, he recalled a makeshift to which he had resorted during his work on the carbon transmitter. Edison was by then already showing signs of deafness and could not trust his hearing to judge the loudness of a sound as it came over the telephone receiver. To by-pass this difficulty, he had attached a short needle to the diaphragm of the receiver. When he let his finger rest lightly on this needle, the pricks would show him the amplitude of the signal coming over the line. Harking back to this experience, Edison reasoned that if the needle could prick his finger it could just as well prick a paper tape and indent it with a record of the human voice. He set about putting his theories to a practical test, and on July 18, 1877, he scribbled in his notebook:

> Just tried experiment with diaphragm having an embossing point and held against paraffin paper moving rapidly. The speaking vibrations are indented nicely, and there's no doubt that I shall be able to store up and reproduce automatically at any future time the human voice perfectly.

The steps of Edison's experimentation—whereby he was led from paraffin paper tape to the tin-foil cylinder phonograph—are not clear. Perhaps some unknown notebook lies immured in the Edison archives which could clarify the development of his work. Pending such information (if it indeed exists), we must rely on the somewhat incredible testimony of E. H. Johnson, an associate, publicist, and intimate friend of Edison's during those early years. In the summer of 1877 Johnson embarked on a lecture tour through upper New York State expounding on the marvels issuing from Edison's laboratory. "In the course of one of my lectures," he later wrote, "it occurred to me that it would be a good idea to tell my audience about Edison's telephone repeater. My audience [in Buffalo] seemed to have a much clearer appreciation of the value of the invention than we had ourselves. They gave me such a cheer as I have seldom heard. . . . The next morning the Buffalo papers announced in glaring headlines: 'A Talking Machine by Professor Edison.' " If Johnson is to be credited, this newspaper account was the genesis of the phrase "talking machine"—indeed, of the very concept of a phonograph. For the story goes that Johnson cut his lecture tour short and returned to Edison's laboratory to report on what had happened. As a result, we are told, Edison progressed from his conception of a telephone repeater to that of a talking machine and forthwith set about designing the tin-foil phonograph. But one is loath to accept this report at face value. Johnson's account * smacks of an attempt to assign to himself—thirteen years after the event—a role in the invention which he did not quite deserve. It seems very unlikely that a man with Edison's quick turn of mind would remain insensible to the potentialities of his experimentations until a headline writer had pointed them out.

The instrument that Edison designed consisted basically of a metal cylinder (with a fine spiral groove impressed in its surface) and two diaphragm-and-needle units—one to be used for recording, the other for reproduction. The cylinder was mounted on a screw, so that turning a handle would make it both revolve and move from left to right. A piece of tin foil was to be wrapped around the cylinder, and thereon the recording needle, following the spiral groove, would indent a pattern of the sound vibrations directed into the mouthpiece. The stylus would move vertically, creating a so-called

* Published in the *Electrical World*, February 22, 1890.

"hill and dale" pattern in the trough of the groove. On re-playing, the reproducing needle was to convert these inden-tations on the tin foil back into sound. Edison made a sketch and gave it to one of his most trusted mechanics, John Kruesi, to build. Within thirty hours Kruesi is supposed to have returned with the finished product. Edison wrapped a sheet of tin foil around the cylinder, set the needle, turned the crank, and shouted into the mouthpiece the nursery rhyme that begins, "Mary had a little lamb." This was hardly the most profound quotation to utter at the birth of a great invention, but it at least gave fair warning of Edison's future lack of discrimination in the quality of phonographic rep-ertoire. Edison then adjusted the reproducer, cranked the cylinder again, and there issued from the machine a recog-nizable reproduction of his voice. He admitted later: "I was never so taken aback in my life."

The "official date" for this event is given as August 12, 1877, but this was fixed upon many years later on the occa-sion of an anniversary celebration. The date is highly questionable, despite the evidence of a rough sketch on which Edison had scrawled the words "Kruesi—Make this—Aug. 12/77." Earlier editions of this book reproduced that sketch but questioned its authenticity. It seemed hard to believe that the tin-foil instrument could have been brought into being less than a month after Edison's initial experi-ments in indenting paper tape with spoken sound (July 18), and even harder to believe that Edison would have waited until December 24, 1877, to file an application for a patent had a practicable instrument been developed four months previously. Since those earlier editions appeared, researchers at the Edison National Historic Site in West Orange, New Jersey, have turned up another sketch that seems much more likely to have been the one used by John Kruesi to con-struct the first tin-foil phonograph (see illustration). It bears the date November 29, 1877, and would seem to establish conclusively that the first working phonograph was made in the late autumn of 1877.

Edison was issued a patent on the phonograph February 19, 1878, less than two months after he applied. Not a single "interference" was registered nor a single "reference" cited against his application. Nothing in the Patent Office files remotely approached the instrument that Edison had devised.

EDISON'S FIRST SKETCH OF THE PHONOGRAPH

And yet Edison at this time was not the only man concerned with the invention of a phonograph—as an event at the Académie des Sciences in Paris demonstrated. For on December 5, 1877, a paper was opened in the Académie which also described a process of recording and reproducing sound. This document had been written by Charles Cros, a minor poet, amateur scientist, friend of Verlaine, Banville, and Manet. In his paper Cros described a process which "consists in obtaining traces of the movements to and fro of a vibrating membrane and in using this tracing to reproduce the same vibrations, with their intrinsic relations of duration and intensity, either by means of the same membrane or some other one equally adapted to produce the sounds which result from this series of movements."

In essence Cros and Edison had hit upon the same idea. In detail there were differences. Cros specified a disc rather than a cylinder; and instead of recording on tin foil, he proposed tracing the sound waves on lampblacked glass and photoengraving the tracings into reliefs or indentations. The prime distinction between the two men, however, was that Edison had actually constructed a working phonograph while Cros dwelt in the realm of theory. But to say as much does not minimize the Frenchman's vision or imply that he would have been unable, given the proper resources, to translate his theory into a workable product. Certainly, he anticipated Edison's researches by several months.

Cros wrote his paper on April 18, 1877; he deposited it with the Académie des Sciences on April 30. During the twelve-day hiatus, it is believed, the impoverished poet tried desperately to borrow enough money to defray the costs of a patent. But as nobody felt inclined to finance him (for Cros was a scientist without portfolio and reputed to be an impractical dreamer), he tried the next best thing to securing a patent. This was to "go on record" at the Académie by depositing a sealed paper embodying his ideas. Several months later the apparatus proposed by Cros was discussed by the Abbé Lenoir, a popularizer of scientific developments, in an article published in *La Semaine du Clergé* of October 10, 1877. Lenoir it was who christened Cros's instrument the "phonograph." Finally, early in December, Cros demanded that the sealed paper at the Académie be opened and publicly read, a move presumably stimulated by reports of Edison's successful experiments in America.

The history of invention shows that minds can and do run in the same direction, and at the same time. That Cros and Edison should both have bethought themselves of an instrument to record and reproduce human speech in the year 1877 is surprising but by no means beyond the bounds of probability. Neither is it unreasonable to assume that Edison and the Abbé Lenoir were drawn quite independently of each other to an identical name for the instrument. We know that Edison had referred to his invention as a "phonograph" by mid-December 1877. We know, too, that he could have acquired a copy of the October 10 issue of *La Semaine du Clergé* before this date and that it was thus possible for him to have borrowed Lenoir's designation. But how much more probable it is that he and Lenoir arrived at the name by an identical process of thought, for the word "phonograph" is compounded of two common Greek roots (it means "sound writer") and is, moreover, obviously inspired by the word "telegraph." No, any argument to prove Edison's dependence on parallel developments in France can be based only on the flimsiest of foundations. To whom, then, should the glory for inventing the phonograph go? This is a question on which much fruitless debate can center. Let it be resolved by giving each his due: Charles Cros for being the first to *conceive* the phonograph, Thomas Edison for being the first to *achieve* it.

That achievement was soon making its way in the world with appropriate éclat. On the morrow of its invention, Edison took John Kruesi's handiwork to the editorial rooms of

Scientific American, Dec. 22, 1877

EDISON'S ORIGINAL PHONOGRAPH

the *Scientific American* at 87 Park Row, New York City. That journal described the event in its issue of December 22, 1877:

> Mr. Thomas A. Edison recently came into this office, placed a little machine on our desk, turned a crank, and the machine inquired as to our health, asked how we liked the phonograph, informed us that *it* was very well, and bid us a cordial good night. These remarks were not only perfectly audible to ourselves, but to a dozen or more persons gathered around.

The "dozen or more persons" were quickly augmented by other onlookers as word of Edison's curious machine sped through the building. The crowd grew so large that the editor had to call a halt to the demonstration for fear that the floor would collapse. Reports of the invention appeared in New York newspapers, and some curiosity seekers made the trip to Edison's laboratory in New Jersey to examine the phonograph for themselves.

What they saw and heard was an instrument of crude design and dubious utility. Edison himself later admitted that the tin-foil record "lasted only a few times after it had been put through the machine" and that "no one but an expert could get anything intelligible back from it." Indeed, it was advisable for the listener to hear the words as they were spoken into the phonograph in order that he might comprehend what the instrument uttered. But at the time no one objected. To hear a recording of the human voice, no matter how faultily reproduced, was enough. The crowds came, listened with astonished incredulity to the phonograph's raucous croak, applauded it with gusto, and asked for more.

No time was lost in exploiting the phonograph's growing notoriety. On January 24, 1878, the Edison Speaking Phonograph Company was formed to control the manufacture and exhibition of the instruments. The company gave Edison $10,000 in cash and contracted to pay him a twenty per cent royalty, in return for which Edison turned over the manufacturing and sales rights of the phonograph. Its commercial value at that time lay solely in its appeal as a curiosity. The company made no false claims for it. An advertisement stated:

> The adaptation of this wonderful invention to the practical uses of commerce not having, as yet, been completed in all its mechanical details, this company is now prepared to offer to the public only that design or form of apparatus which has been found best adapted to its exhibition as a novelty.

James Redpath, the founder of a thriving lyceum bureau in Boston, was put in charge of assigning territories to a group of showmen, who were trained in the technique and care of the phonograph, provided with an instrument apiece and a quantity of tin-foil "blanks," and sent out to cultivate their assigned terrains. The operators were to retain a stipulated percentage of the gate receipts and remit the balance to the company.

For a while business prospered magnificently. As a show property the phonograph won an immediate success. To audiences throughout the country it provided an evening's entertainment always fascinating and usually diverting. It would talk in English, Dutch, German, French, Spanish, and Hebrew. It would imitate the barking of dogs and the crowing of cocks. It could be made to catch cold and cough and sneeze "so believably that physicians in the audience would instinctively begin to write prescriptions." Skeptics would be invited on stage to test the phonograph for themselves; they came and subjected the apparatus to all the different sounds of which the human voice is capable. Then the phonograph would be called upon to demonstrate its musical proclivities. This part of the program would begin soberly enough, but it was likely to end in the kind of high jinks that took place one evening in New York when Edison himself was directing the show and the cornettist Jules Levy was on hand to provide the *materia musica*. A contemporary account described the affair thus:

> Fresh tin foil being adjusted on the cylinder, the bell of the cornet was placed near the mouthpiece, and *Yankee Doodle,* first plain, and then garnished with variations of the most decorative character, assumed the form of dots on the foil. Without the loss of a note, the phonograph repeated it, and not only this, but even the peculiar expression imparted by the player, and the triumphant kind of flourish which brought the tune to a conclusion, were reproduced with wonderful accuracy. After several other popular airs had been similarly replayed, Mr. Edison showed the effect of turning the cylinder at different degrees of speed, and

then the phonograph proceeded utterly to rout Mr. Levy by playing his tunes in pitches and octaves of astonishing variety. It was interesting to observe the total indifference of the phonograph to the pitch of the note it began upon with regard to the pitch of the note with which it was to end. Gravely singing the tune correctly for half a dozen notes, it would suddenly soar into regions too painfully high for the cornet even by any chance to follow it. Then it delivered the variations on *Yankee Doodle* with a celerity no human fingering of the cornet could rival, interspersing new notes, which it seemed probable were neither on the cornet nor any other instrument—fortunately. Finally the phonograph recited "Bingen on the Rhine" after its inventor, then repeated the poem with a whistling accompaniment, then in conjunction with two songs and a speech, all this on one tin foil, though by this time the remarks began to get mixed. Just here Levy returned to the charge, and played his cornet fiercely upon the much-indented strip. But the phonograph was equal to any attempts to take unfair advantage of it, and it repeated its songs, and whistles, and speeches, with the cornet music heard so clearly over all, that its victory was unanimously conceded, and amid hilarious crowing from the triumphant cylinder the cornet was ignominiously shut up in its box.

No wonder that, with such diversion to offer, a single exhibition phonograph could earn as much as $1,800 per week.

During the first half of 1878, while the phonograph was thus showing its mettle, Edison kept busy designing different models—one of them a disc machine with a volute spiral, which anticipated the form of the phonograph as we know it today. He found it far easier to affix a sheet of tin foil to a flat disc than to a cylinder; but because the quality of reproduction deteriorated sadly toward the center of the disc, Edison soon abandoned it and returned to the cylinder. For a while he experimented—also unsuccessfully—with clockwork motors to take the place of the impractical hand crank. And he designed the Parlor Speaking Phonograph for home amusement, which spoke "loud enough to be heard in any

ordinary room," used a tin-foil blank with a capacity of 150
to 200 words, and was sold for $10.

Crude though the phonograph was during those months of
its infancy, there was a general feeling that perfection lay
just around the corner; and along with this conviction went
roseate forecasts of the phonograph's role in years to come.
In an article for the *North American Review* of June 1878,
Edison predicted ten ways in which his invention was to
benefit mankind:

1. Letter writing and all kinds of dictation without the aid
   of a stenographer.
2. Phonographic books, which will speak to blind people
   without effort on their part.
3. The teaching of elocution.
4. Reproduction of music.
5. The "Family Record"—a registry of sayings, reminiscences, etc., by members of a family in their own voices,
   and of the last words of dying persons.
6. Music-boxes and toys.
7. Clocks that should announce in articulate speech the
   time for going home, going to meals, etc.
8. The preservation of languages by exact reproduction of
   the manner of pronouncing.
9. Educational purposes; such as preserving the explanations made by a teacher, so that the pupil can refer to
   them at any moment, and spelling or other lessons
   placed upon the phonograph for convenience in com-
   mitting to memory.
10. Connection with the telephone, so as to make that in-
    strument an auxiliary in the transmission of permanent
    and invaluable records, instead of being the recipient
    of momentary and fleeting communication.

This was a remarkably prescient forecast: every application
except the articulate clocks has come to pass, though several
of them had to wait for fruition until the phonograph was
developed far beyond anything Edison had envisaged. To
a reporter from the New York *World* the inventor elabo-

rated on his ideas for reproducing music. "Orchestral concerts by brass and string bands" were to be recorded. The
phonograph would be attached to a hole in one end of a
barrel, and a funnel "like those used in ventilating steam-
ships" would project from the other end. "This," Edison
explained, "will receive the music from the entire orchestra,
but of course not reproduce it with so great a volume. Piano
music will be phonographed by a hood being placed over the
instrument, and the volume of the reproduction will be one-
fourth that of the piano."

The privilege of speculation was not restricted to the
phonograph's inventor. In that great era of invention, every
mortal exercised his imagination in elaborating on the utility
of science's latest boons. It was suggested that "public
speakers repeat their speeches to the phonograph, and then
twenty-four hours later have the phonograph play their words
back to them that they might prevent themselves from making rash or overheated or silly remarks." An irreverent wag
"didn't see but that now clergymen and choirs were out of
date. The phonograph could repeat service every Sunday
and run off old sermons with wonderful accuracy." Another
proposal was "to erect statues of popular speakers in life size,
Mr. Henry Ward Beecher for instance, reproduce his speech
in tin foil, put a phonograph inside of him (the statue, not
the man), and stand him on a platform to repeat the new lecture on the 'Wastes and Burdens of Society.' "

Everyone had a wonderful time—for about half a year.
Then the bubble broke. For after you had listened to the
apparatus and chuckled over the stunts it could perform,
what was left? The phonograph, in truth, had been launched
prematurely. It was all very well to talk about dictating letters into the phonograph or using it to read *Nicholas Nick-
leby* to the blind, but not when a tin-foil cylinder would play
for scarcely more than a minute and give forth only the

barest approximation of human speech. And it was all very
well to rapturize about the inspiring concerts of music that
the instrument was to provide, but not when the sounds it
emitted were a grating, metallic travesty of what had been
recorded and when the tin-foil records would wear out after
half a dozen playings. In the first flush of enthusiasm writers

SOME ATTENTIVE PHONOGRAPH LISTENERS IN 1878

had prated of the "absolutely perfect reproduction of the
voice," just as they were to continue to do regularly for the
next century. But a hardheaded Britisher, Sir W. H. Preece,
has left us a more accurate description of the tin-foil phonograph's capabilities:

> The instrument has not quite reached that perfection
> when the tones of a Patti can be faithfully repeated; in fact,
> to some extent it is a burlesque or parody of the human
> voice. . . . There are some consonants that are wanting al-
> together. The *s* at the beginning and end of a word is en-
> tirely lost, although it is heard slightly in the middle of a
> word. The *d* and the *t* are exactly the same; and the same in
> *m* and *n*. Hence, it is extremely difficult to read what is
> said upon the instrument; if a person is put out of the room
> and you speak into it, he can with difficulty translate what
> it says.

And so the crowds at the phonograph exhibitions thinned away as quickly as they had once appeared, and the Edison Phonograph Works after producing about five hundred exhibition instruments ground to an abrupt halt. Undoubtedly the inventor could have rescued the phonograph from its decline, could have improved it to the point of commercial feasibility. But by then his mind had struck out on another path. In July 1878, Edison had traveled to Wyoming in company with several eminent scientists to witness a total eclipse of the sun. During that trip the suggestion was repeatedly made that Edison apply himself to the perfection of a cheap and efficient electric light. On his return, Edison was further encouraged by a group of investors who offered to finance his work on the electric light—no matter what the cost. Edison did not delay long. By October 1878, he had cast aside all other work and was immersed in experimentation on the incandescent lamp. The phonograph itself entered into a total eclipse, and the ingenious tin-foil apparatus joined the printing telegraph, the motograph, the electric pen, and numerous other Edison inventions which had experienced brief reigns of glory only to be abandoned and forgotten in the wake of newer scientific marvels.

In its first report on the phonograph the *Scientific American* had averred that "the voices of such singers as Parepa and Titiens will not die with them, but will remain as long as the metal in which they may be embodied will last," the reference being to two famous singers who were recently deceased. But unfortunately voices continued to die during the decade that the phonograph lay dormant. Mankind gained the incandescent lamp, but posterity lost Jenny Lind and Franz Liszt.

2 CYLINDERS IN BUSINESS

WHEN EDISON DESERTED THE PHONOGRAPH, IT WAS INEVITABLE that others would intervene and proceed from where he left off. So auspicious an invention could scarcely be expected to remain forever in an obscure and half-realized state. The wonder is not that the phonograph was subsequently developed outside Edison's laboratory, but that it languished unattended for as long as it did.

From 1879 to 1887 the phonograph went into torpid retirement. The tin-foil apparatus had had its day; the public had lost interest; the glorious prophecies were unfulfilled. But though the phonograph had fallen on dismal days, memories of it and a divination of its promise continued to haunt a few isolated souls. One of these was Alexander Graham Bell, who had applauded its birth and followed its infancy with attentive interest. Through his father-in-law, Gardiner G. Hubbard, one of the original stockholders in the Edison Speaking Phonograph Company, Bell had kept a close watch on the early progress of the invention. It is even possible, though no documentary evidence can be offered in proof, that toward the end of 1878 Bell offered to collaborate in the future development of the phonograph. But this proposal—if indeed it was ever made—could only have met with a cool response from Edison, who was by then concentrating his energies wholly on the electric light.

We know, at any rate, that Bell subsequently proceeded on his own. With the $10,000 Volta Prize, which he received

33

in 1880 from the French government for his invention of the telephone, Bell financed a laboratory in Washington, D. C., to promote research relating to sound and acoustics. In this project he associated with him his cousin Chichester A. Bell, a chemical engineer, and Charles Sumner Tainter, a scientist and instrument maker. One of the goals toward which they aspired was the improvement of Edison's forsaken phonograph.

Their work followed various courses. In searching for the best answer to their problem, they devised and patented elaborate methods for transmitting and recording sound by means of gaseous or liquid jets and by means of radiant energy. One of the air-jet models was deposited in the Smithsonian Institution on October 17, 1881. On this machine Charles Sumner Tainter recorded a quotation rather more apt than the nursery rhyme favored by Edison; he chose a line from *Hamlet*: "There are more things in heaven and earth, Horatio, than are dreamt of in your philosophy." After years of experimentation, Chichester Bell and Tainter discarded their jets of air and beams of light, and settled instead upon a method basically the same as Edison's, though refined in several important particulars. In the place of Edison's tin foil they prescribed cardboard coated with wax, in which the recording stylus engraved the pattern of its vibrations in narrow grooves. And in place of Edison's rigid reproducing needle they devised a loosely mounted stylus which could more easily be guided by the record. On June 27, 1885, Bell and Tainter applied for a patent on this apparatus, which was granted May 4, 1886. It specified a disc record; but in one of those curious vacillations between disc and cylinder which seemed to afflict all the recording pioneers, Bell and Tainter soon after decided upon the cylinder as better suited to their purposes. Early in 1887 the Bell-Tainter cylinder machine was put on public view in Washington, D. C. It was named the "graphophone."

Clearly, Edison's tin-foil phonograph had been outpaced. Judged by the standards of 1920—to say nothing of those of 1977—the Bell-Tainter graphophone was a crude and imperfect artifact; but compared to the raucous phonograph of 1878, it performed with dulcet clarity. The use of wax allowed for sharper, better defined recording, though not so loud; one could hear an early wax recording properly only through ear tubes. Wax also permitted closer grooving than had tin foil and thereby increased the number of words that could be recorded in a given surface. The "floating stylus" represented a distinct forward stride in converting the engraved impressions into recognizable sound. And the constant speed provided by the graphophone's foot-treadle mechanism, or electric motor, did away with the bizarre fluctuations of pitch that prevailed with Edison's hand crank.

Before unveiling the graphophone in public, Bell and Tainter had sent emissaries to the Edison Electric Light Company to apprise the inventor of what they had wrought. Their purpose was to enlist his co-operation in perfecting the instrument and launching it commercially. According to Alfred O. Tate, Edison's personal secretary at the time, the Bell-Tainter representatives acknowledged:

> that their work was merely the projection and refinement of his [Edison's] ideas, and that they now wanted to place the whole matter in his hands and to turn their work over to him without any public announcements that would indicate the creation of conflicting interests. . . . They had named [their] instrument the graphophone to differentiate it from the phonograph, but if Mr. Edison would join them they would drop this name and revert to the original designation.

The proposed entente had no appeal for Edison. He looked upon Bell and Tainter as trespassers and usurpers, and he vowed to improve the phonograph himself and beat the upstarts at their own game.

The incandescent lamp had by then been perfected and a great electric lighting industry established; the time was propitious for fresh endeavor. In Edison's new laboratory in West Orange the phonograph was given priority over all other efforts. By October 1887 enough had been accomplished for Edison to make a public announcement. To a reporter from the New York *Evening Post* he said:

> You know that I finished the first phonograph more than ten years ago. It remained more or less of a toy. When the electric business assumed commercial importance, I threw everything overboard for that. Nevertheless, the phonograph has been more or less constantly in my mind ever since. When resting from prolonged work upon the light, my brain would revert almost automatically to the old idea.

Thus sprouted the carefully nurtured legend that Edison had never deserted his "favorite invention," that he had intended always to improve it. The chronology, however, shows no constructive moves on his part until the Bell-Tainter developments had been announced. What is more, the improved Edison phonograph, as it eventually emerged from his laboratory, bore a strikingly close resemblance to the graphophone. It too employed "wax" (actually a wax-like compound) as the recording material and utilized the principle of the "floating stylus." The prime difference between the two lay in the fabrication of the records—or phonograms, as they were then called—the graphophone's being made of wax-covered cardboard while the phonograph's were of solid wax. In practice, the distinction meant that Edison cylinders could be shaved and used over and over again while graphophone cylinders had to be discarded much more quickly. Solid wax thus represented a decided gain in utility, and the graphophone soon appropriated the idea. Still, the essential modifications had been devised not by Edison, but by Chichester Bell and Charles Sumner Tainter.

While Edison continued to bombard the press with news

of his improved phonograph, the laboratory at Orange concentrated on producing a model adapted to commercial exploitation. This prototype finally emerged on June 16, 1888, after Edison and some associates had labored continuously for five days and nights. A photograph of Edison taken at the conclusion of this travail shows his hair wildly tousled, his expression forcefully determined, his posture dramatically fatigued. The picture summed up convincingly Edison's celebrated credo that genius is ninety-nine per cent perspiration, and for years to come it did duty as propaganda for the inventor and his phonograph. But Edison had not labored five days and nights merely to provide good advertising copy. This toil was rather the crowning episode in an attempt to overtake the progress of the graphophone, which had been sold by Bell and Tainter to a group of capitalists and was being marketed by the American Graphophone Company from its headquarters in Washington, D. C. This company, organized in June 1887, had as yet been unable to exploit its year's head start with much success. Its strategy had been to introduce the graphophone as a dictating machine and to let the instrument win its sovereignty in the vast government offices of Washington. But the apparatus was far from foolproof at the start, and of the few graphophones manufactured even fewer were placed in operation.

By the spring of 1888, after vexatious trial and error, the graphophone was at last beginning to make some headway. Edison had to meet the challenge without delay by producing a competing model. He had also to find financial backing. The investment house of J. & W. Seligman evinced some interest, and a demonstration was scheduled at Edison's laboratory. When the bankers arrived on the appointed day, Edison sat down before the instrument, set it in motion, and dictated a short letter into the mouthpiece. He then lowered the reproducing stylus into place and prepared to let the phonograph sell itself to his assembled guests. But instead of parroting the words he had just spoken, the phonograph emitted nothing more than an ugly hiss. Was it showing its contempt for the leaders of finance? Edison made some small adjustments, inserted a fresh cylinder, and dictated another letter—with the same humiliating result. After some further abortive tries, the Seligman entourage took their leave, promising to return when Edison had the instrument in working order. The defect was quickly repaired, but the Seligman people never paid a second visit. Their lack of enthusiasm was understandable, though in the long run it proved costly. For when J. & W. Seligman and Company finally did buy into the phonograph business, thirty-eight years later, the price of entry was $40,000,000.

If the phonograph would go out of order under Edison's own expert handling, it is no wonder that the instrument made slow progress in securing the esteem of others. Even so partisan an organ as the *Scientific American* had to acknowledge that the phonograph was "not yet reduced to that simplicity and perfection of operation necessary for its general sale and introduction. . . . To get really satisfactory results, we believe it needs the employment of an expert to watch, adjust, and work the instruments." But the waywardness of the phonograph, its habit of performing beautifully on one occasion and breaking down completely on the next, did not deter its early devotees. With stubborn zeal they proceeded to put the phonograph through its paces.

Like the graphophone, Edison's improved phonograph of 1888 employed an electric motor powered by heavy-duty batteries. This assurance of a constant speed for recording and playback, together with the superior qualities of wax as a recording medium, tempted Edison to make a few shies at recording serious music. In 1888 the pianist Josef Hofmann, then a boy of twelve, visited the Edison laboratories to inspect the phonograph and engrave some cylinders. These were the first recordings to be made by any recognized artist. Not long after, the famous German musician Hans von Bülow came to examine the new apparatus. He recorded a Chopin mazurka, then put the tubes to ears and waited for the playback. What he heard caused him to faint dead away—though whether he was laid low by his own playing or merely by the poor reproduction of it has never been divulged. The Bülow cylinder itself, like so many recorded documents of this period, has disappeared. Its musical value was probably slight, for the two-minute playing time of a wax phonogram

CORNETIST RECORDING, 1889

did not encourage musicians to record works of great consequence. But a snatch of Bülow would be better than none at all, and collectors will continue to look for a surviving copy of this Edison test record, probably the only recording that the celebrated pianist ever made. In England that same year an Edison phonograph was set up in the press gallery of the Crystal Palace during the annual Handel festival. According to the *Illustrated London News,* it "reported with perfected accuracy the sublime strains, vocal and instrumental, of 'Israel in Egypt.'"

The celebrities who made their record debuts were not

only musical ones. Henry M. Stanley visited the Edison laboratory and left a waxing of his voice; but he did *not* choose to leave for posterity the words "Dr. Livingstone, I presume." And at the Paris Exposition of 1889, William Ewart Gladstone, an early admirer of Edison's, recorded a message of appreciation to be sent to the inventor.

While the phonograph was being thus rebaptized, Edison and the American Graphophone Company readied themselves for a bitter patent fight. Edison felt himself powerless to sue. His American patent of 1878 specified a process of "embossing or indenting" the recording material. Edison employed those terms because they applied to the tin foil he then used, and by so doing he lost a "basic patent" on the phonograph. For when Bell and Tainter came to patent their graphophone, they circumvented the Edison patent by prescribing a process of "engraving" the recording material. Embossing or indenting merely changed the shape of the recording material, they pointed out, while engraving involved actual removal of material. It was, to be sure, a subtle verbal distinction, but on it Bell and Tainter had erected a patent which Edison considered impregnable. Ten years before, he might have been inclined to fight it. But mounting experience had caused him to lose faith in the efficacy of patent protection. "The burden of proof," he complained, "is now put entirely on the man who holds the patent instead of the man who wishes to infringe it."

But though Edison would not sue for patent infringement, the Graphophone interests were eager for litigation. Edison's improved phonograph they saw as a direct embodiment of the Bell-Tainter principles. Did it not engrave wax in a gouge-cut groove and employ the principle of the "floating stylus"? Lawyers on both sides began preparing briefs to present in court. The arguments they mustered are propounded with heat to this day—for the phonograph-graphophone controversy has refused to die. There are still those who believe that Bell and Tainter "stole" Edison's invention, just as there are others who maintain that Bell and Tainter are the true fathers of the phonograph (Edison's tin-foil instrument being dismissed as an unsuccessful, stillborn first attempt). Neither argument is valid. The partisans of Edison might remember that any patent invites improvements and modifications, and that if the patentee does not make them others undoubtedly will. And the partisans of Bell and Tainter might bear in mind that the graphophone was originally introduced as a refinement of the tin-foil phonograph, with full credit going to Edison for the basic conception.

In 1888 reason on this subject prevailed more readily than it does today. Just as litigation was coming to a head, a third party entered the scene and temporarily harmonized the conflict.

He was Jesse H. Lippincott, a businessman from Pittsburgh who had sold a controlling interest in the Rochester Tumbler Company for $1,000,000 and was looking for a new industry in which to invest his cash. A friend suggested the Graphophone to him as a promising venture.* Lippincott investigated, was impressed with its potential earning power, and negotiated an agreement with the American Graphophone Company whereby he invested $200,000 and became sole licensee of the company with exclusive rights to exploit the Graphophone in the United States. By the terms of this agreement, the American Graphophone Company continued to manufacture the instruments in its Bridgeport plant, while Lippincott assumed control of sales.

Lippincott did not stop there. This was the heyday of the trusts, those giant combines which consolidated allied industries under one over-all management, and Lippincott fol-

---

* Although the word "graphophone" was originally coined by Bell and Tainter to denote a generic piece of equipment, it did not enter the vocabulary as such. Instead, it was understood to refer to a brand of phonographs manufactured by the American Graphophone Company—and hence deserves a capital G from this point on.

lowed the trend of the times. Once he had completed negotiations for the Graphophone, he started dickering for the rights to the Edison phonograph. His proposal was well timed. Edison wanted to begin manufacture of his improved phonograph and needed financial backing. Lippincott provided it in the amount of $500,000, for which he secured Edison's patent rights, leaving the manufacturing rights in Edison's hands. To handle the business, Lippincott formed the North American Phonograph Company, which was organized July 14, 1888.

By the autumn of 1888, Lippincott was in control of the entire talking-machine industry in the United States. Everyone concerned had profited from his largess except the lawyers. For now that the phonograph and the Graphophone were represented by the same company, squabbles between them temporarily ceased and all litigation was canceled. The Edison and Graphophone companies turned from patent suits to the problems of manufacture, and Lippincott began the task of shaping his North American Phonograph Company into an effective sales agency. After ten indecisive years of infancy, the phonograph was ready to prove itself on the open market place.

Alas, it had the misfortune to be launched by a misguided skipper. Jesse Lippincott was blind to the phonograph's great potentialities. A businessman himself, he saw it solely as an implement of business. And he compounded this lack of vision by confusing the phonograph with the telephone. In two disastrous particulars Lippincott modeled his phonograph company on the developing telephone system. First, he divided the country into territories and sold "states' rights" for exploitation of the phonograph to territorial subsidiaries. Second, he adopted the policy of leasing, rather than selling, the instruments—the annual rental of $40 being split between the parent company and the subsidiary in whose territory the instrument was leased. Had the phonograph really succeeded as an office dictating machine, these decisions might not have proved so costly. As it was, they were almost catastrophic.

Throughout its first year of business, the North American Phonograph Company was engaged principally in distributing territorial franchises. Altogether, thirty subsidiary companies were organized, and all but one started off by losing money. Both the Edison and Graphophone factories ran into production difficulties, and what instruments they did manage to manufacture quickly went out of order and had to be recalled. Only the Columbia Phonograph Company (covering Maryland, Delaware, and the District of Columbia) paid a dividend in 1889—mainly because it had inherited the already established business of servicing Graphophones in government offices. The next year began somewhat better. Mechanical kinks had been straightened out, and production in both factories was keeping pace with demand. But that demand stayed far below expectations. The phonograph did not revolutionize the ways of commerce as its proponents had hoped. A few government bureaus, a few professional people, a few scattered offices were loud in its praise; but most of the nation's business continued to be conducted as before, with the aid of flesh-and-blood stenographers. The latter, faced with the prospect of losing their jobs, did their utmost to retard the phonograph's progress. When a phonograph was on trial in a business office, the alarmed stenographers (still predominantly male) would make sure that it developed such serious defects as to make it impracticable for their employer's use. Under these circumstances, phonograph rentals ran far below what Jesse Lippincott had envisioned when he organized the North American combine. After two years of unprofitable operations, the strain on Lippincott's health and finances proved more than he could bear. In the fall of 1890 he was stricken with paralysis. A few months later, being unable to meet his obligations, he lost control of the North American Phonograph Company, and Edison—as its principal creditor—assumed direction of the enterprise.

His first move was to abandon the misguided rental policy. Thenceforth, phonographs could be bought outright, for $150 each in 1891. This was a well-directed step, but Edison went no further. He persisted in Lippincott's mistake of viewing the phonograph primarily as an instrument for office dictation. Edison was no longer the young man of thirty-one who had jocundly entertained large audiences with his tin-foil phonograph. He was now well into his forties, the proprietor of an overstuffed Victorian home, and an aspirant in the world of big business. He could not or would not countenance the potentialities of the phonograph as a medium of entertainment. He insisted that it was not a toy. He resented its use for amusement. And for years he deliberately discouraged the development of the phonograph as a musical instrument.

But there the phonograph was, ready and willing to reproduce the popular airs of the day; and since he would not encourage it along these lines, others did. The major subsidiaries of the North American Phonograph combine took the initiative. One by one, they began to offer the phonograph for coin-in-the-slot operation in public places and to produce professionally recorded wax cylinders of musical selections. The unsung genius who first conceived this prototype of the latter-day jukebox revivified a faltering industry. With its heavy, acrid storage batteries, the phonograph was too troublesome for the average home; it was also far too costly for the average wage-earner. But the demand for recorded entertainment existed, and the nickel-in-the-slot phonograph met it with immediate success. The strains of Sousa marches and Stephen Foster melodies quickened the tempo of phonograph business from Massachusetts to California.

Edison, in his house organ, *The Phonogram,* deplored this turn of events. In its very first issue of January 1891 that journal editorialized:

> Those companies who fail to take advantage of every opportunity of pushing the legitimate side of their business, relying only on the profits derived from the "coin-in-the-slot," will find too late that they have made a fatal mistake. The "coin-in-the-slot" device is calculated to injure the phonograph in the opinion of those seeing it only in that form, as it has the appearance of being nothing more than a mere toy, and no one would comprehend its value or appreciate its utility as an aid to businessmen and others for dictation purposes when seeing it only in that form.

But as the territorial companies would have gone bankrupt pursuing "the legitimate side of their business," such pronunciamentos understandably carried little weight. It was quickly discovered that while business offices took a chill view of the phonograph as a medium of dictation, neighborhood drugstores and saloons welcomed it as a medium of entertainment. The nickels with which the local citizenry commanded renditions of Sousa and Foster mounted up at a most lucrative rate. One coin-operated phonograph installed in a well-situated New Orleans drugstore averaged $500 a month in receipts. In 1891 this was claimed to be the most profitable phonograph in the country. They did not all reach such exhilarating heights. The average nickel-in-the-slot phonograph earned about $50 a week—which was still an excellent return on the original investment.

At last the phonograph had caught the public's ear; and whatever Mr. Edison might say about it, the local companies were going to tout its entertainment value for all it was worth. But what kind of entertainment did it purvey? What did the customer hear when he had deposited his nickel and donned the ear tubes with grinning anticipation?

3 *ENTERTAINMENT FOR A NICKEL*

WHEN COMMERCIAL RECORDING GOT UNDER WAY IN THE YEAR 1890, the phonograph industry was burdened with three grave handicaps. First, the quality of reproduction was extremely poor. Only a fraction of the tonal spectrum could be caught in wax, and even that fraction issued from the ear tubes in so blurred and indistinct a manner as to make any resemblance to real music almost coincidental. Second, the wax cylinders played for a maximum of two minutes, which was too short a playing time to be productive of really satisfying musical results. Third, and most important, there was no method of duplicating cylinders; as a consequence, every recording sold was necessarily a custom-made product.

None of these handicaps was insurmountable—as events a decade or so later proved—and had Edison been disposed to encourage the entertainment side of the phonograph industry, they might all have been overcome much sooner. But because Edison was not so disposed, the industry had to adapt to the *status quo.* Was the tonal gamut limited? Very well, cylinder recordings would be limited to brass bands, cornet solos, and whatever else happened to fit into the phonograph's restricted compass. Was the playing time of scant duration? In that event, two minutes of music would have to do. Had no duplicating process been devised? Then the industry would have to hire artists willing to record the same piece again and again until the demand was satisfied. What resulted from these compromises was not especially noteworthy. But given the dimensions within which the industry had to work, it is difficult to see how anything better could have been expected.

Consider a typical recording session in the early Nineties as it progressed in the headquarters of the New York Phonograph Company, 257 Fifth Avenue. In the center of a large room are grouped members of Cappa's Seventh Regiment Band of New York; they are surrounded by ten phonographs in a circle, each one equipped with a giant metal horn. An attendant has checked all the batteries and has inserted a fresh wax cylinder in each machine. Now the recording engineer steps before the horn of the first phonograph, starts up the motor, and announces in stentorian tone: " 'My Country 'Tis of Thee,' played by Cappa's Seventh Regiment Band, record taken by Charles Marshall, New York City." He stops the motor, steps over to the second phonograph, and repeats the same announcement—and so on, through the group of ten. ("A musical record," Mr. Marshall believed, "is half made by a perfect announcement. Nothing is more gratifying to a listener to a phonograph than a clear and distinct announcement at the beginning of the record.") When every cylinder has been inscribed with an announcement, all ten motors are started up simultaneously. Music pours into the big horns until each cylinder has received as many sound impressions as it can hold, whereupon Mr. Marshall holds up his finger, and the band comes to a full stop at the end of the next musical phrase. If "My Country 'Tis of Thee" has not run its full appointed course, no one seems to worry much. The recorded cylinders are taken off the instruments and put aside in pasteboard boxes, and fresh ones are inserted. Again, the title of the selection is shouted into each horn, the band is given the signal to play, and the process is repeated. Now and then, if there is a little space left at the end of the cylinders, the band indulges in a wild burst of applause, shouting and stamping in fervent approbation of its own performance. The session lasts for three hours; and if all goes well, the New York Phonograph Company will have three hundred cylinders ready for sale the next day, at a dollar apiece.

Similar scenes were taking place at every major subsidiary of the North American Phonograph combine. Each branch had its own specialties, but for range and extent of repertoire none could equal the Columbia Phonograph Company in Washington, D. C. From the very beginning, as an offshoot of the American Graphophone Company, the Columbia firm had pushed ahead of its fellow subsidiaries. Under the aggressive management of Edward D. Easton, an ex-court reporter and one of the original stockholders of the Graphophone Company, Columbia was rapidly assuming leadership in the field of commercial recording. It had signed an exclusive contract with the United States Marine Band, under its brilliant conductor John Philip Sousa, and was busily producing recordings of marches that were to become the most popular cylinders in America. By 1891 Columbia had already issued a catalogue of its recordings, tiny in format and only ten pages long. There were twenty-seven marches listed, beginning with Sousa's *Semper Fidelis* and ending with the *Phonograph* March (by a composer named Campagna); thirteen polkas, including the *Anvil* Polka recorded with "real anvils"; ten waltzes, of which two were by Johann Strauss and two featured Spanish castanets; and thirty-four items listed as "miscellaneous," comprising the major national anthems, some well-known hymns ("with bell tolling"), and one operatic arrangement from Verdi's *Il Trovatore* identified as *"El Misererie."* After the Marine Band recordings came Columbia's next-ranking attraction, John Y. AtLee, the famous artistic whistler. Mr. AtLee spent his days working as a government clerk, his evenings making Columbia recordings in which he sang and whistled an assortment of popular airs. The 1891 catalogue listed thirty-six AtLee selections, among them "The Mocking Bird," "Home, Sweet Home," and "Marching through Georgia." The piano accompaniments were by "Professor Gaisberg," a lad in his teens who would play a leading role in the history of recording for the next fifty years. The remaining recordings listed in this early catalogue were anonymous; there were thirteen selections for clarinet and piano, nine for cornet and piano, and thirty-two songs for voice and orchestra divided into categories labeled: "Sentimental," "Topical," "Comic," "Negro," and "Irish." Finally, there were twenty speaking records under the heading "The Auctioneer"; *Sale of Dime Museum* ("with parrot imitations") and *Sale of Red-Haired Girl* ("with white horse accompaniment," whatever that might have been) were typical items.

By the early Nineties the Columbia Company was disposing of between three hundred and five hundred cylinders daily. Because a singer could record at most three cylinders at a time and a band at most ten (the circle of recording horns could be enlarged in proportion to the greater volume), selections had to be repeated without end in the recording studio—no matter how weary the United States Marine Band must have grown of *Semper Fidelis* and John Y. AtLee of his popular "Mocking Bird." Only thus could the company keep stocked with the titles listed in its catalogue. Cylinders were sold mostly by mail, were warranted to be loud, clear, and free from defects, and could be returned when worn out as partial payment for new ones. They went principally to operators of coin-in-the-slot phonographs. There was, to be sure, a certain market among individuals who owned phonographs and employed them for purposes of amusement; but until 1895 home listeners were in a small minority. The phonograph of 1889–95 was priced far beyond the means of most householders. Edison's Electric Motor Phonograph of 1893, equipped with batteries, ear tubes, blanks, and sundries, sold for $190. In 1893, with the dollar worth many times its present value, that seemed a lot to pay for a phonograph.

To make the price seem less onerous, imaginative minds worked overtime thinking of new and wonderful functions for the phonograph to perform. A go-getter in the Columbia firm dreamed up the idea of an "advertising phonograph," for which the company made cylinders that interspersed spoken advertisements with musical selections, humorous anecdotes, et cetera. The passer-by whose attention was captured by an advertising phonograph would hear something like this: "Good morning. Are you aware that John Smith is today selling the cheapest and best spring overcoat ever offered; only $10 each? You will now hear the celebrated United States Marine Band playing 'Marching through Georgia.'" Then the band was heard to play a few snatches, after which the cylinder continued: "You like that music, I am sure. Well, you will be just as much delighted with Mr. Smith's overcoats. For quantity and quality they cannot be excelled. Listen now to a bit of artistic whistling by John Y. AtLee, the world-renowned whistler." Then came a few strains from the *Chirp, Chirp* Polka before the cylinder continued: "Can't he whistle, though? Yes, indeed; but he is no more satisfactory in his line than is Mr. Smith in the clothing line." Phonographs to play such cylinders could be installed either inside or in front of a store and were operated simply by pressing a button. (One was not required to pay a nickel for an advertisement.) According to a Columbia brochure, "the men who have machines state that they have greatly increased their business by this novel way of advertising. The throngs who come to see the instrument leave so much money for purchases that the slight cost of the machine and supplies cuts a small figure in the calculation."

Another idea man in the Columbia organization put out an appeal to the illiterate businessman. Instead of writing ungrammatical letters, he was urged to communicate by inscribing a phonograph cylinder and mailing the cylinder itself to the addressee. In this way, it was stressed, "poor writers and spellers are enabled to communicate by mail without disclosure of their educational defects."

"Signor Foghorni, the great Hibernian basso-tenore robusto-profondo, is so disgusted at the frivolity of contemporary musical taste (which is not ripe enough to appreciate him), that he gives up all attempts to please the present generation: he buys a phonograph, *instead, and devotes his energies to singing for posterity. By applying his ear to this marvellous instrument immediately after singing into it, he not only hears his song echoed back to him out of the dim future, but he also hears the rapturous applause of unborn millions!"*

"THE REAL MUSIC OF THE FUTURE" AS DEPICTED BY *Punch* IN 1888

Someone suggested using the phonograph as a musical composing machine by playing favorite airs backward on it. "A musician could get one popular melody every day by experimenting in that way."

A leading medical journal asserted that the phonograph opened up vistas delightful to contemplate. It painted a picture of the future in which the phonograph would:

> reproduce the sob of hysteria, the sigh of melancholia, the singultus of collapse, the cry of the puerperal woman in the different stages of labor. It will furnish the ring of whooping cough and the hack of the consumptive. It will be an expert in insanity, distinguishing between the laugh of the maniac and the drivel of the idiot. It will give the burden of the story of the old lady who recounts all the ills of her ancestors before proceeding to the era of her own. More than this, it will accomplish this feat in the ante-room, while the physician is supposed to be busying himself with his last patient. Last, but not least, it will simultaneously furnish to the medical philosopher the grateful praises and promises of him who is convalescent from dangerous illness, together with the chilling accents in which, later, the doctor is told that he must wait for his remuneration till the butcher and baker have been paid.

These intriguing side lines notwithstanding, the phonograph was striding ever more boldly into the arena of entertainment. By 1893 the Columbia catalogue had grown to thirty-two pages. The number of marches recorded by the United States Marine Band had jumped from twenty-seven to eighty-two, representative of a like increase throughout the catalogue. George H. Diamond was augmenting an expanding list of vocal records with such gems as "You Will Never Know a Mother's Love Again" and "Have One on the Landlord with Me." Foreign-language courses recorded by Dr. Richard S. Rosenthal were offered; the price included fifty cylinders, a set of books, and the right to correspond with the good Herr Doktor. And "to meet a growing demand," Columbia had added to its catalogue a whole new section of recitation records. Charles B. Hanford, a leading tragedian of the day, was represented in twenty selections, among them twelve snatches from Shakespeare.

By the mid-Nineties speaking records were in great vogue. Unquestionably the most popular pre-1900 recording artist was the monologist Russell Hunting, originator of the famous Casey series, who recorded first for the New England Phonograph Company and later for a multitude of others. To this day veteran record collectors will chuckle, in recollection, over Hunting's *Casey as a Judge,* which—like most of his recordings—consisted of rapid-fire exchanges between two Irish characters. Hunting was a young supporting player in the Boston Theater Company when he first began to make cylinders. He was an early enthusiast of the phonograph and had leased one for his private amusement before he thought of making records for sale. When the Boston Theater was empty, he would set up his phonograph on stage, attach a large horn to the reproducing stylus in place of the usual rubber ear tubes, and test its efficacy in reaching the farthest rows of the gallery. Hunting realized during these experiments how well suited his own voice was to phonographic reproduction. Not everyone could make successful speaking records in the 1890s. The record of an unpracticed speaker, a contemporary account complained, "will consist of a confused medley of harsh, grating, unintelligible sounds." One needed a voice with a timbre susceptible of intelligible recording; one needed, too, to learn how to enunciate and modulate the voice, and to know at what speed to talk and at what angle the voice should strike the horn. Part of Hunting's success lay in the audibility of his cylinders, part in the virtuosity of his performances. He covered a wide range, from the boisterous humor of his Casey recitations to the tearful pathos of *The Dying Soldier.* His recordings were extraordinary one-man shows; in *The Steamboat,* for

instance, he assumed ten different voices in addition to supplying all the sound effects, and even Edison—prejudiced as
he then was against such efforts—acknowledged this to be the
most remarkable record ever made on a phonograph. Russell Hunting, like Fred Gaisberg, was to enjoy a long career
in the phonograph industry. He was active, first as a performer and later as an entrepreneur and recording engineer,
until the 1920s.

Second only to "Michael Casey" in popularity was a mythi-
cal phonograph character called "Pat Brady," as recorded by
Dan Kelly for the Ohio Phonograph Company. Kelly was an
old-timer in show business who had begun his recording
career with some cylinders of Shakespearean recitations and
unaccompanied songs. It then occurred to him that an imitation of a courtroom scene he had witnessed as a boy might
be suitable for the phonograph. He called it *Pat Brady's
Plea in His Own Defense.* This cylinder far outsold the
Shakespearean recitations and the songs, and soon Kelly's
rich brogue was to be heard in dozens of Pat Brady scenes,
such as *Pat Brady before the Election,* in which Pat dispensed
some extravagant promises to the electorate, or *Pat Brady
and the World's Fair at Chicago,* in which he exposed his
views on what countries should send representatives and who
should stay away. In 1893 an encomiast wrote that "wherever mankind appreciates the peculiar wit and humor of
Irish character, that comical Irishman, Pat Brady, is always
in demand, and it is not at all uncommon to see ladies and
gentlemen standing in line before an automatic phonograph
in many of our larger cities to hear him sing and talk."

There were many singers, too, building up reputations by
way of the phonograph: Will F. Denny, "a tenor of pure tone
and much pathos," who recorded popular songs of the day;
Len Spencer, a son of the handwriting expert, who specialized in Negro songs interspersed with shouts, humorous
asides, and touching sayings according to the temper of the

verse; George J. Gaskin, a tenor whose forte was pathetic ballads; Dan Quinn, a specialist in musical comedy hits; George W. Johnson, a Negro with an infectious laugh, who became famous for his record of "The Whistling Coon." Such were the major musical personalities of the phonograph during the decade of the Nineties.

But where were the celebrated divas and symphony orchestras? And what happened to the operas and concertos that were to be captured by the phonograph for the edification of the present and the benefit of the future? Since 1878 the press had been predicting for Edison's invention a vital role in the forward march of musical culture. "The voice of Patti," was a phrase that fell easily from the editorialist's pen when it was called upon to praise the wonders of the phonograph. But one will search uselessly through the catalogues of those early years for mention of any Patti cylinders. This is saddening but hardly surprising. Who could have expected Patti to make commercial recordings in the 1890s. That temperamental lady would certainly have boggled at the proposal to sing *"Casta Diva"* several hundred times over before the recording horn—even if the phonograph had been capable of doing justice to her voice, which it was not. The time was not yet right for enterprises of serious musical substance. Major technical drawbacks combined with a lack of vision to form the restricted repertoire of the Nineties. For a decade the chattering of a Michael Casey and the lachrymose balladmongering of a Dan Quinn were to rule the record grooves.

Whatever the ultimate artistic value of their efforts, these recording artists of the early Nineties succeeded in casting the phonograph in its rightful role. By 1894 Edison had to admit that his objectives needed an overhauling. After having opposed the idea for years, he finally agreed to promote the phonograph as a medium of entertainment, and he began to outline the design of a simpler and far cheaper model—

one that would fit the means of the average American family. But before he could proceed with these plans, Edison felt obliged to liquidate the North American Phonograph Company. Jesse Lippincott's cumbersome sales organization had been discredited by sad experience. Most of the subsidiaries were quiescent, and the active ones kept invading each other's territories and cutting each other's throats. Edison deemed it essential to regain the right to sell phonographs directly from his factory instead of having to deal through thirty autonomous subsidiaries; and to this end, early in 1894, he threw the North American Phonograph Company into bankruptcy.

For two years the phonograph industry fell into turmoil. Edison was restrained by law from selling phonographs to anyone, pending settlement of the receivership. With the important exception of Columbia, the territorial companies —cut off from a fundamental source of supply, and each with a huge investment tied up in the bankrupt parent company —began to founder one by one. While Edison struggled to extricate himself from the ruins of Lippincott's empire, the American Graphophone Company seized the opportunity to till the field singlehanded. Having dealt originally with Lippincott as an individual and not with the North American Phonograph Company, the Graphophone enterprise was exempt from the legal restraint imposed upon Edison. The close relationship between the Columbia and Graphophone companies was now cemented under the over-all management of Edward D. Easton, and together they prepared to capitalize on Edison's enforced retirement.

Like Edison, the Graphophone people had finally concluded that the future of the talking-machine industry lay down the avenue of mass entertainment. The manager of the Graphophone factory in Bridgeport, Connecticut, was a brilliant Scotsman by the name of Thomas Hood Macdonald who saw, long before Edison did, that the phonograph needed a far cheaper form of motive power. While Edison remained wedded to his expensive electric motor and his inefficient storage batteries, Macdonald went ahead and developed a machine with a reliable clockwork motor. It was called the Graphophone Grand and was on sale in 1894, retailing for $75, when the Graphophone-Columbia coalition began its large-scale assault on the phonograph market.

Thus, by trial and many errors, the Edison-Bell-Tainter phonograph had at last evolved into a form acceptable to the public. Its primary function as a medium of entertainment was finally recognized and it was about to enter its years of glory. Yet they were to be few in number; for a new development already gaining momentum was shortly to relegate the cylinder phonograph to the backwoods and eventually to render it obsolete altogether.

4 *EMILE BERLINER'S DISC*

THE NEW DEVELOPMENT THAT WAS TO CUT OFF THE CYLIN-
der phonograph in its prime owed its impetus to a young immigrant from Germany named Emile Berliner. He had
landed in New York in 1870, aged nineteen and in the pro-
verbially penniless state, and for three years had clerked in
a Washington, D. C., dry-goods store owned by a fellow immigrant from Hanover. Then he quit, and for three more
years he drifted from one job to another in various parts of
the country. During his travels he worked for a time as a
bottle washer in the laboratory of Constantine Fahlberg, the
man who later compounded saccharin. These surroundings
evidently imbued Berliner with a taste for science. He began
to spend his evenings in the library of New York's Cooper
Union Institute, where he educated himself in the basic
principles of chemistry and physics.

In 1876 his former employer in Washington persuaded
him to return at a higher salary and in a more responsible
position. But though Berliner went back to earning money
in the dry-goods business, his enthusiasms were irretrievably
removed from the world of drapery. Like many other young
men of his time, he had acquired an appetite for invention.
He built a small laboratory in his boardinghouse and began
to make practical experiments in the two fields that interested him most: electricity and acoustics. Specifically, he addressed himself to the problem of improving Alexander
Graham Bell's newly invented telephone. In his home exper-

iments after store hours Berliner worked out the principle
of an improved telephone transmitter. He applied for a patent and took his model to the Bell people. Berliner's visit
could not have come at a more auspicious moment. Edison
had also invented an improved telephone transmitter and
had sold it to Bell's biggest competitor. The Bell interests
were compelled to counterattack, and Berliner's invention
became their weapon. In 1878 they paid him a large sum for
his telephone transmitter and put him on a monthly retainer
to continue his researches.

Berliner's association with the Bell Telephone Company
was not very fruitful: his first invention for the telephone
proved also to be his last of any consequence for that instrument. In 1881 he took a leave of absence and with his
brother Joseph set up in Hanover the Telephon-Fabrik Berliner to manufacture telephone apparatus for the German
market. Two years later, back in the United States, he severed his connection with the Bell company entirely, built a
large house on Columbia Road in Washington, D. C., and
began to work on his own.

Just when his thoughts turned to an improvement of the
phonograph is not clear. We know only that his interest was
first aroused by the phonautograph of Léon Scott. Edouard-
Léon Scott de Martinville, to give his full name, was a French
amateur scientist who had invented an instrument to tran-
scribe a visual record of sound vibrations—hence its name
phonautograph, or sound writer—on lampblacked paper. It
dated from 1857 and for some years was manufactured by a
Paris firm for use as a laboratory instrument in measuring
and analyzing sound; however, its career had been short-
lived, and in Berliner's time it was relegated to the display
case of a Washington museum.

The characteristic of the phonautograph that attracted
Berliner was its laterally moving stylus. He reasoned that if

he could devise a talking machine employing a lateral zigzag system of recording instead of the vertical "hill-and-dale" system then in use, he might get greatly improved results— and he would certainly have a patentable invention differing in essential particulars from Edison's phonograph. Berliner's first steps were to carry out in practice what Charles Cros had suggested in theory. He covered a disc of heavy plate glass with lampblack, set it revolving on a turntable in contact with a stylus, and mounted the stylus on a feed screw so that it would create a spiral pattern on the disc. When actuated by sound waves, the stylus vibrated laterally and left a visual tracing on the lampblacked disc. Berliner "fixed" this delicate tracing with varnish and had the record photoengraved in metal. As Cros had predicted, when this photoengraved record was played back through a stylus-and-diaphragm reproducer, the original sounds were re-created. Not very well, it is true, but sufficiently so that Berliner could apply for his first patent. The date of his application was September 26, 1887—ten years after Edison's tin-foil phonograph and one year after the Bell-Tainter graphophone.

To differentiate his invention from its predecessors, Berliner named it the "gramophone." Today the terms "gramophone" and "phonograph" have become synonymous. They were not so in the nineteenth century. "Gramophone" then referred specifically to a talking machine employing *lateral-cut discs,* "phonograph" to a talking machine employing *vertical-cut cylinders.* For reasons that will be explained later on, the word "gramophone" was eventually dropped from the American vocabulary (though not from the English) and "phonograph" began to do verbal duty for all types of talking machines. But the distinction between the two terms was a useful one, and it will be observed in this book up to the chronological point where it ceases to have any significance.

Although Berliner's photoengraved record may have been

patentable, it was far from practical. It depended on a complicated manufacturing process, and it sputtered forth with a grating, almost indecipherable approximation of the human voice. Nevertheless, Berliner had the wit to perceive elements in his crude gramophone that were of vast potential promise, and he persevered in its improvement. A prime weakness of his invention lay in its reliance on photoengraving, at that time a slow, intricate, and imperfect process. If Berliner's gramophone were to have any practical utility, a better method of engraving the disc would have to be developed.

In his original patent specifications, Berliner had mentioned the possibility of engraving a gramophone record by chemical action; he turned toward the realization of this idea in the winter of 1887–88. Berliner proposed to coat a zinc disc with some workable substance, inscribe a recording on that surface, and then immerse the disc in an acid bath; the acid, he reasoned, would eat away the metal where the recording stylus had made its tracings, leaving a thin shallow groove of even depth etched into the zinc. It took several months of experimentation to find a suitable coating. Lampblack would not do; for, though it registered the delicate vibrations of the stylus, it did not resist the acid solution. At length, Berliner developed a method of coating the zinc disc with a thin fatty film that responded to the stylus and yet was impervious to acid.

By March 1888 he had begun making test records by this direct chemical process. To his home came a procession of local musicians—pianists, violinists, singers—who gladly performed into the recording horn in the interests of scientific progress. What they heard on the playback (and it took only fifteen or twenty minutes for the acid bath to produce a finished record) seemed excitingly loud and lifelike—and doubtless it was, for 1888.

On May 16 of that year Berliner demonstrated his gramophone before members of the Franklin Institute in Philadelphia. At this session he began by describing his inven-

RECORDING APPARATUS FOR ACID-ETCHED DISCS

tion; then he played some discs previously recorded in his Washington laboratory and proceeded to dilate on the potentialities of the gramophone. Much of what he said merely echoed the rosy prognostications then current about the talking machine. He invoked the magic name of Patti, prophesied vast musical and educational boons, and pictured the happy day when "future generations will be able to condense within the space of twenty minutes a tone picture of a single lifetime: five minutes of a child's prattle, five of the boy's exultations, five of the man's reflections, and five from the feeble utterances of the death-bed." It is significant that he made no claims for the gramophone as a dictating instrument. He viewed it solely as a medium of home entertainment, and he looked to the day when the mass distribution of first-rate musical recordings would be technologically and economically feasible. It was possible, Berliner explained, to "make as many copies as desired" from an original zinc recording. This being so, "prominent singers, speakers, or performers may derive an income from royalties on the sale of their phonautograms."

Home entertainment, duplication, and royalties: these were all novel concepts at a time when the phonograph and Graphophone entrepreneurs still thought principally in terms of office equipment, and they were to prove powerful forces with which to combat the competing wax cylinder.

Yet many years passed before the gramophone was developed to a competence that offered any real threat to the phonograph and Graphophone. Although Berliner did not abandon his invention as Edison had abandoned the phonograph in 1878, he hardly pressed its perfection with excessive haste. Berliner later acknowledged the slow development of the gramophone, explaining that he had not been concerned at all with time. "Fortunately," he said, "I have been spared the spur of commercial rivalry to add to the complexity of the situation, and could, with due leisure and caution, feel my way through the various technical problems and their labyrinthine courses."

The chief problems centered on the question of duplication. When Berliner spoke at the Franklin Institute of making as many copies of a gramophone record as desired, he had in mind metal duplicates manufactured by the cumbersome process of electrotyping. Indeed, one of the discs he demonstrated at Philadelphia was a copper duplicate made in this fashion. But soon thereafter he conceived of a far more feasible way of producing duplicates. It involved making a reverse metal matrix from the original acid-etched recording, and then using this "negative" matrix to stamp "positive" records in some suitable material, very much as a metal seal stamps an impression into molten sealing wax. Upon this conception, which provided for an almost illimitable supply of duplicates from one master recording, a great industry was erected. But Berliner's method of duplication, for all its commercial potentialities, evolved at a sluggish pace. Six years of painstaking research elapsed before he was ready to put his gramophone on the American market.

In the interim Berliner went to Germany to demonstrate his invention, and it was there that the gramophone made its world debut as an article of commerce. In 1889 a toymaker (Kämmerer & Reinhardt) in Waltershausen obtained a license from Berliner to manufacture miniature hand-propelled gramophones for the novelty gift trade. They were flimsy affairs, and the five-inch celluloid or hard rubber discs that went with them were not calculated to inspire much faith in the gramophone's artistic capabilities. The instruments from Waltershausen turned up all over Europe. In England they were sold for two guineas, including six records. Most of the selections were in German, though a small number were recorded in English, French, Spanish, Italian, and Russian. *The Lord's Prayer* and *Twinkle, Twinkle, Little Star* became the big sellers in England. Kämmerer & Reinhardt manufactured gramophones for two or three years, then dropped them in favor of more lucrative products.

By 1893 Berliner felt that the gramophone was ready for commercial exploitation in America. He was at last able to produce an adequate stamping matrix, and he thought he had found in hard rubber a suitable material for the records. In conjunction with a few friends and relatives, Berliner formed the United States Gramophone Company, of 1410 Pennsylvania Avenue N.W., Washington, D. C., the main assets of which were the Berliner gramophone patents. Its cap-

Thomas Alva Edison, aged thirty-one, photographed
beside his tin-foil phonograph by Levin Handy
of the Mathew Brady studio in Washington, D.C., on
April 18, 1878. Edison was there to demonstrate
his invention to President Rutherford B. Hayes.

The Miracle of the 19th Century.

The Talking

WONDER.

WONDER.

The Talking

Edison's Phonograph.

THE DREAM OF THE INVENTOR REALIZED.

It will Talk, Sing, Laugh, Crow, Whistle, Repeat Cornet Solos, imitating the Human Voice, enunciating and pronouncing every word perfectly,

IN EVERY KNOWN LANGUAGE.

This wonderful machine, which has attracted the attention of thinking men all over the civilized world, and who have pnonounced it without a dissenting voice, the most Marvelous Acoustical Phenomenon of the Century. Will be exhibited in Grand Rapids, at

FRIEDRICH'S MUSIC HALL,
No. 80 CANAL STREET,
Commencing WEDNESDAY, JULY 3d,

Exhibited Daily July 3d, 4th. 5th and 6th.

To accommodate those who desire not only to hear the Phonograph speak, but to inspect and examine it closely, it will be exhibited every day from 10 to 12 a. m., from 2 to 5 p. m., and from 8 to 10 evenings. The operator will fully explain the machine and test its powers at every entertainment.

Special attention paid to Ladies and Children.

ADMISSION, only 25 Cents,   **Children, 10 Cents.**

Eagle Steam Job Rooms—W. C. Dennis & Co.

As a show property the phonograph won an immediate success. This poster announces four days of exhibitions in Grand Rapids, Michigan, during the summer of 1878.

Edison listens to his wax-cylinder phonograph at 5:30 A.M. on June 16, 1888. Genius, he said, was one per cent inspiration and ninety-nine per cent perspiration.

Entertainment for a nickel in 1891.

Gianni Bettini posing beside his Micro-Phonograph
in the Bettini studio, 110 Fifth Avenue,
New York City.

Sarah Bernhardt recording a cylinder for
Bettini in the same studio during the mid-1890s.

The Berliner gramophone, circa 1894. Its turntable was rotated manually, like an egg beater, to play seven-inch discs at a speed of 70 rpm.

Emile Berliner, 1851–1929, the inventor of the gramophone.

Eldridge R. Johnson, 1867–1945, founder of the Victor Talking Machine Company.

Johnson's machine shop in Camden, New Jersey, as it
appeared when he began supplying motors and parts
to the Berliner Gramophone Company.

The Improved Gramophone, circa 1898,
immortalized in a famous trademark
(see overleaf).

GRAMOPHONE

An advertisement of the London-based Gramophone Company from the early 1900s. The artists featured were well-known music hall performers.

An unidentified singer (Felia Litvinne?) in the Gramophone Company's Paris studio, circa 1905. When actually recording, the singer would of course face the horn jutting out from the rear wall. *Below,* top-hatted Parisians sample the latest cylinders in Pathé's Salon du Phonographe on the Boulevard des Italiens.

Alfred Lester, Violet Loraine, and George Robey—stars of *The Bing Boys*—record excerpts from the show for Columbia in London, 1916. *Below,* a home recording session in America at about the same time.

Ernestine Schumann-Heink poses with a Victor
talking machine, vintage 1904.

The rapt auditor is Feodor Chaliapin, listening
to an HMV "pleated diaphragm" gramophone
of the early 1920s.

Enrico Caruso with Calvin G. Child, Victor's director of artists and repertoire. The photograph shows them at the entrance to Victor's headquarters in Camden, New Jersey, February 1917.

italization in dollars and cents was small. Neither Berliner nor his associates had the funds to launch the gramophone with proper éclat. They proposed to manufacture gramophones on a small scale and to begin a program of recording, but the operation was to be a token one aimed principally at demonstrating the gramophone's potentialities and attracting outside capital.

For the position of accompanist and talent scout Berliner hired twenty-one-year-old Fred Gaisberg, who had been employed previously in a like capacity for the Columbia Phonograph Company. Gaisberg knew many experienced recording artists of professional caliber, and he persuaded several of them to come to Washington and record for the gramophone. Toward the end of 1894 the first gramophone records (or "plates," as they were then called) appeared on the market. They were pressed in hard rubber and embodied all "the Latest Improvements regarding Articulation and Freedom from Friction." The United States Gramophone Company released a new batch of records every month and printed regular listings of the latest titles. Many of the recordings were anonymous, being listed merely as "Songs (baritone)" or "Songs (basso)" followed by a few popular titles—"The Old Folks at Home," "Marching through Georgia," "Rocked in the Cradle of the Deep," and the like. These anonymous recordings were the products of local Washington talent whose names possessed no sales appeal. But along with their journeyman efforts went a leavening of stellar fare: "Casey" recitations by Russell Hunting, for example, and tearful ballads by George J. Gaskin. They were all single-sided seven-inch discs, with a playing time of two minutes, and they sold for fifty cents each, or $5.00 a dozen.

To play these records, the United States Gramophone Company manufactured three types of gramophones. The cheapest and most popular model was the Seven-Inch Hand Gramophone. Its turntable was rotated manually, like an egg beater, and it was no easy task to keep it going at the correct speed. A manual accompanying each Hand Gramophone explained that "the standard velocity for seven-inch plates is about 70 revolutions a minute." * "A more rapid motion," it warned, "will raise the pitch and sharpen the sound; a slower motion will deepen the same." How was the operator to know when he was turning at the right speed? On this point the manual was not too helpful; it merely suggested that "the handle should be turned with a *wrist* movement, resting the elbow on the table, and at a uniform speed." Once the operator got the record revolving at about 70 rpm, he would use his free hand to "place the reproducer and needle into the outer groove," the "reproducer" in question consisting of a sound box and a small metal horn coupled directly to it, both mounted on a swinging wooden arm. Metal needles were to be inserted into the sound box and held tight by a screw. It was necessary to change them periodically; and if no regular gramophone needles were available, the manual was ready with excellent alternative suggestions: "If a magnifying glass of about 4 diameter power and a small Kansas oil-stone be handy, the worn needles can easily be reground to the rounded point of a darning needle. In fact, the broken-off end of darning needles ('Thorpes' No. 14), which are of the same thickness as our standard needles, are excellent substitutes."

The Seven-Inch Hand Gramophone, which sold for $12, was by far the lowest-priced talking machine on the market in 1894. But very few people beyond the vicinity of Wash-

* This speed represented a compromise between fidelity and playing time. Had Berliner recorded at a faster speed, say 100 rpm, his records would have sounded better but their playing time would have been impractically short. Had he recorded at a slower speed, say 40 rpm, he would have achieved a record of fairly long duration but impossibly bad sound. Later the speed of gramophone records was somewhat increased. From 1900 to 1925 it hovered between 74 and 82 revolutions per minute, then became stabilized at 78 rpm with the introduction of electrically powered turntables. The synchronous motor ran at 3600 rpm. With a 46:1 gear this produced a speed of 78.26 rpm, which became the standard.

ington knew of its existence, or of the more expensive electrically powered gramophones that were also offered by the United States Gramophone Company. There was no national advertising to tout the new gramophones, no system of distribution, no organized sales effort. Berliner and his associates were conducting a trial business geared only for local sales in the District of Columbia. They were looking not for customers but for backers.

And for a while it seemed as though no backers were to be found. Investors could be induced to take a good-natured interest in the gramophone, but not to part with any money on its behalf. Berliner hired a former Methodist preacher, named B. F. Karns, to promote his invention and sent him to the Bell Telephone Company in Boston. The Bell directors did not pounce on Berliner's gramophone as they had on his telephone transmitter back in the 1870s. They were amused by it—especially by the recording of *Twinkle, Twinkle, Little Star* rendered by Berliner himself in pungent German-American—but they refused to consider it a musical instrument worthy of serious exploitation. "Has poor Berliner come down to this?" one of them asked. "How sad! Now if he would only give us a talking doll perhaps we could raise some money for him." The talking-doll motif was echoed by the toy dealer F. A. O. Schwartz and other potential investors in New York to whom the gramophone was demonstrated. But Berliner, like Edison, resented the implication that his invention should be treated primarily as a toy.

Finally, in the autumn of 1895, Karns got together a syndicate of Philadelphia investors who were willing to put up a total of $25,000. The syndicate was headed by Thomas S. Parvin, a jobber of structural steel. Other investors were Max H. Bierbaum, Parvin's partner; Joseph Goldsmith, a clothing manufacturer; and William J. Armstrong and Thomas H. Latta, contractors. Under the auspices of this group, the Berliner Gramophone Company was established to manufacture instruments and records under license from the patent-holding United States Gramophone Company. It was incorporated in Philadelphia on October 8, 1895.

From this date began a lively contest between gramophone and phonograph, the issue of which was to remain in doubt for several years. When we review the struggle with all the benefits of hindsight, the outcome seems foreordained. The gramophone was a simpler, more rugged mechanism than the phonograph; it could lay claim to the immense superiority of easily duplicated records made of tough, resistant material; it reproduced sound with far greater volume and, consequently, was better suited for home entertainment. But these advantages were much less evident to the onlooker in 1895 than they seem today. The gramophone was a crude and untried upstart, the phonograph an established invention bearing the valued imprimatur of Edison. In its coin-in-the-slot manifestation, the wax-cylinder apparatus had swept the country and fixed itself in the minds of most Americans as *the* talking machine. Since then, two large companies had been developing it steadily so that at last it could be offered at a reasonable price for home use. Viewed side by side, the gramophone seemed a poor relation, the phonograph a bejeweled *grande dame*. All eyes were turned on her as she moved forward into her years of glory.

5 AT HOME WITH THE
PHONOGRAPH

A READER OF LARGE-CIRCULATION AMERICAN MAGAZINES IN
the winter of 1895–96 could not fail to notice the ubiquitous
advertisements sponsored by the Columbia Phonograph
Company. They pictured a family in a moment of rapt delight: grandfather sitting relaxed in an easy chair, his son
and daughter-in-law standing attentively to his either side,
and his grandson—clad in knee breeches and a Little Lord
Fauntleroy jacket—hopping up and down between his knees.
The attention of all four was directed to the horn protruding
from a small phonograph on a near-by table. They were
clearly being entertained in imposing fashion by "the machine that talks—and laughs, sings, plays, and reproduces all
sound," a machine "so simple that even a child can make
it pour forth the most enchanting selections of the world's
greatest Musicians, Singers, Actors, and Speakers." Prices
began at $50. An illustrated catalogue and a "list of thou-
sands of cylinder records" were free for the asking.

The talking machine's assault on the American home had
begun—with the Columbia Phonograph Company, as sole
sales agent for the American Graphophone Company, leading
the attack. It trumpeted its message through the pages of
McClure's and *Cosmopolitan*, *Munsey's* and *Harper's*. The
happy family enraptured by the phonograph was unavoid-
able. And apparently irresistible. Columbia's business
soared; the company moved from its original headquarters
in Washington, D. C., to New York City and set up branches

in Chicago, Philadelphia, St. Louis, Baltimore, and Buffalo. As sales advanced, prices dropped. For the Christmas trade in 1897, Columbia introduced an instrument retailing for $10. "It is the Eagle Model," the ads proclaimed, "and an Eagle will buy it. A new Graphophone run by clockwork that will reproduce music as loudly, brilliantly, and delightfully as the highest priced machine. . . . Ten dollars invested in this machine will yield pleasure without limit. . . . The infinite variety of the Graphophone, which brings into the home all the pleasures of music, reproducing the performances of bands, orchestras, and operatic choruses, as well as of vocal and instrumental soloists, makes it an entertainer of which one never tires." A larger and sturdier model, the Columbia Home Graphophone, sold for $25. It was described as "the Prince of Entertainers."

Edison followed close behind. He had finally extricated his affairs from the legal morass of the bankrupt North American Phonograph combine and, in January 1896, had formed the National Phonograph Company to manufacture and distribute phonographs for home use. The spring-driven Edison Home Phonograph, retailing for $40, appeared in the autumn of 1896. A year later came the $20 Edison Standard Phonograph, which was indeed to be a standard model—with minor modifications—for over three decades. It was a rugged, well-engineered, carefully crafted machine, and with it Edison eventually became the dominant power in the cylinder phonograph field. But his hegemony was not established overnight. Throughout the 1890s Edison's National Phonograph Company ran second best behind the aggressive, virtuosic Columbia-Graphophone alliance.

Neither company, however, had cause to complain about the state of the phonograph business. Large dividends and expanding markets were the order of the day. *The Phonoscope,* a trade magazine published from 1896 to 1900, attributed the rise in phonograph sales to three factors:

"reduced cost of machines, improvement in sound amplifying horns, and improvement of records." The first two were indubitable. Phonographs were certainly cheaper: in 1893 Edison's least expensive model had sold for $140; six years later there was a serviceable Edison phonograph ("The Gem") for $7.50. And they were assuredly louder: the rubber hearing tube had given way to a metal horn that provided adequate volume at short range, if hardly an overpowering plenitude of sound.

As for the records, the extent of improvement was debatable. Mechanically, there had been some slight gains. Articulation was clearer, surface noise had been reduced, and a rudimentary duplicating process was in general use. The method of duplication involved "playing" a master cylinder on one mandrel and transferring the sound vibrations pantographically onto a wax blank revolving on an adjacent mandrel. Although it was slow and inadequate—not to be compared to the gramophone's stamping process—at least it allowed the mass production of records without imposing intolerable strain on the performers. Recording artists were obliged, nevertheless, to do many "repeat performances" before the recording horns, for one master cylinder would yield only a limited number of pantographed duplicates. Harry MacDonough, a veteran tenor of early cylinder days, recalled that Edison recording engineers in the late Nineties would make five master cylinders at each performance of a song and that each one of these masters would produce at least twenty-five duplicates before the original wax impressions wore out. A single "take" before five recording horns would thus yield 125 cylinders; but that would not begin to meet the demand for a fast-selling selection, and MacDonough remembered having recorded his popular songs again and again at the Edison studio in West Orange, New Jersey.

The improvement in recorded repertoire had also been of small dimension. For the "pleasures of music" promised in the advertisements, one could choose among the catalogues of at least a dozen different companies. The Norcross Phonograph Company, of New York City, listed numerous recordings by the Metropolitan Band, conducted by Signor G. Peluso, with the accent on potpourris from Italian opera. Reed & Dawson, of Newark, publicized the efforts of T. Herbert Reed, "maker of the only successful violin records." Edison's National Phonograph Company tendered a varied assortment of popular ballads, marches, and talking records— both humorous and inspiring. But in this field, again, Columbia for a time eclipsed all competitors. The catalogues published by this company read like a *Who's Who* of the recording stars of early cylinder days; its pages are a manifest gauge of what the phonograph owner of the late Nineties was likely to hear when he gathered together a selection of cylinders, grouped his family or some friends in a small semicircle before the metal horn, and quieted the room for an evening of recorded music.

There were marches by Gilmore's Band and Sousa's Grand Concert Band, piccolo solos by George Schweinfest, banjo solos by Vess L. Ossman, "Casey" dialogues by Russell Hunting, and songs by George J. Gaskin, Steve Porter, Dan Quinn, and Minnie Emmett. There were over eighty cylinders by the Columbia Orchestra, an ensemble that specialized in "Descriptive Records." If you ordered No. 15064, *Down on the Suwanee River,* from the "Descriptive" category, you were certainly getting your fifty cents' worth, for in the space of two minutes it spun out the excitement of "Pulling in the Gang Plank, Steamboat Bells, Whistle, and Dance on Board with Negro Shouts and Clogs." But with all the talent marshaled together in Columbia's 1898 catalogue—and there is no belittling the particular artistry of a Russell Hunting or a Vess Ossman—only one performer represented in its thirty-two pages could claim serious musical standing. He was Bernard Bégué, a young baritone from France who had already sung minor roles at the Paris Opéra and was later to have an uneventful career at the Metropolitan Opera. Among Bégué's ten Columbia cylinders were some honest-to-goodness operatic arias: *"Vision fugitive"* from *Hérodiade,* *"Adamastor, roi des vagues"* from *L'Africaine,* the Prayer *("Je te bénis")* from Rossini's *Guillaume Tell,* and the Toreador Song from *Carmen.* Here was a beckoning musical oasis, but its fruits could hardly be described as "the most enchanting selections of the world's greatest singers"—this being the verbal bait with which Columbia tried to lure prospective buyers of the Graphophone.

In truth, however much the advertisements prated of "a musical education to the young" or of a "repertoire as limitless as the realm of melody itself," the phonograph still showed all the earmarks of a cultural pariah. Columbia and Edison had made a few tentative infiltrations into the giant domain of great music that was supposed to envelop the American home in an aura of uplifting art, but the bulk of their efforts pointed in the direction of pure home-grown "corn." With one exception, the early entrepreneurs of the phonograph demonstrated no more than a cursory interest in the musical potentialities of the wax cylinder, being content that it amused and gratified a not too discriminating public. A latter-day commentator has no cause to berate them for this attitude, but he may be excused for by-passing their work and concentrating instead on the one man (the exception noted above) who took a loftier aesthetic view of Edison's invention.

A less likely candidate for the part could hardly be imagined than Gianni Bettini. Born in 1860 in Novara, Italy, the scion of a wealthy land-owning family, he had left school early, after failing to show any glimmerings of scholastic aptitude, and had been sent off to the army. There, he was commissioned an officer in the cavalry. Army life for him was not very rigorous. Bettini spent much of his time in

Paris, parading up and down the boulevards in his splendid uniform and attending the elaborate social functions to which his family status gave him admission. At one of these *soirées* in Paris he met a rich young American socialite named Daisy Abbott, whom he followed to New York and married. Just how he terminated his army career is not clear; he was known, at all events, as Lieutenant Bettini for long after he had settled in the United States.

In 1888 Bettini acquired an Edison wax-cylinder phonograph, one of the first that had been manufactured. Being a member of New York's high society as well as an Italian, he was a confirmed and enthusiastic opera-goer, and he listened to the phonograph with a trained, critical ear. What he heard did not please him. But instead of putting the phonograph aside and finding another diversion, Bettini surprised everyone by setting out to improve on Edison's apparatus himself. He had had no scientific training and had shown no special technical talent. Nevertheless, in 1889 Bettini was able to patent an "Apparatus for the Recording and Reproduction of Sounds" based on Edison's wax-cylinder phonograph but embodying several important modifications. He called his machine the Micro-Phonograph, and in June 1890 described it in a short article, which he wrote—being a good Continental—in French.

He began by detailing the defects of the early phonographs and Graphophones: one could never be sure of getting an audible impression in the wax cylinders; and even if one did, the quality of reproduction lacked the clarity of timbre that enables a listener to distinguish one voice from another. Furthermore, he complained, it was unpleasant to listen to music through rubber hearing tubes; and if one discarded them and substituted a metal horn, the reproduction was entirely without character, the tones being faint, indistinct, and lacking in musical quality. In the Micro-Phonograph, Bettini wrote, he had endeavored to obtain "a clearer, more natural reproduction, with a volume sufficient to obviate the necessity of using hearing tubes" and he had tried especially to "avoid a metallic timbre" in the reproduced sound. His researches had taught him that the results he desired could not be obtained with the recording and reproducing elements supplied by Edison. Edison employed a crystal diaphragm with a single stylus projecting from its center; Bettini favored a mica diaphragm, and in place of Edison's straight stylus he substituted a "spider" with radial legs of varying length bearing against the diaphragm at a number of points and culminating in a single recording pin. He justified his innovations in this way:

A diaphragm vibrates over its whole surface, but at varying degrees at different points. The study of acoustics teaches us that a diaphragm contains dead points where the vibrations will be feeble or nonexistent. If the stylus is anchored to only one point of the diaphragm [as in Edison's apparatus], that point may often be dead, or nearly so; such a diaphragm might sometimes make a good recording, but there would be many other times when it would record very imperfectly. Suppose, however, that a "spider" with legs of different lengths be anchored to a diaphragm at several points; two or three of these points may be dead points at times, and consequently incapable of transmitting sound vibrations, but the other legs will be able to actuate the recording pin nevertheless. The "spider" has other advantages: it transmits more force to the recording pin, and because of its many supports that pin is held more rigidly. To sum up, I catch the vibrations of a diaphragm at several different points, and with the aid of independent conductors I concentrate these vibrations on a single recording pin.

The results he modestly described as "perfect." The same "spider" principle was employed in the reproducing attachment, and with the same indicated results.

Such was the Micro-Phonograph. What Bettini did with it matters very much more than the invention itself. At the time the Micro-Phonograph was developed, Bettini and his wife lived in the Sherwood Studios at the corner of Fifty-seventh Street and Sixth Avenue, a building much frequented by musicians. The Bettinis kept open house there for visiting stars of the opera and the theater; they were vivacious, agreeable hosts, and their elaborate parties attracted many great stage personalities of the day. Inevitably, at these parties the Micro-Phonograph would be brought out and made to perform. And since it was a remarkably good apparatus for its time, Bettini's famous guests would want to make recordings on it themselves. Slowly the young Italian inventor accumulated a valuable collection of celebrity recordings. He kept them for himself; they had been made on a friendly basis, with no thought of commercial use.

Late in 1891, or early in 1892, Bettini decided to go into the phonograph business. He rented offices in the Judge Building, 110 Fifth Avenue, and invited members of the press to hear his Micro-Phonograph and his recordings. A reporter from *Leslie's Weekly* wrote an adulatory account of the "bright and cultured young Italian" who, "working patiently for three years, unassisted by skilled mechanics, and himself untrained in the mechanical arts, has seen his Micro-Phonograph improve day by day until at last it has reached a startling degree of perfection." A writer from *The Microcosm* was "enchanted with the matchless exhibition of this new acoustical wonder. Compared with this latest and grandest of all talking machines, the Edison phonograph, even as recently perfected, becomes a second-rate device." Bettini's first move was to manufacture his "spider" recording and reproducing attachment for use either with the phonograph or the graphophone. "To obtain perfect reproductions from your talking machine," he advertised, "use the Bettini Micro-Attachment. It refines the sound, eliminating all metallic resonance, screech, rasp and harshness. It is the clearest and loudest made. A novice makes perfect records with this attachment. Try it."

Bettini's Fifth Avenue studio became a favorite meeting place for his musical friends. They found it convenient to exchange gossip and talk shop there, and it was useful to make recordings. Useful because a singer could thereby listen to his own voice, analyze its strengths and its weaknesses, and compare it with the voices of other artists who had similarly recorded for Bettini. A reporter from *The Phonoscope* visited the studio in 1896 and came away dazzled by the cylinders he had heard:

> The collection [he wrote] is unequaled anywhere. There are songs by Yvette Guilbert, who sang into the phonograph on her recent visit to this country. When the writer visited the studio lately, Yvette's voice sounded from the phonograph, one of her English songs, "I Want You, My Honey." Then the voice gave "La Soularde" and an imitation of Bernhardt's style of delivery in a favorite character. Then followed a selection from "Izeyl," by Bernhardt herself, with all the passion in which the passage was recited on the stage. . . .
> The next cylinder was one labeled "Melba," which was truly wonderful; the phonograph reproducing her wonderful voice in a marvelous manner, especially on the high notes which soared away above the staff and were rich and clear. Mark Twain interrupted the singer with a few remarks on the experience he had had in trying to make practical use of the instrument. The humorist is now on his lecturing tour around the world and the record he made in the phonograph was taken in December 1893. . . .
> It would be tedious to name all the artists represented in the collection. Some, however, should be mentioned. Among them were Victor Maurel, the well-known baritone singer; . . . Tomaso Salvini, who rolled out a grand passage from "Othello" in the Italian translation; M. Coquelin, the famous French actor, whose visit to this country will be remembered; Pol Plançon and Mme. Saville, the beautiful Frenchwoman who warbled a bit from the opera of "Rigoletto," and another from the opera of "Carmen." . . . Signor Nicolini has a cylinder to which he sang on his last visit to this country with Mme. Patti three years ago. Nicolini was

never much of a singer and the phonograph of today does not give him even justice as it has been considerably worn from repetitions given to those who wanted to hear Mme. Patti's husband sing. Sigrid Arnoldson's voice was heard in a cylinder to which the artist sang three years ago.

All in all, *The Phonoscope* called Lieutenant Bettini's cylinders "a revelation to those who have only heard the phonograph in the ferry houses and saloons."

Sometime in the mid-Nineties, when pantographic duplication became feasible, Bettini began to offer cylinder recordings for sale. He published a twelve-page catalogue in 1897 and a thirty-two page catalogue in 1898—the latter listing over two hundred recordings of serious music (many by artists of celebrity rank) and another two hundred in the popular category. Bettini's performers included some from the Metropolitan Opera, among them the sopranos Frances Saville and Marie Engle, the tenor Dante del Papa, the baritones Mario Ancona and Giuseppe Campanari, and the basso Pol Plançon. Yvette Guilbert was represented by six songs; there were four cylinders by the violinist Henri Marteau; and there were dramatic excerpts read by Bernhardt, Réjane, and Salvini. Prices ranged from $2.00 to $6.00 per cylinder—at a time when other companies were offering cylinder recordings at fifty cents each. The 1899 Bettini catalogue, fifty-five pages long, presented a few more Metropolitan singers: the contralto Eugenia Mantelli, the tenors Albert Saléza and Ernest van Dyck, and the baritone Anton van Rooy. At the end of the listing came an appetite-whetting announcement: "We have in our collection many records from celebrated artists, not mentioned in this catalogue, and we are constantly adding new ones." Perhaps this implied that, for a consideration, Bettini would make duplicates of his rarest recordings. It is believed, from documentary evidence, that in addition to the artists listed in his catalogues Bettini owned recordings of Sigrid Arnoldson, Emma Calvé, Nellie Melba, Lillian Nordica, Marcella Sembrich, Ernest Nicolini, Italo Campanini, Francesco Tamagno, Jean and Edouard de Reszke, Jean Lassalle, and Victor Maurel.

Bettini did not aspire to a mass-production business. He duplicated cylinders to order, and he was at pains to make clear that his specialty was "High-Grade Records, High-Class Music, and only by Leading Performers and World-Famed Artists." At the prices he charged, only the most affluent music-lovers could afford Bettini merchandise. An item in *The Phonoscope* for May 1897 reported that William K. Vanderbilt (one of the original Metropolitan Opera stockholders) had purchased three Bettini Micro-Phonographs and "over 100 records of famous artists." This represented a total investment of at least $500. Mr. Vanderbilt could afford it; the average phonograph owner in the 1890s could not. Considering Bettini's prices and the small scale on which he operated, it is doubtful whether he sold more than a few hundred copies of any one recording. In no other way can the fact be explained that today Bettini cylinders are even rarer than Gutenberg Bibles or Shakespeare quartos. A group of them was discovered in 1945 in Mexico City—none, unfortunately, by singers of eminent stature—and sold to a collector in Boston. I know of no other authenticated Bettini cylinders in existence; * Gianni Bettini's own collection of "originals" was stored in a French warehouse in 1914 and destroyed by bombing during World War II. Thus, barring a lucky find in an attic or junk shop, posterity will never hear the voices of those singers who recorded only for Bettini, or hear in their prime those singers whose later records give evidence only of declining vocal powers (such as Ernest van Dyck). But we must not romanticize unduly the legacy

* Since writing this, an important Bettini recording has been discovered (in New Zealand, of all places): a five-inch wax cylinder of Marcella Sembrich singing Johann Strauss's *Voci di primavera*. Luckily, it was still in playable condition and has been "dubbed" onto a 45-rpm disc. The brilliance and presence of the sound speak well for Bettini's technical expertise.

that has been lost. Some writers, employing imagination instead of prosaic research, have ascribed a dazzling galaxy of recording artists to Bettini's enterprise: Richard Wagner, Jenny Lind, Pauline Lucca, Milka Ternina, Etelka Gerster, Adelina Patti, and Queen Victoria among them. The first two were chronologically unable to oblige Bettini, having died before his recording career. The others were indeed alive, but there is no evidence other than wishful thinking that Bettini ever recorded them.

In 1902 Gianni Bettini sold his American patent rights in the mica diaphragm to Edison, closed his Fifth Avenue studio, and moved to Paris, where he established the Société des Micro-Phonographes Bettini, with headquarters at 23 Boulevard des Capucines. For a few years he continued to make and sell recordings, phonographs, and attachments. Among his last coups was a series of recordings of Pope Leo XIII, made at the Vatican shortly before his death in 1903. But Bettini as a businessman was neither determined nor astute. As the cylinder phonograph declined in public esteem, so did Bettini's interest. By 1908 he had left the phonograph business altogether and was busily promoting two new inventions —the Bettini Motion-Picture Camera and the Bettini Multiplex Camera—neither of which proved to be very successful. In 1914 he served as a front-line war correspondent for *Le Gaulois*. Three years later he was back in the United States, with a military mission of the Italian Government, and there he stayed until his death in 1938. Bettini's inventive faculties never ceased to function. A mirrorlike surfacing for cloth, a golf-practice device that measured the distance, height, and curve of a hit ball, a cigarette lighter (manufactured and sold for some time by Cartier)—his creative ingenuity yielded new ideas to the end. He did not seem unduly bothered that not one of his inventions had ever struck real pay dirt. He was an indifferent entrepreneur; and by the time he died, the

combined Bettini-Abbott fortune had suffered serious deple-
tion.

However much he interests us today, Bettini cut a small
figure in the phonograph business of the 1890s. Edison and
Columbia were the ruling powers, and their competition was
brisk and tempestuous. To satisfy the demand for a louder
wax-cylinder talking machine, Columbia introduced the
Graphophone Grand, which utilized a cylinder four and a
half inches in diameter instead of the standard two-inch
cylinder. It was a cumbersome apparatus and expensive
($150), but it did, as the ads claimed, reproduce music "with
many times the volume of the smaller styles." Columbia
brought out the Graphophone Grand in September 1898.
Three months later Edison was in production with a similar
instrument, called the Edison Concert Phonograph, which
was "strong and vibrant enough to fill the largest auditorium" and sold for $125. Columbia countered with a
cheaper version of the Graphophone Grand at $100 and with
the exhortation to "get the *genuine* improvement; avoid the
imitation." But despite extensive advertising by both companies, the large-cylinder machines did not find a secure
footing in the American market. After a few years they disappeared entirely.

All the while, both companies were bending every effort to
perfect a practical method of molding duplicate cylinders
from a negative matrix. The more the phonograph business
increased, the more did the limitations of the pantographic
copying process assert themselves. And yet for years the
Edison and Columbia companies had to rely on it for the
whole of their recorded output. It was only in 1901 that a
successful process was perfected for molding cylinders. But
the jubilant announcements could not mask the fact that it
had come too late. Already the cylinder was fast losing
ground to the flat disc. It had attained its summit at the turn

of the century; and though it was to linger until 1929, the cylinder phonograph had had its day. Edison had made the choice between cylinder and disc back in 1877. He had favored the cylinder by reason of its acoustical superiority—and on that ground he was right. But he had forgotten to consider the disc's simplicity, its ease of handling and storage; and, being intolerant of the phonograph as a medium of entertainment, he had undervalued and neglected mass duplication of recordings. Edison, who had invented the cylinder phonograph, lived to see it repudiated by the great public it was meant to serve and enlighten.

6 *THE IMPROVING GRAMOPHONE*

In Philadelphia the newly formed Berliner Gramophone Company established its headquarters and assembly plant in a red-brick building at 1026 Filbert Street. Not far away, on Chestnut Street, the company opened a retail store under the management of a young man named Alfred Clark. But a world hungry for recorded entertainment did not beat a path to its door, nor did the postman seem excessively laden with replies to the advertisements for gramophones that began to appear in magazines and newspapers. There was every good reason for the sluggish rate of sales. So long as the gramophone had to rely on manual power, its prospects were not very good. The hand-propelled instrument looked like a toy, and sounded like one too. Even the most practiced operator could not keep the turntable speed constant; and as the gramophone record joggled fitfully round and round, the pitch would soar and tumble in diverting but hardly satisfying cacophony.

It was easy to prescribe a remedy: obviously, the gramophone would have to follow the wax-cylinder phonograph's example and adopt a spring motor. But to translate the prescription into practical terms was rather more difficult. The gramophone motor had to be efficient, noiseless, and cheap—especially cheap, for Berliner realized that he could edge into a field dominated by Columbia and Edison only by offering superior value at lower price. Several spring motors had been tried out experimentally on the gramophone, but all had fallen short in one way or another. Among the unsuccessful designs for a motor was one submitted by an old Philadelphian who had advertised clockwork motors for sewing machines in the Philadelphia *Ledger*. His specifications were sent on to Eldridge R. Johnson, a twenty-nine-year-old mechanic who operated a small machine shop in Camden, New Jersey, and built experimental models for inventors as a side line. When the old man's design proved impracticable, the Berliner directors turned it down and thought no more about it.

However, they had not seen the last of Eldridge Johnson, for in building the model, the Camden mechanic had become infected with a severe case of gramophonitis. Johnson was certainly not one to be gulled by novelty; as a busy model-maker, he was used to seeing new inventions pass through his shop. Yet there was something different about the gramophone. "It sounded," he later wrote, "like a partially educated parrot with a sore throat and a cold in the head, but the little wheezy instrument caught my attention and held it fast and hard. I became interested in it as I had never been interested in anything before." To Johnson, harried by the bitterly competitive and unrewarding wire-stitching machinery business, in which his workshop specialized, the gramophone seemed exactly what he was looking for. He began to tinker with a gramophone motor of his own design and found that if the motor handle was left to unwind itself as the machine played, he could dispense with some expensive parts. By pruning costs here and improving performance there, he finally produced a motor that satisfied him. Moreover it satisfied the Berliner directors when it was demonstrated to them—so much that they gave Johnson a contract, in the summer of 1896, to manufacture two hundred motors. It was not a very big order, to be sure, but the Berliner business was not very big either.

The gramophone, indeed, required more than a cheap and

workable spring motor: it needed someone to promote and sell it. The men who ran the Berliner Gramophone Company were sorely inexperienced in the art of marketing and were loath to finance a program of aggressive promotion. Casting about for help, the Berliner directors discussed their problem with an energetic New York promoter and advertising man named Frank Seaman. Seaman talked convincingly and took an optimistic view of the gramophone's future. Better still, he suggested a *modus operandi* that would cost the Berliner group nothing. He proposed that they make him the exclusive United States selling agent for the gramophone, in return for which he would set up his own company to advertise and distribute gramophone merchandise. This sounded reasonable, and in 1896 the Berliner Gramophone Company signed a fifteen-year contract with Seaman along the lines he had suggested. The gramophone's affairs were thence to be partitioned among three separately owned and managed enterprises: Seaman's National Gramophone Company, of New York City, would have charge of advertising and selling; the Berliner Gramophone Company, of Philadelphia, was to manufacture instruments and records; the United States Gramophone Company, Berliner's own patent-holding company of Washington, would continue to control the gramophone patents. It was a complicated system of alliances, and it was due for entanglements and trouble.

Seaman opened an office at 874 Broadway and proceeded to saturate the newspapers and appropriate magazines with bold full-page advertisements of the gramophone. A headline extolled it as the "Talking Machine That Talks Talk!" (which was catchy if not very meaningful), while the finer print explained that the instrument was not adapted for office work but was intended "simply and solely for the entertainment of the home circle or for public exhibition." For the first few months of its existence the National Gramophone Company was able to offer only the hand-propelled model, which it sold for $15, including two records, express prepaid to any address east of the Rocky Mountains. By November 1896, however, Eldridge Johnson had delivered enough spring-motor gramophones for Seaman to take advantage of some Christmas gift business. At $25 the gramophone outdistanced all competition (the cheapest spring-driven cylinder machines were then twice as expensive), and orders began to come in faster than Seaman could handle them. Indeed, business spurted forward so quickly and unexpectedly that National Gramophone had to apologize in large advertisements for falling behind in shipments:

> Since November [Seaman explained in the spring of 1897] we have been doing our best to keep up with the increasing demand for gramophones. Our manufacturing facilities have been steadily extended; work has been carried on night and day; much foreign business has been declined, yet we find ourselves with hundreds of orders unfilled. But one conclusion can be drawn from this unprecedented demand: the gramophone is without question the most popular, as it is the simplest and most wonderful, talking machine.

Eldridge Johnson's "partially educated parrot" was exceeding his fondest hopes, and the Berliner Gramophone Company, hard-pressed by Seaman's demands for more and more merchandise, began ordering motors by the thousands instead of the hundreds. Meanwhile, Johnson came up with two new pieces of equipment. One was an improved sound box, developed jointly by Alfred Clark and himself; the other was an improved motor, which was to be mounted at the rear of the gramophone instead of underneath the turntable. It took no little persuasion for the Berliner group to relinquish their sound box in favor of Johnson's; but Johnson's superior craftsmanship prevailed, and in mid-1897 his shop began to manufacture both the new sound box and the new motor. The instrument embodying these two pieces of equipment was called the Improved Gramophone. It is certainly the most familiar single piece of talking-machine equipment that the world has ever known (although it was already out of date in the early years of the twentieth century), for the Improved Gramophone achieved immortality in a picture, thanks to a chubby black-and-white fox terrier who peers wistfully into its horn and listens to "His Master's Voice." But in 1897 Frank Seaman could not possibly have guessed that the Improved Gramophone was to gain such notoriety. As yet there was no picture of dog and gramophone; words alone were employed to paint its virtues, and Seaman implored readers not to "make the mistake of thinking you have ever heard a *real* Talking or Singing Machine till you have heard the Improved Gramophone, with its *new* sound box, *new* motor, and *new* records; it is positively and preeminently without a rival."

As sales increased, Seaman's National Gramophone Company clamored for more and better recordings. Under Fred Gaisberg's youthful stewardship a recording studio was set up in Philadelphia; soon after, a second studio was opened in New York with Calvin Child, a renegade from the Columbia Phonograph Company, in charge. Neither studio could have been called elaborate; in those early days, a recording machine, an upright piano, and four walls sufficed. Seven-inch master discs were recorded on zinc plates and etched by the chemical process described in Chapter 4. These masters were then dispatched to Washington for the manufacture of negative matrix stampers. Matrix making was the critical step in the production of flat discs, and it was one aspect of gramophony that Berliner continued to supervise personally. For many years the inventor refused to let outsiders learn his intricate and painstakingly developed metallurgical technique.

The discs themselves were pressed at first in vulcanized rubber, which had the great advantage of being "indestructible" (a persuasive selling point vis-à-vis the delicate wax cylinders). Unfortunately, the rubber records tended to flatten out in spots, and this would send the needle skidding across the disc. In the latter half of 1897 Berliner switched to a shellac composition manufactured by the Durinoid Company of Newark, New Jersey. Although this material had its own complement of deficiencies, it at least held the impress of the stamper and was relatively cheap.

In building a recorded repertoire for the gramophone, Gaisberg and Child faced fewer difficulties than their opposite numbers who worked with wax cylinders. For the gramophone impresarios, record making was not a multiple-production affair. There was no need for the same selection to be recorded by the same artist *ad infinitum*. Let a good recording once be made, and nothing more was required except to process a matrix and send it to the Durinoid Company for manufacture. Thousands of discs could be pressed before the stamper showed signs of serious wear. Theoretically it was possible to obtain gramophone records from artists who would not have dreamed of subjecting themselves to the tiring, repetitive wax-cylinder routine. But a sizable gap separated the possible from what actually was accomplished. In its early years the gramophone showed small awareness of its superior potentialities. The philosophy of the coin-slot bonanza still ruled the industry. Familiar names abounded in the gramophone catalogue: Dan Quinn, Len Spencer, George J. Gaskin, Will F. Denny, Vess Ossman, Cal Stewart, Russell Hunting; one by one, the stalwart phonograph entertainers now visited the gramophone studios and refurbished their old routines for the new medium. The gramophone was nothing if not imitative. Like the phonograph, it made a specialty of "Descriptive Records," such as the one entitled *Morning on the Farm*, a realistic farmyard scene "so real and exact that it requires but a slight stretch of the imagination to place one's self in that delightful position, the result of which is the drinking in of copious drafts of fresh air and numerous other pleasures attainable only on the farm."

Musically, the gramophone repertoire kept a step ahead of Columbia and Edison, though it nowhere approached the level of the great Bettini. A tenor named Ferruccio Giannini was responsible for most of the operatic arias in the gramophone catalogue. Fred Gaisberg, who had heard Giannini sing in a small touring Italian opera company, persuaded the tenor to make some discs in the Philadelphia studio. Giannini recorded truncated versions of the big arias from *Rigoletto, Traviata, Trovatore,* and *Cavalleria,* as well as a group of popular Neapolitan songs of the *"Santa Lucia"* variety—all with piano accompaniment. He was not a musical artist of great distinction, especially in that day of virtuosic singing, and his records today have a curiosity value only. Giannini's most sought-after disc is the *"Miserere"* duet from *Trovatore,* No. 930 in the Berliner catalogue, in which an anonymous cornetist intones the music that Verdi allotted to a soprano.

Such celebrities as the gramophone could boast of in the 1890s were drawn mainly from the stage and the orator's platform. By 1898 one could hear via gramophone records the voices of Dwight L. Moody, the tub-thumping evangelist; Chauncey Depew, railway magnate and after-dinner speaker extraordinary; Joseph Jefferson, the American actor famous for his playing of Rip van Winkle; Robert Ingersoll, a militant freethinker with a gift for oratory; and Ada Rehan, a brilliant comedienne who divided her time between the London and New York stage. Other eminent names listed on the gramophone roster were John Philip Sousa, whose band now recorded exclusively for Berliner, and Maurice Farkoa, a music-hall entertainer of international reputation.

In the fall of 1898 Seaman's advertisements reminded readers: "The long winter evenings are coming on. Now is the time to buy a gramophone." It was stated proudly that an instrument "was recently ordered for the Imperial Palace in Constantinople; even the Sultan apparently recognizing the fact that for Making Home Attractive, there's nothing like the Gramophone." To make the picture even more enticing, the National Gramophone Company began selling on the installment plan: $5.00 down and $3.00 per month for seven months. The constellation of long winter evenings, the Sultan's taste in domestic furnishings, and $5.00 down combined to move gramophones as never before. At the end of 1898 the ledger books were pleasant to behold. National Gramophone claimed that its total sales topped the million-dollar mark. Eldridge Johnson alone showed a $40,000 profit that year; by then Johnson's shop was manufacturing complete gramophones, taking up overflow from the busy Berliner factory in Philadelphia.

The wax-cylinder companies watched this activity with undisguised alarm. In its advertisements Columbia began to make tart references to the gramophone. It referred to "other so-called talking machines" that would "reproduce only specially prepared cut-and-dried subjects," and reminded readers that "the Graphophone does much more; it repeats your voice; your friend's voice; songs sung to it or stories told to it." Along similar lines Columbia made it known that "makers of machines limited by their mechanism to imperfect reproductions of specially prepared records attempt to persuade intending purchasers that it is one of the merits of their invention that it will not make records of sound. Much of the pleasure, however, of a talking machine in the home is derived from its power of recording favorite musical selections, songs sung by loved ones, or the voices of friends." Even *The Phonoscope,* which was supposedly an unbiased periodical for the whole talking-machine trade, took a virulently anti-gramophone stand in the fall of 1898. A gramophone record, it editorialized, "sounds first like escaping steam. You listen more attentively hoping for better things and you are next reminded of the rumbling of a horseless carriage. Finally, when the attempt to reproduce a voice is begun, you are forcibly compelled to liken the noise from the Gramophone to the braying of a wild ass." To add insult to injury *The Phonoscope* observed that the gramophone's "looks are not very inspiring" and that "its blasty, whang-doodle noises are not desired by citizens of culture."

Seaman was not the kind of man to let these aspersions go unchallenged. He rushed into print with large advertisements carrying the considered opinion of "the celebrated cornetist" W. Paris Chambers that "the Phonograph reproduces only one-fifth of the true tone quality of the Cornet, while the improved Gramophone reproduces practically all of the tone quality and volume of the instrument." Another advertisement reproduced a joint testimonial by five soloists from Sousa's band: "We consider the Gramophone the *only* Talking Machine which perfectly reproduces the true tone qualities of our respective instruments." And picking up Columbia's claim for home-recorded entertainment, Seaman fired right back with the assurance that the gramophone "has never brought discredit upon itself by amateur or fraudulent records."

The warfare between cylinder and disc galloped from the copywriter's pen into the lawyer's briefcase. It was a litigious industry to begin with, and the American Graphophone Company especially had the reputation of racing into court at the slightest provocation. Indeed, many people held that the chief asset of the prosperous Columbia-Graphophone alliance lay in the person of Philip Mauro, a shrewd, forty-year-old Washingtonian who as principal legal counsel for the Graphophone had defended the Bell-Tainter patents for all, or perhaps more than, they were worth. In 1898 he turned his attention to this new form of competition which was beginning to threaten the Graphophone even more than the archenemy Edison. Mauro subjected Berliner's patents

to the most assiduous legal scrutiny. Superficially, the Berliner disc patents and the Bell-Tainter cylinder patents were
miles apart, both in concept and in execution. But was there
not some point of friction, some obscure but vital transgres-
sion for which the menacing gramophone could be called to
account in court? Mauro burrowed deeply and emerged
with one of his typically ingenious stratagems. It hinged on
a mainstay of the original Graphophone patent, the provision
for the so-called "floating stylus," which had been one of
Bell and Tainter's chief improvements over the Edison tin-
foil phonograph. As Mauro played a gramophone and observed how its sound box was propelled by the grooves of a
record, it suddenly occurred to him that the gramophone's
stylus could be said to "float" also. If this could be proved,
then the gramophone patent most certainly invaded the
Bell-Tainter domain.

Mauro went to court, but he sued neither the patent-
holding United States Gramophone Company nor the
manufacturing Berliner Gramophone Company. Instead, he
directed his attack against the National Gramophone Company and Frank Seaman personally. On October 22, 1898,
as counsel for the American Graphophone Company, he entered suit in the United States Circuit Court for the Southern
District of New York, demanding that the defendants be en-
joined from the further sale of any talking machine that
employed a floating-stylus sound box.

In leveling his blow against Seaman, the Graphophone
lawyer was functioning at his Machiavellian best. Seaman
and the Berliner group had been getting on very badly. The
flaws in the tripartite division of the gramophone business
had grown increasingly evident. Too many people were
cutting a slice out of the profits, and Seaman argued that
National Gramophone's slice was too thin. In reply, the
Berliner group blithely took the position that Seaman had

signed a contract in good faith and should live up to its terms.

That was far from the last word on the matter, as the Berliner people were to learn to their dismay. An entrepreneur as self-assured and knowledgeable as Frank Seaman, who was well accustomed to picking his way through the involutions of business practice and relished the rough-and-tumble of the market place, was not likely to take no for an answer, especially when it came from men who were relative amateurs in the world of commerce. But for a time he was preoccupied with fighting the American Graphophone Company. Philip Mauro's subtle, expert bill of complaint had convinced Judge Lacombe of the Circuit Court in New York. In November, delivering an opinion that the gramophone infringed a fundamental patent of the American Graphophone Company, he granted a temporary restraining order against Seaman to go into effect on January 25, 1899. Seaman appealed Lacombe's decision without delay, and two months later the Court of Appeals set aside the preliminary injunction so as to permit the whole case to be heard in greater detail. A full-scale legal battle impended; meanwhile, business could be carried on as usual.

If one considers Seaman's position in the spring of 1899 from his own vantage point, his subsequent actions become more understandable. Largely through his own merchandising genius, he had built up the gramophone business in three years to a thriving million-dollar industry. Nevertheless, he was entirely dependent on the Berliner Gramophone Company for his source of supply and was obliged to purchase merchandise at what he considered an inflated price. So long as Berliner controlled the gramophone patents, Seaman's hands were tied. But the basic validity of those patents was being questioned; and if the gramophone patents were indeed to be disallowed by the courts, what need was there to deal any longer with the Berliner group or to suffer any further from their inhibiting monopoly?

In March 1899, Seaman transformed the National Gramophone Company, of New York, into the National Gramophone Corporation, of Yonkers, raising the capitalization from $200,000 to $800,000. He assumed the office of treasurer; Frank J. Dunham was president and Orville D. LaDow secretary. Next, a subsidiary called the Universal Talking Machine Company was organized, with the same Orville D. LaDow as president. Under the supervision of a mechanic named DeValque, Universal set up a factory in New York City for the manufacture of gramophones. In mid-summer *The Phonoscope* reported that "they are rushing machines through for the fall business and expect to be able to commence deliveries about September 15th."

While these machinations were in progress, Seaman continued to do business in Berliner gramophones from his old offices at Broadway and Eighteenth Street. Throughout 1899 he carried on the same barrage of advertisements eulogizing the virtues of the Improved Gramophone. That year Seaman opened branch offices in Boston, Chicago, Cincinnati, Cleveland, Philadelphia, and Providence. Business was better than ever; the Berliner assembling plant in Philadelphia and the Johnson shop in Camden were hard put to keep pace with the demand. Indeed, the gramophone had proved such a profitable venture that Johnson was erecting a new four-story factory in Camden to take care of the ever increasing orders.

Suddenly, in October 1899, the orders from Seaman stopped. The blow could not have been unexpected in Philadelphia. Had not *The Phonoscope* given advance notice that the Universal Talking Machine Company was in production and would begin deliveries in mid-September? It seems that the Berliner company had neglected to foresee the consequences of this activity. While Berliner's business came to a headlong and unwelcome halt, Seaman—livelier than ever—began advertising his new machine, which he called the Zonophone. It was a heavier instrument than the Improved Gramophone (its designer put more emphasis on gingerbread decoration than Johnson did), and the spring motor was enclosed within the case instead of being mounted at the rear. These were minor deviations; essentially, the Zonophone was an imitation gramophone. But this fact did not deter Seaman from advertising in bold letters that the "Zonophone is substituted for the Gramophone, which is abandoned, including its name." Curiously enough, the National Gramophone Corporation, which sold the Zonophone, left *its* name intact.

Seaman had not yet done his worst to the dazed and incredulous Berliner people. The *coup de grâce* was to come in the courts. Since January 1899, the American Graphophone Company had been threatening Seaman's very existence with its suit over the validity of the Berliner patents. Now that Seaman had deserted Berliner, there was no longer need to contest the action. He threw in the sponge and on May 5, 1900, accepted an injunction by consent: Seaman admitted in court that his erstwhile opponents were in the right, that the gramophone patents *did* infringe the "floating stylus" principle. Two weeks later came the announcement that an important alliance for legal protection and commercial advantage had been consummated between the National Gramophone Corporation and Universal Talking Machine Company on the one hand and the American Graphophone Company and Columbia Phonograph Company on the other; thenceforth the Zonophone would be manufactured and sold under the protection of the joint patents of all parties to the agreement, exclusive rights to its manufacture having been granted by the American Graphophone Company. The announcement further claimed that, without the patents rights controlled by the parties to the agreement, no disc talking machine could be legally marketed in the United States.

The claim was justified: by June 25, Seaman had persuaded the court to issue an injunction against the Berliner Gramophone Company restraining it from dealings in gramophone merchandise.

The redoubtable Frank Seaman had thus not only withdrawn his business from the Berliner company and commenced manufacture of a competing instrument, but had also made it legally impossible for the Berliner people to sell their own merchandise. Down in Washington the gramophone's inventor, Emile Berliner, spluttered with indignation. The patent-holding United States Gramophone Company took advertising space to tell its side of the story:

> We own the Letters Patent for the Gramophone and its Indestructible Record Discs. These patents have never been attacked, nor have Gramophones and Records made under them ever been declared infringements, except through judgments *confessed* by a former agent of the Gramophone; such judgments have no legal value. The Gramophone patents cover all Talking Machines in which the record groove propels the stylus, and in which hard-pressed discs are used.

But fume as Berliner would, his patents were commercially worthless so long as the injunction was on the books. In league with stockholders of the Berliner Gramophone Company, he instituted lawsuits against the Universal Talking Machine Company, the National Gramophone Corporation, and Frank Seaman personally, for infringements of patents, damages, and an accounting. Berliner and the Philadelphia stockholders could afford to wait until the matter was adjudicated: none of them was dependent on the gramophone for a livelihood. For Eldridge Johnson, on the other hand, the situation was infinitely more precarious. Not only had he just completed a large factory for manufacturing gramophones, but he found himself with $50,000 worth of unpaid-for merchandise that had been ordered by the Berliner Company before the secession of Seaman. Johnson had put his every penny into the gramophone business; if he was to stave off bankruptcy, he had to start selling gramophones himself.

For some time, Johnson had been keeping a trump up his sleeve. Like any listener with critical ears, he had been dissatisfied with the gramophone's quality of tone and powers of articulation. At first he had reproached the sound box; but though he developed an improvement over the original Berliner sound box, the trouble was only partly ameliorated. He decided in due course that the poor tonal quality inhered more in the records than in the reproducing apparatus; and in 1897 he began making secret experiments in the art of recording, employing a process that combined the wax engraving method of Bell-Tainter with the lateral-cut disc of Berliner. Berliner himself had always shied clear of wax; he felt that the wax recording medium clearly pertained to the Bell-Tainter patents; besides, he believed that his method of recording on zinc was every bit as good. Johnson did not agree; he had examined Berliner's master records under the microscope and had seen the jagged acid-etched grooves that were largely responsible for the gramophone's raucous, scratchy sound. Altogether, two years of slow progress were to elapse before he could develop a satisfactory method of converting an original wax recording into a reverse metal stamper. It was time well spent. When Johnson heard the brighter, smoother sound of his wax-recorded pressings, he knew that—whether he had trespassed on other patents or not —this was the only satisfactory way of making gramophone records.

Faced with the problem of breaking into the gramophone business singlehanded, Johnson decided to play the trump he had been hiding. He set up his own business, the Consolidated Talking Machine Company, and hired Leon F. Douglass, a high-strung promoter with ten years' experience in the talking-machine business, to sell the goods. Douglass pro-

posed to splurge half of Johnson's $5,000 capital on advertis-
ing. Although a great gamble, the campaign Douglass
envisioned had much to recommend it, and Johnson gave
his assent. He was always to be a fanatical believer in advertising. In the fall of 1900, Consolidated's advertisements
appeared in the large national magazines. "Gramophone
Records FREE," the headline of one read, and then in
smaller print: "A Marvelous Discovery has just been made in
our Laboratory in the art of making records. The results are
so startling and the improvements so great that we have
decided to give every owner of a Gramophone one of these
new records free. Send us the number of your Gramophone
and we will send you by return mail a record that will surprise and please you." The advertisement also established
Consolidated's credentials: "Our factory has made all the
genuine Gramophones sold in the world." In other advertisements, Douglass touted the Johnson line of gramophones,
which ranged from a hand-driven toy model at $3.00 to the
well-tried Improved Gramophone at $25. Slowly, the large
inventory in Camden began to be translated into cash. At the
end of 1900, Consolidated's business was still just gaining
momentum, but its intake was sufficient to keep Johnson
from the hands of his creditors.

With the arrival of the new year came a fresh blow from
Seaman. In the courts he charged that Johnson's business
was a thinly disguised subsidiary of the Berliner Gramophone Company; he asked for an injunction halting Consolidated's manufacture of gramophones and preventing its
further use of the word "gramophone." Johnson himself
went before the judge to plead against the granting of the
injunction. His entire enterprise was at stake, and he presented his case in his deliberate Yankee drawl with profound
conviction. This time, in a Philadelphia court, the decision
went against Seaman. The injunction halting manufacture
was refused. Only in one particular did Seaman get his way:

the court did agree to enjoin Johnson from use of the word "gramophone." Even that decision was reversed in the Court of Appeals two months later. But Johnson did not take advantage of the reversal. The word "gramophone" really belonged to Berliner, and at the moment Johnson's relations with Berliner were uncertain. He decided to use a name all his own and he chose Victor—Victor Talking Machines and Victor Records. It was euphonious and evocative of success.

No one could have guessed it at the time, but as Eldridge R. Johnson strode out of that Philadelphia courtroom on March 1, 1901, the talking machine in America had come of age.

7 EUROPE WELCOMES THE TALKING MACHINE

WITHIN THREE MONTHS OF THE PHONOGRAPH'S DEBUT IN America, a tin-foil instrument had been sent to Paris for exhibition to incredulous members of the Académie des Sciences. At about the same time another tin-foil phonograph was demonstrated to equally incredulous Londoners at the Royal Institution. Throughout that intoxicating spring and summer of 1878 periodicals in France and England filled their pages with articles describing the new invention and limning its celestial potentialities. But Europeans proved to be just as inconstant in their affections as Americans. Once its novelty had been dissipated by repeated demonstration and a surfeit of publicity, the phonograph was forgotten; interest in it did not revive until the arrival of the improved wax-cylinder apparatus a decade later.

In the renaissance of 1888, Edison again took care that his phonograph should be well introduced to European society. His British agent, Colonel G. E. Gouraud, put the new model on display at that prime rendezvous of Victorian art and industry, the Crystal Palace, and tempted several illustrious Englishmen to immortalize their voices in wax. Among Gouraud's willing victims were William Ewart Gladstone (an Edison admirer of long standing), Cardinal Manning, Alfred Tennyson, and Robert Browning. In Germany, Edison had an agent no less ambitious, who brought off a private demonstration before the Kaiser and induced the aging Bismarck to record a cylinder. One day in 1889, Edison's German agent set up his apparatus in a music room at No. 4 Carlsgasse, Vienna, and recorded Johannes Brahms playing a *Hungarian Rhapsody*. This cylinder came to light in Germany in 1935; but according to those who heard it then, the sound of Brahms's piano was barely audible.

Such coups were more a testimonial to the zeal of Edison's missionaries than an indication of any widespread European interest in the wax-cylinder apparatus. Until the mid-Nineties, Europe remained on the periphery of phonographic affairs and depended solely on exports from American factories. These exports were funneled through the Edison-Bell Company, of London, which was licensed to import both Edison and Graphophone merchandise. This firm did not succeed in endearing the phonograph to the British masses. An American correspondent writing for *The Phonoscope* in 1898 reported a dearth of phonograph displays in store windows and the utter absence of coin-slot parlors in the large cities of England and Scotland. He blamed the dreary situation on Edison-Bell's exorbitant price scale. Phonograph merchandise imported into England was pegged at almost twice the price of the same equipment in the United States. The Edison Standard Phonograph at £7 sterling did not appeal greatly to the average British householder, who was glad to bring home £2 a week.

In France things were livelier by far. An industry that took root in a *bistro* near the rowdy Place Pigalle in Paris was bound to be lively. The establishment was run by Charles and Emile Pathé, two enterprising brothers in their twenties who were firm believers in the "better mousetrap" theory of business. One day the elder brother, Charles, saw an Edison phonograph, in action at the annual Vincennes Fair, surrounded by a crowd of wide-eyed onlookers. The Pathés decided to use the same bait in their *bar américain;*

if the phonograph drew crowds at Vincennes, perhaps it could also draw them on the rue Fontaine. The new acquisition, which they imported from England, did indeed attract customers—but not only for alcoholic potables. Many a patron who began by ordering a Pernod ended by offering to buy the phonograph. This turn of events was unforeseen, but not unwelcome. In Belleville, an outlying *faubourg,* the brothers located a machine shop that could turn out a reasonable facsimile of the Edison phonograph at a reasonable price, and they soon gave up dispensing Pernods in favor of merchandising Les Phonographes Pathé. That same year, 1894, the Pathés built a small factory in the suburb of Chatou to meet an increasing demand for cylinder blanks. Chatou remains to this day the center of the French record industry.

At the end of the century, Pathé's Belleville plant was employing two hundred workmen in a vain attempt to keep up with orders for "Le Coq," a cheap cylinder instrument modeled closely on the Eagle Graphophone. So popular did the "Cock" become that the swaggering bird was adopted as Pathé's trademark. It could be seen and heard for years at the beginning of Pathé newsreels. As the "Cocks" multiplied, so did orders for cylinders; out in Chatou some hundred and fifty factory hands were busily manufacturing wax blanks and shipping them all over Europe. The headquarters at 98 rue de Richelieu, from which the Pathés governed their fast-expanding empire, served also as a recording studio. Singers from the near-by Opéra and Opéra-Comique paid regular visits to the Pathé studio from 1896 on. Few of them had international reputations (French opera singers rarely do), but they were respected figures in the musical life of Paris— Gustarello Affre, Maximilien-Nicolas Bouvet, Adolphe Maréchal, Léon Melchissédec, and Albert Vaguet. Music-hall entertainers trooped into the rue de Richelieu studio also, among them the rising young star at the Gaîté-Rochechouart,

Charlus, who would record forty songs in the morning, take time out for a revivifying lunch, and then record forty more in the afternoon. Pathé cylinders, duplicated pantographically as in America, ranged from 1.25 francs to 2 francs (25¢ to 40¢ at the time); by 1899 there were fifteen hundred titles to choose from in the catalogue.

Every one of them could be heard in Pathé's remarkable Salon du Phonographe on the Boulevard des Italiens. Nothing like it existed elsewhere. The Salon was a palatial emporium, beautified by thick carpeting, red plush, and polished mahogany, in which top-hatted *boulevardiers* could be found day and night sampling the latest tunes. There were rows of richly upholstered easy chairs, each facing an ornate mahogany cabinet from which protruded a pair of hearing tubes, a coin slot, and a dialing device. When the customer had chosen a title from the catalogue, he dropped a fifteen-centime token in the slot, dialed the desired record number, and put the tubes to his ears. A minion below ground would scurry to the record bins for the appropriate cylinder and put it on a phonograph connected to the ear tubes. The whole process, from dropping of token to beginning of music, was supposed never to exceed ten seconds. This high-class automat of music was patronized alike by easygoing gentlemen with an hour or more to kill and frugal *midinettes* with an eye for inexpensive entertainment. Its takings on an average day amounted to a thousand francs.

Thanks to the influence of Pathé Frères, wax cylinders flourished in France as nowhere else in Europe. As early as 1897 the Columbia Phonograph Company had acknowledged the French predilection for cylinder merchandise by locating its first foreign office in Paris. By the turn of the century, phonograph factories were springing up hopefully all over Germany; but they soon ran into competition from the gramophone and were to wither as quickly as they had sprouted. In Italy, phonographic activity was confined at first mainly to the *bar automatico*—or coin-slot parlor—where popular *canzoni* and standard opera arias could be heard for ten centesimi each. Later the Anglo-Italian Commerce Company was formed, with offices at 6 via Dante in Milan, and for several years it played an important role in cisalpine phonograph history. This company, of which tantalizingly little is known today, relied for its operatic repertoire on members of Milan's several opera houses. One of these was a tenor in his late twenties who had made a wondrous impression on the Milanese public in Giordano's *Fedora*. His name was Enrico Caruso. No one has been able to say with assurance just when Caruso recorded his three A.I.C.C. cylinders; most experts incline to late 1900 or early 1901. Whatever their date, the cylinders are competent reproductions of a voice which, though light and immature, is unmistakably Caruso's. Anglo-Italian had a reciprocal agreement with Pathé Frères, giving the French company permission to issue A.I.C.C. recordings outside Italy on the Pathé label. Caruso's subsequent fame prompted Pathé to keep his early cylinder recordings in the catalogue long after all other A.I.C.C. titles had been deleted and forgotten, and long after the Anglo-Italian Commerce Company itself had gone out of business.

By 1901, in Europe as in America, the wax cylinder was fast losing ground to the advancing gramophone disc. Indeed, the disparity between the two media was even more noticeable in Europe, for with the exception of France the wax cylinder had never really taken firm root, whereas the gramophone—after the abortive Waltershausen "toy" venture of 1890—had met with instantaneous and widespread approval. Much of its early success must be credited to the vision of an ex-lawyer turned promoter who journeyed to England in 1897 with the grand plan of organizing there a company to control the sale of gramophones throughout the whole of Europe. He was William Barry Owen, the son of a New Bedford whaling captain, who had worked for a while with the National Gramophone Company and had learned the ins and outs of the business under the volatile aegis of Frank Seaman. Armed with permission to negotiate the European sale of Berliner's patent rights, Owen sailed for London and established himself in high style at the Hotel Cecil. Potential investors came and saw the gramophone but were not conquered. Probably memories of the crude Waltershausen instruments discouraged British capitalists, though Owen—with Eldridge Johnson's Improved Gramophone to demonstrate—must have presented powerful counterarguments. After nearly a year of unsuccessful efforts, Owen was introduced to E. Trevor Williams, a young man of means and connections who saw a future in the gramophone and was able to gather together a group of willing investors. In May 1898, the Gramophone Company was formed with a working capital of £15,000 and the exclusive rights to sell gramophone merchandise throughout Europe. William Barry Owen was named managing director, and headquarters were established in the basement of a small building at 31 Maiden Lane, just off the Strand and within easy walking distance of the Hotel Cecil.

The new company was not disposed to fritter away its small capital on expensive installations. Gramophone parts were to be manufactured in Camden by Eldridge Johnson, shipped to England, and assembled in London under the supervision of Belford Royal, one of Johnson's close friends and an experienced mechanic. The Gramophone Company would make its own recordings, but the discs were to be pressed in a plant erected at the Berliner family's expense. In July 1898, Fred Gaisberg and Joseph Sanders, a nephew of Berliner's, sailed for England, the one to take charge of recording, the other to build a pressing plant. Both were in their twenties, and both were already veterans in the infant gramophone business. On arrival in London, Gaisberg claimed a small room in the Maiden Lane building and began converting it into a recording studio. Sanders went on to Hanover, where Emile Berliner's brother Joseph, the proprietor of the Telephon-Fabrik Berliner, had agreed to put up a pressing plant. (There had been some talk of locating the plant in England, near the headquarters of the company, but young Sanders feared the strongly organized British trade unions and was in addition a staunch supporter of German efficiency.) Four hydraulic record presses, imported from America, arrived in Hanover in the autumn of 1898, before even German efficiency had been able to finish erecting the factory. Sanders set them up beneath a large tent and began manufacturing shellac discs alfresco from zinc masters that Fred Gaisberg had already recorded in London. Early in 1899 the Hanover plant was ready for full-scale operation; equipped with fourteen presses and ancillary apparatus, it was the first factory in the world to be devoted solely to the manufacture of gramophone records. The German-made discs looked very much like their American counterparts. They were seven inches in diameter, and the information as to title and recording artist was etched into the center of the record. Paper labels were still to come.

With the arrival of shipments from Hanover and Camden in the fall of 1898, William Barry Owen proceeded to treat Great Britain to the kind of shock tactics he had learned at home from Frank Seaman. He was one of the first advertisers to take full pages in London newspapers, and he observed none of the customary British reticence in his layouts and copy. The Owen frontal assault introduced the British to the gramophone with a minimum of social punctilio; once the two were acquainted, it became a matter of love at first sight. Never had the gramophone been so well received. Sales billowed mightily as Christmas approached, and by mid-December the Gramophone Company was completely sold out of machines and records. Buoyed by prosperity, Owen lost no time in expanding the size of his domain.

While the Hanover factory was still half built, a branch—
Deutsche Grammophon A.G.—opened up in Berlin, and
from this two subbranches in Russia and Austria were soon
formed. In May 1899, the Compagnie Française du Gramophone was organized in Paris, and it too spawned a sub-
branch, in Spain. At the head of the French branch was
Alfred Clark, whose gramophone career had taken him far
afield since the days when he presided over the Berliner Company's retail store in Philadelphia.

One day in 1899 a slim, bearded gentleman, shabby but
proper, ventured into the Gramophone Company's Maiden
Lane office and inquired if he might borrow a brass horn.
He wanted it, he said, for a picture he was painting and
would return it within a fortnight. The caller was sent up
to see Owen. He introduced himself as Francis Barraud and
told Owen that he was an artist by profession and a frequent
exhibitor at the Royal Academy; his painting "An Encore
Too Many" had been purchased not long before by the Liverpool Art Gallery. There was, he confided, a little story
attached to his request for a brass horn. Several years earlier
he had painted a picture of his fox terrier listening to an
Edison phonograph. He called it "His Master's Voice." An
appealing scene, he had always thought—but no one had
shown much interest in it. The canvas had been gathering
dust for years when a friend of his saw it and suggested that
he bring it up to date by substituting one of the new brass
gramophone horns for the old-fashioned black japanned horn
on the Edison machine. It would brighten the picture considerably. Owen asked the artist to bring along his picture
when he returned the horn. A few days later Barraud duly
arrived with the painting under his arm. The picture, Owen
agreed, was certainly appealing, and he offered to buy it if
Barraud would paint out the Edison phonograph and substitute an Improved Gramophone. Barraud was only too
glad to oblige, but he did not quite eradicate all traces of

his original brushwork. The painting hangs today in the Gramophone Company's head office in Hayes, Middlesex, and a close scrutiny of it will reveal a phantom phonograph buried deep in the impasto beneath the glistening gramophone that took its place.

It was typical of William Barry Owen's erratic brilliance that he should have purchased this memorable *objet d'art* only to leave it hanging on the wall. The Gramophone Company already had a trademark, an angel writing with a quill on a gramophone disc. Every record pressed in Hanover carried an image of the "recording angel"; so did the literature and advertisements sponsored by the company. Owen did not fancy changing trademarks in midstream, and his philosophy so influenced the Gramophone Company that the dog was not permitted on its records until 1909.* For Eldridge Johnson, on the other hand, Barraud's little fox terrier seemed eminently promotable. Emile Berliner had seen the picture in London and had taken out a United States copyright on it in July 1900. Johnson began using it soon thereafter in his very first advertisements for the Consolidated Talking Machine Company. He also put the dog's picture on his records, printing it on the new paper labels that he introduced in 1900 as an improvement over the old Berliner method of molding record information right into the shellac. Barraud's dog did not live to see the whole civilized world appreciate him at his true worth. Nipper had died in 1895, *aetat.* eleven, four years before his picture was purchased by the Gramophone Company. But as is man's way, a later generation tried to make amends for previous neglect. The dog had been buried under a mulberry tree on Eden Street, Kingston-on-Thames, and in 1949 the Gramophone Company belatedly decided to honor the site with a plaque. Today Nipper is properly eulogized in brass, on

* In 1953 the "recording angel" trademark was revived for an export brand, Angel Records, manufactured by the British company.

the façade of a bank which has since displaced the mulberry tree of hallowed memory. As for Francis Barraud, he lived another quarter century to the age of sixty-eight and earned a comfortable competence painting replicas of "His Master's Voice."

The purchase of Barraud's picture, whatever its future implications, was of small moment when William Barry Owen and his backers examined the total reckoning for the year 1899. They had cause for jubilation. Within twelve months of its founding, the Gramophone Company had expanded so greatly that it was necessary to take over the entire building at 31 Maiden Lane. During the Christmas rush of 1899 even this space proved inadequate, and the employees often were obliged to work from eight in the morning until midnight to cope with the press of business. With sales accumulating at such a giddy rate, the Gramophone Company could finance a recording program of unprecedented scope. Gaisberg's first recordings, issued toward the end of 1898, had been made in London; appropriately enough, the band from Owen's favorite Hotel Cecil tooted away on many of the early seven-inchers. By the time the initial English issues were on the market, Gaisberg and an assistant, another young American, had set off with their zinc disc recording equipment on a trip through Europe—the first of many similar trips. They went to Paris, Madrid, and Milan, to Leipzig, Vienna, and Budapest, recording a bewilderingly varied repertoire with profligate abandon. No sooner had the etching acid done its work than the zinc masters would be rushed to Hanover, where stampers would be made and great batches of records pressed, boxed, and shipped to the markets for which they were intended. By 1900 the Gramophone Company was advertising a choice of five thousand recordings. They were listed in a series of small catalogues printed on cheap colored paper, each one covering a particular segment of the gramophonic prism; there were separate lists of English, Scotch, Irish, Welsh, French, German, Italian, Spanish, Viennese, Hungarian, Russian, Persian, Hindi, Sikh, Urdu, Arabic, and Hebrew records. Unlike its ally in America, the Gramophone Company evinced a high regard from the very start for serious music, especially operatic music. The Italian catalogue put special emphasis on opera: by early 1900 all the major arias and duets—and a fair number of minor ones too —could be found in its pages. They were performed, as were the A.I.C.C. cylinders, by singers of established reputation in Italy, though not of international celebrity. Familiar names in the turn-of-the-century Italian lists were Bice Adami, soprano, Giovanni Cesarani, tenor, and Ferruccio Corradetti, baritone. The German and French catalogues also gave more than a cursory nod to the operatic repertoire, with Rudolf Berger and Paul Knüpfer represented in the one, Léon Melchissédec, Jean Noté, and Hubert Paty in the other. The coarse and wayward sound of these acid-etched recordings greatly vitiated their musical significance. Moreover, the short playing time of the seven-inch discs necessitated merciless curtailment of all but the briefest arias; and even in truncated form, they were subject to such further assaults of musical mayhem as a profusion of wrong notes or the utter incompatibility of soloist and accompanist. The queasy music-lover of 1900, once he had been unnerved by a croaking montage of *"Celeste Aida,"* might well have turned with relief to the less exacting repertoire in the Gramophone Company's lists—racy *chansonettes* from Paris, waltzes and assorted varieties of vocal *Schwärmerei* from Vienna and Berlin, gypsy music from Budapest, and music-hall songs from London.

Eldridge Johnson, whose American-made gramophones were being marketed throughout Europe, was discovering that in the burgeoning English firm he had a prime source of revenue. The Gramophone Company bought the rights to his secret wax recording process for $15,000 and soon thereafter adopted his paper record-label. Both began to be used in Europe in 1900. One of the early results of the wax recording process was a series of operatic excerpts recorded in Milan by the tenor Carlo Caffetto, the baritone Aurelio Viale, and the basso Franchi with orchestral accompaniment. They were issued in the autumn of 1900. Acoustically they were so imperfect that the company quickly reverted to piano accompaniment. Six more years elapsed before recordings with orchestral accompaniment were attempted on a large scale.

In 1900 William Barry Owen began to wonder how long this profitable business could keep up. He became obsessed with the certainty that the gramophone craze was a bubble about to be punctured. As a hedge against disaster, he persuaded his associates to branch out into another field totally unrelated to the talking machine. Their choice ultimately fell on the Lambert Typewriter, a device that employed a rotating disc in place of the normal keyboard. On December 12, 1900, the company was renamed the Gramophone & Typewriter Ltd. and was recapitalized at £600,000. Among its assets was the factory in Hanover, which Joseph Berliner made over to the new company in return for a substantial block of shares. The subsidiary business that Owen had recommended turned out to be both unsuccessful and unnecessary. The Lambert's sole superiority lay in price: it sold far more cheaply than any other typewriter on the market. But the typist needed so much more time and energy to twirl its dial than to depress the keys of an ordinary machine that the commercial world paid it small heed. Eventually, the principle of the rotating dial was adopted for toy typewriters, but this was small comfort to the Gramophone Company, which had given up the Lambert as a bad job in 1904. The unsound venture was one of several *gaffes* that forced Owen's resignation from the company he had formed. By 1905 he was back in the United States raising chickens on Martha's Vineyard. He died a poor man.

Fortunately, the income from gramophones and records was so great that the company could easily absorb a loss on the typewriter. Some of its biggest dividends emanated from the branch in Russia, which had been organized in 1898 as an offshoot of the Deutsche Grammophon Company and which showed such signs of vitality that a separate pressing plant was erected in Riga solely to service the needs of the Russian market. By 1900 there were gramophone shops in every large Russian city, among them a particularly lordly establishment on Nevsky Prospect in St. Petersburg run by a shrewd merchant named Rappaport. His store was softly carpeted and equipped with richly ornamental furniture, potted palms, and other sybaritic appurtenances. Everything had an air of the *haut monde*—except the merchandise. Rappaport implored the Gramophone Company to record leading singers from the Imperial Opera and to sell their recordings in a de luxe—and costly—edition. To achieve the proper patrician air in all details, he suggested that the discs bear red labels, setting them off from the ordinary black-label issues by gypsy singers, comedians, and the like. The company took his advice and in 1901 issued the first examples of what were to become known as Red Label Records. They were ten-inch discs (among the first of this size to be made) and were sold for the equivalent of $5.00 each. Among the singers chosen to launch the new series were Feodor Chaliapin, then twenty-eight years old and already a leading basso at the Imperial Opera, and a husband-and-wife team, Medea Mei-Figner and Nicola Figner, mezzo-soprano and tenor, who recorded both singly and in duo. The Figners were Italian-trained singers who had settled in Russia in 1887 and remained for years reigning favorites at the Imperial Opera. The role of Lisa in Tchaikovsky's *Pique Dame* was created by Medea Mei-Figner, whose 1901 recording of the

Act III aria constitutes an early example of a "creator's record," that is, a record by an artist associated with the first performance of a musical composition. The link with Tchaikovsky is not the Figners' only claim to the attention of posterity. A year before they went to Russia, the Figners had toured in South America as members of a traveling opera company. Midway in the tour, in Rio di Janeiro, one of the company's cellists made an astounding last-minute debut as a conductor. He was Arturo Toscanini. When the troupe returned to Italy, it was Nicola Figner who arranged for Toscanini's first assignment in his native land (in Alfredo Catalani's *Edmea*, November 4, 1886). Unfortunately, the metal masters of the historic recordings by the Figners have disappeared, and there are precious few remaining copies of the original shellac pressings.

News of the successful Red Label venture in Russia was soon forwarded to the head office in London, and plans were drawn up to extend the issue of high-priced celebrity records throughout all of Europe. It was with this in mind that Gaisberg and Owen set off in March 1902 for Milan and a rendezvous with the man who was to become the gramophone's most precious asset.

8 *A MUSICAL INSTRUMENT*

AT THE TEATRO LA SCALA IN MID-MARCH 1902 THE MAIN topics of conversation were Baron Franchetti's new opera *Germania,* which had its world *première* on March 11, and the tenor Enrico Caruso, who sang the part of Frederico Loewe. In his thirtieth year Caruso was on the threshold of international celebrity. He had already sung at St. Petersburg, Monte Carlo, and Buenos Aires, and would shortly make his debut in London's Covent Garden opera house. Reports of his prowess had been relayed to William Barry Owen and Fred Gaisberg, and they were both in the audience at the second performance of *Germania* to judge the young tenor for themselves. They did not delay coming to a conclusion. Early in the opera Frederico Loewe makes a stirring appeal to his assembled cohorts in the aria *"Studenti, udite."* Caruso carried it off magnificently; and as the audience at La Scala stamped their feet in tumultuous approval, the two gramophone scouts were convinced they had found a singer full worthy of a place on the Red Label roster. "We went backstage," Gaisberg has related, "and talked to Caruso. There were many hangers-on present and each had a word to say or obstructions to raise just as we were on the point of coming to an agreement. Actually, once terms were fixed the greatest difficulty was to steal a few hours in the tenor's busy program to record the ten songs selected."

Early in the afternoon of March 18, Caruso presented himself at the Hotel di Milano, in company with a pianist, Sal-

114

vatore Cottone, and the Gramophone Company's Milan agent, Alfred Michaelis. There a room had been turned into an improvised recording studio and equipped with an upright piano, set up high on packing cases, which faced a tin bell-shaped horn suspended five feet from the floor. Caruso dispatched the ten arias as fast as Gaisberg could put wax blanks on his machine, and they were rushed to Hanover for processing. The records were an immediate success, both artistic and commercial. It is generally agreed today that Caruso's Milan series of March 1902 were the first completely satisfactory gramophone records to be made. Caruso's strong voice and slightly baritonal quality helped drown out the surface noise inherent in the early discs, and his vocal timbre seemed peculiarly attuned to the characteristics of the acoustic recording diaphragm. "He was," Gaisberg says, "the answer to a recording man's dream." Even on the inadequate reproducers of the time, his records sounded rich and vibrant; and in addition they offered performances of surpassing beauty and artistic refinement. Five of the ten masters made at this session have remained in perfect condition, and records from them are still being manufactured by the Gramophone Company in England. For his ten records in March 1902, Caruso was paid a flat sum of £100. Before his death in 1921 he was to earn over $2,000,000 from the gramophone.

Other singers, even more famous at the time, were making recordings in the Gramophone Company's home studio in London. They had been persuaded to do so by Landon Ronald (later Sir Landon Ronald), an English accompanist and conductor then in his late twenties whose association with the company began when he recorded a piano transcription of the *"Liebestod"* on a seven-inch disc in 1900. Even as a young man he was closely connected with many prominent musicians. He had an extraordinary flair for accompanying and coaching, and was consequently much in demand. William Barry Owen, relying on one of his more successful intuitions, marked him down as a man pre-eminently suited to combat the prejudice of serious musical artists against the gramophone. In 1901, Ronald began working for the Gramophone Company as musical adviser, a post that he held until his death in 1938. The first musician of note whom he corralled into the recording studio was the Welsh tenor Ben Davies, "the robust and eupeptic Ivanhoe" of 1891 (according to Bernard Shaw), who by 1901 had given up opera in favor of oratorio and recital. Davies clung longer to an active career than almost any singer in the history of music; his last records were made in 1933, when he was seventy-five.

But bigger game was in store for the decisive year 1902, when the Gramophone Company committed itself intensively to the Red Label program. In the spring of that year Landon Ronald was able to secure recordings from a group of Covent Garden's most illustrious stars: Pol Plançon, the French basso with coloratura agility and great elegance of style; the baritones Maurice Renaud and Antonio Scotti; the sopranos Suzanne Adams and Emma Calvé. Madame Calvé, who endowed opera roles with an abundance of Latin temperament, did not abate her vivacity when it came time to make recordings. Taken to the door of the Maiden Lane building in a luxurious four-wheeler by Landon Ronald, she at first refused to budge from the carriage. Dismayed at the shabby appearance of the building and the sinister atmosphere of the narrow street, she cried out: "Never in my life will I enter such a place. It is a tavern—not a manufactory. I shall be robbed there. You have brought me to a thieves' den." Ronald was inured to the outbursts of prima donnas and knew well how to cope with this one; he excused himself for a moment, ran into the accountant's office, and returned bearing the company's payment for Calvé's services (one hundred guineas for six records). This acted as a strong restorative, and soon she was upstairs—ready to perform for the gramophone. But the troubles had only begun. She had the disconcerting habit of commenting on her performance in the midst of a recording—even uttering shrieks of joy or groans of disgust, depending on whether she had turned a particular phrase to her liking—and in the *"Séguedille"* from *Carmen* she insisted on dancing in front of the recording horn just as she was wont to do on stage. Despite her antics, Calvé's 1902 recordings came off fairly creditably, though their improvisatory quality seems rather grotesque beside the studio-perfect renditions that we are accustomed to hearing on records today.

In September 1902, the Gramophone Company published its first Red Label catalogue, an expensive-looking brochure printed on heavy paper and generously illustrated with pictures of Red Label artists. Except for the violinist Jan Kubelik, the musicians represented therein were all opera singers. It was, after all, the Golden Age of Opera, an epoch when no mere instrumentalist could approach the glamorous aura of a cherished singer. Moreover, the recording technique then in use dealt far more kindly with the human voice than with musical instruments, either solo or in ensemble, a fact which the company was quick to perceive and exploit. Not every operatic celebrity of the day could be found in the first Red Label catalogue, but there were enough spine-shivering names to show that the talking machine had finally found respectability as a medium of musical communication. Recordings made before 1902 can be classified as incunabula—much of it experimental, some of it interesting, only a little of it valuable in musical terms. Beginning with Caruso's recordings in March 1902, the instrument at last began living up to the claims that had been made for it with such reckless generosity during the preceding quarter century. It was no longer an ad writer's fancy, it was demonstrable fact: "the most enchanting selections of the world's greatest singers" could in truth be heard in the home—and for only ten shillings a record.

The list of Red Label recording artists burgeoned glitteringly throughout 1903. While Fred Gaisberg was off in the Far East spreading the sound of the gramophone from Bombay to Tokyo, his fellow recorders were covering the Continent and capturing trophies of the loftiest musical order. In Warsaw they secured a series of records from the baritone Mattia Battistini, a wonderful exponent of *bel canto* whose antipathy to sea travel made him refuse all offers from America. Sessions in Milan yielded further records by Caruso and by another tenor of equal *réclame*, Fernando de Lucia, the original Canio in *Pagliacci* at London's Covent Garden and at the Metropolitan Opera, who sang with a strong sense of personal style if not always with scrupulous regard for the composer's markings. In Rome the recording apparatus was taken to the Sistine Chapel, and there the last of the great *castrati*, Alessandro Moreschi, bequeathed to unborn generations the eerie bleat of the male soprano. Felia Litvinne, a statuesque diva noted for her intense projection of the more robust soprano roles (she was the first Isolde in Paris), went before the recording horn to commit nine songs and arias to wax; her accompanist in the Paris studio was twenty-six-year-old Alfred Cortot, who was still making records for the Gramophone Company a half century later. From Paris also came a series of discs by the baritone Victor Maurel, a singing actor of uncommon elegance and intelligence, who had been chosen by Verdi sixteen years earlier to create the role of Iago in *Otello;* one of his 1903 Red Label records was the aria *"Era la notte"* from that opera. In London the Gramophone Company enticed into the studio the veteran Charles Santley, a baritone with a history of opera and oratorio performances dating back to 1857. A mint copy of *"Non più andrai"* recorded by Santley in 1903 at the age of sixty-nine was sold shortly after World War II to a collector in California for $400.

The greatest coup of all that year was the series of recordings made by Francesco Tamagno, the prototype of the *tenore robusto* and the singer who had created the role of Otello in Verdi's penultimate opera, a massive man with a massive voice somewhat nasal in quality but powerful and distinctive. In 1899 he had given his last opera performance and thereafter lived in semiretirement, restricting himself to a few concerts a year. Despite his bull-like physique, Tamagno developed a bad heart early in life; he died in 1905 of angina pectoris, at the age of fifty-four. Alfred Michaelis negotiated a contract with him in December 1902. It was the first gramophone contract embodying the royalty principle which Emile Berliner had forecast in his Franklin Institute address years before. Tamagno insisted that his records sell for £1 each and be affixed with a special "Tamagno Label"; he was to collect ten per cent of the retail price on each record sold, and in expectation of a rapid turnover the Gramophone Company paid him a cash advance of £2,000. Tamagno further stipulated that the recording sessions were to take place in his own villa so as to minimize the physical strain on him. Early in 1903, Fred Gaisberg's brother William, who had assisted at the Caruso session a year before, arrived at Tamagno's home in Ospedaletti and set up his equipment. During the course of three weeks Tamagno made thirty-five records, of which he approved nineteen for issue to the public. Five of them were the new twelve-inch records, which extended the playing time of a gramophone disc to four minutes.

The Tamagno records made their debut in April. William Barry Owen, with his flair for effective advertising, determined to make a selling point of their high price. He took a full page in the *Daily Telegraph* and lined the borders with a parade of £1 figures. The copy explained that the original seven-inch records were brought out at two shillings sixpence and had remained at that price, that the ten-inch "Concert" records had always been five shillings and the Red Label se-

ries ten shillings. But now came the great Tamagno and a
truly luxury record at £1; you could not expect to pay less
for it. To its dealers the Gramophone Company offered encouragement and advice:

> The £1 record has raised the whole tone of the gramo-
> phone business. It has brought into the trade new customers
> who will remain, if carefully nursed and judiciously at-
> tended to, a constant source of income to the dealer. In a
> nutshell, it has broken new ground. We have sowed the
> seed. Let us both reap the harvest.

The tone of the gramophone was indeed on the rise, both
literally and figuratively. A year later, in March 1904, the
Gramophone Company invited the London press to a re-
corded concert at the Hotel Metropole. The reports were
uniformly friendly. According to the *Westminster Gazette,*
"The records are not yet free from mechanical defects, but
they are marvellously better than they were a year ago."
Among the selections played at the press party was the aria
"Ah! fors è lui," which Nellie Melba had recorded privately
for her father in Australia only a few days before. Soon the
Gramophone Company, aided by the persuasive Landon
Ronald, had convinced Melba that her private recordings
should be issued to the public. The famous diva capitulated,
but on her own opulent terms. Fourteen twelve-inch discs
were put on sale in July 1904 at one guinea each (a shilling
more than Tamagno!) and with special "Melba Labels"
printed on mauve paper. Each record came in an individual
printed jacket, and the whole series was described in a handsome mauve booklet entitled "Melba and Her Gramophone
Records." Melba was forty-three at the time. She continued
to record for the Gramophone Company regularly until 1926.

The presence of Melba and Tamagno in the catalogue persuaded another astral member of musical society that the
gramophone merited serious attention. This personage was
the Baroness Cederström, better known to devotees of sing-

ing as Adelina Patti, an artist who truly deserved the much-abused appellation "legendary." Her operatic debut dated back to 1859 (at the Academy of Music, New York), and her subsequent musical dossier encompassed all the great opera houses of the nineteenth century. At the time of her first gramophone recordings Patti was living in seclusion in a drafty Welsh castle, Craig-y-Nos, enjoying the fortune she had amassed in the days when her services would cost an impresario $5,000 a performance. Toward the end of 1905, after two years of arduous negotiations, Patti agreed to make a series of records for the Gramophone Company. Like Tamagno, she insisted that the recording equipment be brought to her home and kept in readiness until she felt inclined to sing. This session, with Landon Ronald accompanying, yielded fourteen records of songs and arias. They were launched with great fanfare on February 8, 1906. The Gramophone Company placed advertisements announcing the event in two hundred British newspapers, and record stores festooned their windows with long streamers spelling out the news that "Patti Is Singing Here Today." Needless to say, the records carried a special "Patti Label" (pink) and were sold at a special price (twenty-one shillings). But all the hoopla could not disguise the fact that at sixty-two Patti was far more liberally endowed with reputation than with vocal ability.

The bastions of musical resistance were falling one by one. In France the energetic Alfred Clark set out to woo some of the composers prominent in Parisian musical life, sending them each a gramophone and a supply of hand-picked Red Label discs. Among those who responded with friendly attestations were Claude Debussy, Reynaldo Hahn, and Jules Massenet. Debussy expressed his appreciation of the gramophone's ability to confer on music *"une totale et minutieuse immortalité."* Indeed, he thought so highly of the invention that he ventured into the Gramophone Company's Paris studio in 1904 and accompanied the young Scottish soprano Mary Garden in some of his songs and in an excerpt from *Pelléas et Mélisande*.

The dividends of the Red Label program were not only artistic. Financially, the Gramophone Company prospered as no other talking-machine enterprise ever had. In 1901 the annual report showed a net profit of £79,348, in 1902 the figure had jumped to £137,268, and in 1903 it reached £252,285, or well over $1,000,000. To suggest that these mounting profits were directly attributable to the new emphasis on serious music and celebrity artists would overstate the case. Then as now the bulk of record sales were confined to ephemeral, popular music. But the Red Labels established the company and its trademark, gave it status, and pushed it well to the forefront of the talking-machine industry in Europe.

Its leadership did not go unchallenged for long. As might have been expected, competition came first from that arch-rival of the gramophone, the Zonophone. No sooner had Frank Seaman seceded from the Berliner group in 1899 than he began eying the transatlantic market with more than casual interest, and his attention strengthened as reports came in of the Gramophone Company's initial successes in England and on the Continent. Seaman realized that an invasion of Europe required an expert tactician, and he found one in the person of F. M. Prescott, a mild-mannered New Yorker in his mid-thirties who in the space of a few years had built up a thriving business exporting Edison phonographs. Swayed by Seaman's blandishments, Prescott withdrew his allegiance from the Edison machine and transferred it to the Zonophone, for which he was named exclusive export agent.

Prescott made the grand tour of Europe in 1899 and again in 1900, signing up local distributors and preaching the virtues of the Zonophone to all who would listen. But operating as he did from New York, it was difficult for him to make much headway against the Gramophone Company with its own European factory and its growing network of branches and subbranches. To join battle directly with the Gramophone Company, the Zonophone had to set up shop on the former's terrain; and for this purpose the International Zonophone Company was incorporated in 1901 with Prescott as managing director and Seaman as a principal stockholder. In May of that year Prescott sailed for Germany with three assistants: John D. Smoot, recording engineer, Raymond Gloetzner, matrix foreman, and Edward Pancoast, machinist. Each member of this trio had been employed previously by Berliner or Johnson and was thus initiated in the "secrets" of the wax recording process.

Prescott located the headquarters of International Zonophone in Berlin, at 71 Ritterstrasse, and lost no time in building up a repertoire of recordings to challenge the Gramophone Company's erstwhile monopoly of discs. He worked out an ingenious method of amassing an extensive catalogue with no great capital outlay. Zonophone agencies were appointed all over Europe; in France, for example, Prescott came to terms with Ch. & J. Ullmann Frères, a musical instrument firm, and in Italy the agent he chose was the Anglo-Italian Commerce Company, which saw its cylinder sales declining and wanted to break into the growing disc business. These various agents took charge of all matters relating to artists and repertoire in their respective territories and financed all recordings made under their auspices. International Zonophone manufactured the discs in its German factory and allowed a rebate on the wholesale cost to the agent until the recording expenses were repaid.

This scheme enabled Prescott to accumulate a representative catalogue in remarkably short time. Like the Gramophone Company, International Zonophone could boast of its own special roster of celebrity artists, whose records were graced with light-blue labels instead of the ordinary black labels of the less exalted, and less expensive, Zonophone regulars. The Light-Blue Zonophone series made its debut at about the same time as the Red Label series of the Gramophone Company; and since exclusive recording contracts were still to come, it is not surprising that the Zonophone and Gramophone lists often featured the same artists. Aïno Ackté, Emma Calvé, Enrico Caruso, Alice Cucini, Jean François Delmas, and Pol Plançon all recorded for both Zonophone and Gramophone during the same general period. Caruso's seven recordings, along with the other Italian records in Zonophone's catalogue, were made at the behest of the Anglo-Italian Commerce Company, Zonophone's Italian agent, which hired him, chose the repertoire, and underwrote the expenses. It was A.I.C.C. also which marketed the records throughout Europe; a contemporary advertisement in a German magazine urged readers to "order the Italian Catalogue of Zonophone Records direct from the Anglo-Italian Commerce Company, via Dante 6, Milano." Just when Caruso made his Zonophone records has never been established with finality, though most indications point to the late spring of 1902, or just after he made his first batch of Red Labels. Technically, they are inferior to the March 1902 series recorded by Fred Gaisberg; the voice is more distant and sounds curiously constricted. As with so many records that fetch fabulous prices in today's market, the worth of the Caruso Zonophones lies more in their rarity than in their intrinsic musical value.

By 1903 the Gramophone Company had started to feel the pinch of competition. Zonophone was not yet a serious rival, but it had potentialities for generating future trouble. At first the Gramophone Company tried to kill Prescott's business by patent litigation. When these tactics stalled, it turned to the alternative expedient of purchasing the Zonophone enterprise *in toto*. Seaman and his fellow stockholders in America were inclined to listen to any reasonable proposal. From

Berlin, F. M. Prescott had been sending letter after letter pleading with them for more capital; only by constant expansion, he warned, could the Zonophone keep up with its formidable competitor. To the stockholders in New York, however, an immediate short-term profit seemed infinitely preferable to the risks of a protracted foreign entanglement, and in the summer of 1903 they sold out their majority interest in the International Zonophone Company. The Gramophone Company thereafter operated Zonophone's thriving European business, but on a noncompetitive basis, the Zonophone celebrity records being taken out of circulation and the label used exclusively for low-priced discs. The American portion of the Zonophone empire was sold to Victor; it had never amounted to much except as a troublemaker, and after a short career as a Victor subsidiary it was liquidated. In Europe the Zonophone label survived until the 1930s. When it was ultimately retired, after three decades as a poor relation of the Gramophone Company, few people remembered the Zonophone's onetime eminence and its valiant attempt to rival the artistic distinction of the Red Label catalogue.

The demise of the International Zonophone Company left its managing director, F. M. Prescott, without a job. He created one forthwith by forming another record business, the International Talking Machine Company. His principal backer was the erstwhile Paris agency for the Zonophone, Ch. & J. Ullmann Frères; and in deference to the preponderance of French capital in his enterprise, he named his records after a famous theater in Paris, the Odéon. Prescott erected a factory in Weissensee, near Berlin, for there was no getting around Germany's superiority as a manufacturing center, and began marketing Odeon records and Odeon talking machines in 1904. The records made a profound impression when first exhibited to the trade at the Leipzig Fair that spring. They were double-faced. Up to then, gramophone records had been stamped on one side only. The reverse was wasted; it was either left entirely blank or embossed with a trademark. By pressing both sides of a record, Odeon offered double the amount of recorded entertainment per disc. It proved to be quite a selling point. Throughout Europe the double-faced Odeon records caught the public fancy beyond Prescott's most sanguine expectations, and his competitors were soon paying him the compliment of imitation. But the double-faced disc was not Odeon's only claim to distinction. Its early catalogues were affluently endowed with operatic excerpts expounded by leading artists of the French and German opera houses. Outdistancing all other Odeon artists in sheer renown was the soprano Lilli Lehmann, a singer of astonishing versatility who could cope equally with the florid roulades of Bellini and the robust heroics of Wagner. She had taken part in the first Bayreuth performances in 1876 and was a revered legatee of a past tradition when she recorded an extensive repertoire for Odeon between 1905 and 1907. Despite Lehmann's age (she was nearing sixty at the time), her voice still retained its supple, mercurial quality, and her records bear impressive testimony to the technique and musicianship that won such acclaim from her contemporaries. Another Odeon artist who recorded at about the same time as Lilli Lehmann was a young and very impecunious tenor from Ireland who would shortly blossom into a box-office attraction of magnificent dimensions. His name was John McCormack. Only glimmerings of the artistry he later developed can be detected in his Odeon discs.

One further European record company of consequence deserves mention: the Societá Italiana di Fonotipia, which began operations in Milan during the latter part of 1904. Fonotipia enjoyed the status of being the world's first record company to concern itself exclusively with serious musical repertoire. It was a purely European enterprise (as distinct from the Gramophone, Zonophone, and Odeon companies, with their American-born managers and technicians) and its board of directors was composed of men active in the high councils of European musical life: Harry Vincent Higgins, director of the grand opera syndicate at Covent Garden; Duke Umberto Visconti di Modrone, the president of La Scala, Milan; Tito Ricordi, the powerful Italian music publisher; and Baron Frédéric d'Erlanger, a composer of minor talent and a banker of major resources. For its artistic direction Fonotipia obtained the services of Umberto Giordano, the composer of *Andrea Chénier, Fedora,* and other operas of the *verismo* persuasion; and for its managing director the company secured the experienced Alfred Michaelis, formerly the Gramophone Company's Milan agent. With such talent in charge of its destinies, Fonotipia set an artistic standard that, record for record, has rarely been equaled. Its catalogue bristled with singers of the highest rank: the baritone Victor Maurel and the soprano Felia Litvinne, both renegades from the Gramophone Company's Red Label series; the French tenor Ernest van Dyck, who was nearing the end of a brilliant career that had started in 1888 with his portrayal of Parsifal in Bayreuth; the sopranos Rose Caron and Aïno Ackté. Fonotipia's greatest strength, however, lay with the Italians, the luminaries of La Scala *ante* World War I; among the notables in its Italian wing were the sopranos María Barrientos, Eugenia Burzio, and Giannini Russ, the tenors Giuseppe Anselmi, Alessandro Bonci, and Giovanni Zenatello, the baritones Pasquale Amato, Giuseppe de Luca, and Mario Sammarco. These singers were not obliged to perform only the regulation operatic arias when they entered Fonotipia's recording studio. Such they recorded in abundance, it is true, but they also delved into operatic fare well off the beaten track—arias from rarely performed operas and lesser-known solo and ensemble passages from the standard repertoire. Often Fonotipia would devote an entire side to the recitative preceding one of the familiar arias, a striking artistic advance in an industry that more often than not saw fit to abbreviate music whenever it ran inconsiderately long. Altogether, Fonotipia was a company to gladden the heart of any true music-lover. Unfortunately, if understandably, its records never sold on the epic scale of the Red Labels. They are exceedingly rare today. Fonotipia's two most famous records, as a matter of fact, have never turned up at all. They are the *"Scène du Tombeau"* from Gounod's *Roméo et Juliette* and the aria *"O souverain"* from Massenet's *Le Cid,* sung by the Polish tenor Jean de Reszke. We know that they were recorded in Paris on April 22, 1905, assigned catalogue numbers, and listed in the announcements of forthcoming Fonotipia discs. Yet they never made an appearance in the record stores. It is assumed that De Reszke was displeased with the test pressings of his recordings and would not consent to their publication. If such was indeed the case, he showed a keener regard for the verdict of posterity than many of his *confrères.* Jean de Reszke was the foremost singing actor of his time, perhaps of all time, a musician of intelligence and elegance and a stage personality with the power to electrify an audience. Even so demanding a critic as Bernard Shaw commended "the beauty of his voice, his sensitively good pronunciation, and the native grace and refinement of his bearing, all of which makes his manliness, his energy, and his fire quite irresistible." But by 1905, three years after his retirement from opera, De Reszke's "beauty of voice" had declined, and his magnetic personality and skillful deportment were wasted on the blind, impersonal recording horn. He decided to be remembered by the encomiums of his contemporaries rather than by the imperfect deposition of a gramophone record, vintage 1905. Posterity, however, with pardonable curiosity, has tried to outwit him. In 1937 an intensive search for the master stampers of De Reszke's recordings was made by the Carl Lindström Company, which had fallen heir to the assets and chattels left by the long-defunct Societá Italiana di Fonotipia. Nothing of De Reszke's could be found, and the projected posthumous issue of his records had to be given up. Shortly after World War II word got around of a collector in Paris who had somehow obtained a copy of De Reszke's *Roméo* recording. Inquirers were permitted to see the disc and examine its seemingly genuine label, but no one was allowed to hear it played. Until that happens, its authenticity must be open to question.

Do the pulses of mid-twentieth-century readers quicken at the very mention of these operatic personages who ruled supreme when the century was in its infancy? If not, the events just related must perforce lose the impact they had on those who experienced them directly. Today the opera singer has fallen precipitously from his erstwhile regal heights: as the reigning representative of the musical muse, he has been displaced by the virtuoso orchestra conductor; and as the awesome figure of glamour and arbiter of fashion, he has given way to the Hollywood movie star. But at the turn of the century the opera singer was at the peak of his glory. Adelina Patti, Nellie Melba, Lilli Lehmann, Francesco Tamagno, Victor Maurel, Mattia Battistini, Pol Plançon—these were more than gifted vocalists, they were objects of adoration, creatures who inhabited an exhilarating and resplendent society. That by the end of 1905 they had been enticed into the recording studio to perform for the lowly "talker" was a fact of immeasurable significance. They mellowed the gramophone with the patina of high art. Emile Berliner's invention had arrived in Europe in 1898 a raw and uncultured immigrant, full of promise and inherent ability, but lacking polish and refinement, and denied access to the higher reaches of society. In seven years it had been transformed by the Old World which adopted it. The impact of European civilization had turned the gramophone into a musical instrument.

9 VICTOR MAKES A DEBUT

THE TRANSATLANTIC METAMORPHOSIS OF THE GRAMOPHONE into a machine of respectable musical attainments was to have far-reaching repercussions in America. But before this influence could take effect, the American gramophone industry had to resolve its patent troubles and settle down into some kind of orderly commerce. Certainly the tumultuous atmosphere of 1901 was not conducive to wooing the muse. It was a time of intense legal scrimmaging. In March of that year the United States Circuit Court in Philadelphia had sustained Eldridge Johnson's right to manufacture and sell gramophones, and in so doing had delivered a telling blow to Frank Seaman's ambitious plans for the piratical Zonophone. Soon after, the Zonophone fortunes had declined even further when Emile Berliner's lawyers succeeded in raising the infamous Seaman injunction of June 25, 1900, that shrewd piece of legal legerdemain masterminded by the Graphophone lawyer, Philip Mauro, who had wrested control of the gramophone from the very man who invented it. Thanks to the redress of legal justice, Emile Berliner could once again call his patent his own.

But was he really in a position to exercise sovereignty over the embattled gramophone? A new power in the person of Eldridge Johnson had emerged during Berliner's year of enforced idleness and was now to be reckoned with. Johnson's relations with Berliner had always been cordial; never was there any question but that Johnson recognized Berliner's

130

patent and his rights to royalties. Still, the situation in mid-1901 was skitteringly delicate. Although Berliner owned the basic patent, Johnson had contributed substantially to the invention. He had furnished it with a motor and an improved sound box and had developed a successful process for recording discs in wax. Overriding all other considerations were the physical facts of Johnson's factory and sales organization: he controlled a going business, Berliner merely controlled a patent.

While the two men negotiated, Johnson's sales surged steadily upward. He was at last beginning to reap the benefits from his unquestioned genius for manufacture. Half of his production was contracted for by the Gramophone Company in London, at terms of cost plus twenty-five per cent profit. Booming sales in America were easily keeping the rest of the Camden plant working at capacity. By September 1901, a year after Johnson had started selling gramophones on his own, his twelve-month net profit had reached the staggering total of $180,000.

In six years the Camden modelmaker had come a long way. And he was content to call a halt. Johnson had never wanted to become an industrial tycoon; the pressures of big business were not to his liking, and he welcomed the chance to sell out and retire on the proceeds. But it was not to be. Although he offered his business in its entirety to the Berliner group, they could not (or would not) raise sufficient funds to purchase his interests. A multitude of counterproposals were entertained and rejected. At last Berliner and Johnson agreed on a plan calling for the formation of a new corporation under Johnson's management in which the Berliner people were to receive forty per cent of the common stock and Johnson most of the remainder. For their share in the company, Berliner and his associates contributed the gramophone patents; for his share, Johnson contributed the plant, a flourishing business, and his own services. The new enterprise was incorporated on October 3, 1901, and named the Victor Talking Machine Company.

Victor was no sooner launched than it struck a reef in the treacherous waters of the Patent Office. The news that came from Washington could not have been more unexpected, or more disquieting. On December 10, 1901, the Patent Office announced the awarding of Patent No. 688,739 to Joseph W. Jones for a method of recording sound that was, in all essential details, identical to Johnson's own wax recording process. Johnson himself had never applied for a patent; his lawyers had advised against it on the assumption that the basic Bell-Tainter patent of 1886 covered all types of recording in wax. Now a fledgling in his early twenties had proved the lawyers wrong and become the patentee of a crucial Victor asset. Joseph W. Jones had spent a summer vacation back in the mid-Nineties, in the early days of the gramophone, working as a chore boy in Berliner's Washington laboratory. While there he had kept his eyes open and had been quick to perceive that wax, and not zinc, was the predestined medium for effective gramophone recording. Being young, unencumbered, and audacious, he wrote out a patent claim for engraving a groove of even depth on a wax blank and filed it on November 19, 1897. Four years and twenty-one days later the Patent Office acted favorably upon it.

Immediately, the cunning wizardry of Philip Mauro burst again upon the scene. Mauro had lost the first round in his fight with the gramophone and its inventor; the injunctions against Berliner and Johnson had failed, and in the aftermath of that defeat the Graphophone-Zonophone alliance had been dissolved. Seeing that the gramophone could not be stopped in the courts, the Graphophone Company had decided to manufacture a competing gramophone-type instrument and to challenge Victor in the market place. In view of the vaulting sales of Victor talking machines and the decline of cylinders in the public esteem, there was no time to lose. But the patent problem remained to be hurdled. Any disc machine manufactured by the Graphophone Company was sure to invade Berliner's gramophone patent. Mauro had attempted for three years to upset the validity of that patent, and he had failed to convince the courts. Undaunted, he looked about for another truncheon; and with a sage appreciation of its ultimate worth, he fastened on Patent No. 688,739 and bought it from young Joe Jones for the sum of $25,000.

By January 1902, the Graphophone factory in Bridgeport was in full production turning out the Columbia Disc Graphophone in three models ranging from $15 to $30. Records were also being manufactured, the seven-inch size selling for fifty cents, the ten-inch for a dollar. "They are," said the ad writer, "the sweetest, smoothest, and most brilliant records ever heard. Until you listen to them you can form no accurate idea of the progress that has been made in bringing the disc records to the point of perfection. Their excellence is fully equalled by their durability." Needless to say, the Columbia Disc Graphophone was a flagrant violation of the Berliner-Victor gramophone patent. On the other hand, Victor records now clearly infringed the Jones-Graphophone wax recording patent. Each side prepared to sue the other in a legal battle to the finish. But the suits never got to court. Instead, Victor and the Graphophone Company agreed to compose their legal differences and pool their patents. It was the only sensible course to take. Together, the two companies controlled every important patent bearing on the manufacture of disc machines and records. To fight out each patent on its merits would have meant long and costly litigation. The Victor-Columbia patent pool allowed each company to concentrate instead on more productive pursuits, and between them they achieved a dominance in the American phonograph industry that endured for more than half a century.

The attentive reader will have noticed in the last sentence the word "phonograph" in a context that clearly points to the disc talking machine, or "gramophone." The usage was intentional, for it reflects the increasingly confused talking-machine terminology that prevailed in America from about 1902 on. During the 1890s the vocabulary had been precise. "Gramophone" had referred to the apparatus employing flat discs, "phonograph" to the apparatus employing cylinders, while "Graphophone" was the trade name for the phonographs manufactured by the American Graphophone Company and sold by its subsidiary, the Columbia Phonograph Company. These clear verbal distinctions were soon muddied. In 1900, Eldridge Johnson decided to drop the word "gramophone" from his advertising and to refer to his product instead as the Victor Talking Machine, or simply the Victor. As a result, "gramophone" eventually disappeared from the American language.* Shortly after Johnson's rejection of the word "gramophone," the Columbia Phonograph Company confounded the terminology still further with its advertisements of a "Disc Graphophone"—which was a "gramophone" sold by a "phonograph" company and called a "graphophone." The terms introduced by Edison, Bell-Tainter, and Berliner to designate their particular inventions having lost their pristine meanings, the way was clear for usage to assert itself. In time the American language adopted the word "phonograph" and applied it indiscriminately to all varieties of talking machines—in which generic sense it will be used hereafter in these pages.

Any doubts left about public acceptance of the flat disc in America were dispelled by the tide of business in 1902.

* Though not from the English.

There were certainly no grounds for complaint at Victor, where—despite competition from Columbia—sales continued to expand at a hurtling pace; the company boasted of more than ten thousand dealers, and at the end of 1902 its ledgers showed a profit of close to $1,000,000. That year saw the first appearance of a new Victor instrument embodying one of Eldridge Johnson's prime refinements: the tone arm, a device which allowed the sound box to be coupled to the metal horn without having to support its weight. This made for easier handling and reduced record wear. The tone arm contributed also to improved sound, according to advertising copy which insisted that the new Victor "has become, more than ever, a musical instrument."

But there was still little of musical consequence to play on it when Victor compiled its first cumulative catalogue in 1902. There were the beginnings, it is true, of a diversified vocal repertoire in its pages. For example, Signor Carlos Francisco, baritone, was represented by some well-loved Italian opera arias and songs; the baritone Herbert Goddard was to be heard in English song repertoire; and another baritone listed merely as M. Fernand had recorded a good selection of French opera arias and songs. Any similarity between the voices of these gentlemen was distinctly not coincidental, for they were all pseudonyms of a young man from Brooklyn named Emilio de Gogorza, who was to become one of the great recording artists of all time. Listening to De Gogorza's records of 1902 and before, it is easy to understand why he was so prominently featured (albeit under various *noms de disque*) in the early Victor catalogue, for his recordings have a vibrancy and a clarity unusual for their time. Like Caruso, he had the kind of vocal projection that seemed ordained for the recording horn. In addition to De Gogorza's efforts, several soprano arias had been rendered for Victor by Rosalia Chalia, a Cuban singer who was one of Bettini's lesser lights, and specimens of the tenor literature were available in performances by the old Berliner stand-by Ferruccio Giannini. But all this was a pale echo of what was being accomplished in Europe by such glamorous artists as Caruso and Calvé, Scotti and Plançon, and it was at best only an insignificant side line in Victor's over-all operation, not to be compared to the contributions of Harry MacDonough (whose fervent renditions of "The Holy City" and "Lead Kindly Light" were among Victor's all-time best sellers), Dan Quinn, the Haydn Male Quartet, and—most important of all—Sousa's Band. Apropos of Sousa, it is worth recording here his testimonial, the apotheosis of understatement, which Victor plugged for all it was worth:

> DEAR MR. JOHNSON: Your Victor Talking Machines are all right.
>
> JOHN PHILIP SOUSA

Columbia—Victor's new competitor—was at first equally laggard in its attention to the higher reaches of musical endeavor. But early in 1903 this company took bold steps to repair that dereliction. Some of the most highly paid singers from the Metropolitan Opera were to be seen in the vicinity of Columbia's recording studio, and rumors began to circulate of intoxicating musical glories entrapped in wax. By mid-March the factory in Bridgeport was producing finished records and in April the company took full-page advertisements to "announce a most extraordinary achievement marking an epoch in the art of recording and reproducing sound." The achievement was not quite so epochal as Columbia intimated, for the Gramophone Company in Europe had done the real pioneering more than a year before, but it was still an important venture: a series of Grand Opera Records, selling at $2.00 per ten-inch disc, which called on the services of Edouard de Reszke, Marcella Sembrich, Ernestine Schumann-Heink, Suzanne Adams, Charles Gilibert, Giuseppe Campanari, and Antonio Scotti, all of them luminaries at the opera house on Broadway and Thirty-ninth Street. Columbia's publicity spoke of "long experiment and vast expenditures of time and money." Of the latter there is no doubt. Columbia was made to pay dearly for the services of its stars. Marcella Sembrich, who recorded arias from *Ernani* and *La Traviata* together with a vocal arrangement of Johann Strauss's *Voices of Spring,* received $3,000 for three discs; and the basso Edouard de Reszke was paid $1,000, also for three discs. Unfortunately, in view of the investment involved, Columbia was to learn that the talent for producing a clear and resonant disc did not automatically come with a four-figure fee. None of the thirty-two records issued was a downright fiasco, but the general level of Columbia's Grand Opera series did not do justice to the musicians involved and the money disbursed.

The Grand Opera series had been on sale for less than a month when Victor parried with a rival line of celebrity discs, announcing it with characteristic *panache* in a double-spread advertisement in the *Saturday Evening Post.* The matrix-exchange agreement that Johnson had previously negotiated with the Gramophone Company was now bearing fruit; Victor's opening celebrity release of May 1903 consisted entirely of Gramophone Company recordings. Like their counterparts manufactured in Hanover, the pressings from Camden bore red labels, or "red seals" as Victor preferred to call them. Seven of Caruso's Milan recordings were offered, along with some of the 1902 London recordings of Calvé, Plançon, and Renaud.

In addition to issuing these imports, Victor initiated a celebrity recording program of its own based in America. For the convenience of musical artists, a small, high-ceilinged room in Carnegie Hall (Studio 826) facing on Seventh Avenue was rented and converted into a recording studio; and there on April 30, 1903, the first Victor Red Seal recording session took place. For this historic event Victor inconsiderately engaged a singer who turned out to be one of the most inconspicuous of Red Seal artists. She was Ada Crossley, an Australian contralto of the sturdy oratorio persuasion who turned up regularly at choral festivals in England and Australia. Her debut recital in New York on February 6, 1903, had elicited critical praise for her "large fresh natural voice" plus the observation that "for temperament Miss Crossley substitutes intelligence." She recorded four sides for Victor with C. H. H. Booth playing the piano accompaniments: Giordano's "Caro mio ben," Reynaldo Hahn's "Paysage," and two English songs of ephemeral interest. They were excellent discs, artistically sung and—for their period—well recorded; but Ada Crossley was never recalled to the Victor studio (later on she made a few recordings in England for the Pathé label) and never achieved much of a reputation in the United States, save posthumously for her historic role as the first Red Seal recording artist.

The singer engaged for the second Red Seal session on May 17, the mezzo-soprano Zélie de Lussan, had a similarly unproductive history as a recorder—only five sides for Victor and four for a minor German concern of pre-World War I vintage named Beka—this despite De Lussan's connection with the leading opera companies and despite her international reputation (second only to Calvé's) as an interpreter of Carmen. Beginning in September, however, with the resumption of Red Seal recording sessions after a summer recess, the Carnegie Hall studio was visited by some singers who were to be Victor "regulars" for years to come, among them Louise Homer, Johanna Gadski, Antonio Scotti, and Caruso. Victor signed its first contract with Caruso on January 28, 1904, just two months after his Metropolitan debut, and made a series of recordings (ten sides altogether, including Caruso's first twelve-inch discs) in the Carnegie Hall studio on February 1.* For his ten recordings Caruso was paid $4,000; in addition, the contract stipulated that the tenor was to receive $2,000 a year for the next five years in consideration whereof he agreed to make records for no other firm (the associated Gramophone Company excepted). Very obviously, Victor was in the celebrity record business to stay.

Meanwhile, Columbia had sailed into foul weather with its much-touted Grand Opera Records. Buyers had responded to the hallowed names of Sembrich, Schumann-Heink, *et al.* far less enthusiastically at $2.00 a disc than was expected, and sales were further deterred by the poor tonal quality of the recordings. Considered solely from an accounting standpoint, the series was a failure: a substantial cash investment was paying most insubstantial cash dividends. Edward D. Easton, the hardheaded president of Columbia, drew the hardheaded conclusion that high-priced celebrity records were an unsound commercial proposition. By his edict, the Grand Opera series of recordings ground to an abrupt halt and the thirty-two discs issued with such ambitious plans were allowed to fall into oblivion. Easton's decision could not have been more ill-advised. He could not have known, of course, that the Edouard de Reszke records which sold for $2.00 in 1903 would be valued at $150 a half century later, but he should have realized that the dollars-and-cents value of a celebrity series could not be measured solely in terms of the records themselves. The fact that De Reszke had recorded for Columbia was worth far more to the company than the immediate profits from his discs; his name in the Columbia catalogue lent an aura to its entire line of phono-

---

* Two months later the Victor engineers decided that a room flanked on either side by noisy vocal studios was no place to make records. The Carnegie Hall lease was canceled and the recording equipment moved to 234 Fifth Avenue. Most Red Seal sessions were held there until 1907, when a special recording studio was opened on Victor's home territory in Camden. Many, many years later Victor sent its engineers back to Carnegie Hall to record another great Italian musician, Arturo Toscanini, whose professional career antedated Caruso's by eight years and who was still performing, and making records, thirty-three years after the tenor's death.

graphs and records. Easton, failing to perceive this, dropped his high-priced artists with undisguised haste and thereby surrendered—to Victor—Columbia's precious head start. It was a costly mistake. Easton's company re-entered the celebrity record business five years later and endeavored to make up for lost time, but not until the 1940s did Columbia offer troublesome competition to its formidable rival in the American market.

10 *THE RED SEAL EPOCH*

ALTHOUGH THE VICTOR RED SEAL ISSUES OF 1903 AND 1904 were recorded more successfully than the Columbia Grand Opera series, there is no reason to believe that Victor's early sales were much more remunerative than those of the opposition. But to Eldridge Johnson this was a matter of small concern. Unlike Columbia's Edward Easton, he did not boggle at the discrepancy between cash investment and immediate return that, superficially, made celebrity recording appear to be a losing proposition. An immediate return was not Johnson's primary interest. To be sure, he felt reasonably certain that the Red Seal Records would in time show a profit strictly on their own account. But even if they did not, he knew he was getting his money's worth. For Johnson was determined to turn his company into an American institution, to make the Victor pre-eminent among phonographs as the Steinway was pre-eminent among pianos; and in this exaltation the Red Seal Record was to play a leading role. "Caruso, the greatest tenor of modern times, makes records only for the Victor," an early advertisement rejoiced. Reading this, how could a prospective customer doubt the corollary, that the Victor was "the greatest musical instrument in the world"?

The rationale of the Red Seal Record was plainly set forth in a series of four advertisements that appeared in the October 15, 1905, issue of *Talking Machine World*, a trade monthly. Bordering each of these advertisements were pho-

141

tographs of Victor recording artists. "Three show pictures of operatic artists," the Victor Company explained; "one shows pictures of popular artists. Three to one—our business is just the other way, and more, too; *but there is good advertising in Grand Opera.*" And what ambitious advertising it was! No matter what magazine or newspaper one opened, there was sure to be a large picture of the "Victor Dog" and an announcement of the latest operatic issues. On the roof of an office building at Thirty-seventh Street and Broadway in New York, Victor erected a huge facsimile, fifty feet square, of Barraud's "His Master's Voice" painting. Hundreds of electric light bulbs made it visible at night; and it was not purely by accident that Victor located its sign in the immediate neighborhood of the Metropolitan Opera House. Advertising became almost a mania with Johnson. The more his business improved, the more he relied upon it. By 1912, Victor's annual advertising budget was to surpass $1,500,000.

Throughout 1904 and 1905 Victor sales leaped higher and higher. In August 1905 (the dullest month of the year), Victor reported a $275,000 increase in sales over August 1904, and at the end of the year the books showed a total business in excess of $12,000,000. Profits were plowed right back—into advertising, plant expansion, and the record catalogue. Bit by bit Victor's engineers had been improving the acoustic recording process, making records that were louder, smoother, and less scratchy. Indeed, the wax-process discs that had sounded so lifelike in 1901 and 1902 seemed almost antediluvian by 1905. In April of that year Victor was able to announce a thorough revamping of its catalogue:

> We began more than a year ago to remake or withdraw every record in our catalogue which failed to come up to the new Victor standard. This work, which has cost us more than $100,000, is now completed. . . . The Victor Company has made it possible, for the first time in talking-machine history, for a buyer to order a record and be absolutely certain that it is a perfect one.

Perfect? Not if compared to the recordings of a half century later. But at a time when successful recording was still in the hit-or-miss phase, the "Victor standard" meant a great deal. Caruso's records quickly became the mainstay of the Red Seal series. His second visit to the Victor studio, in February 1905, netted five more discs—again with piano accompaniment—and his fruitful collaboration with Victor encouraged other artists to join the Red Seal enterprise: Marcella Sembrich, the "intelligent, ladylike, and somewhat cold" American soprano Emma Eames,* and the French basso Marcel Journet, all of whom were in the Victor catalogue by the end of 1905. Another Victor artist of this period deserving of mention is the Russian singer Marie Michailowa, of whom a Victor copy writer maintained that "no soprano in the world, perhaps, has a voice so perfectly adapted to the work of record-making." He was right; purely in terms of tonal quality her records were far superior to those of Sembrich or Eames. Michailowa never came to America (Victor made domestic pressings from masters recorded by the Gramophone Company in St. Petersburg), but she was a familiar singer to thousands of collectors who bought her best-selling recordings of *"Caro nome"* and the *Lucia* "Mad Scene." She was the first, but by no means the last, European musician to attain a transatlantic reputation by means of the phonograph.

The history of a burgeoning commercial enterprise resembles in many ways the growth of a plant: there is a period when it takes root and sends up a sturdy, healthy stalk, and then there is a period when it breaks into bloom. The flowering of the Victor Company can be assigned to the year 1906. It began in February when Caruso made his first recordings with orchestral accompaniment, five operatic arias—*"Di quella pira"* from *Il Trovatore,* *"Spirto gentil"* from *La Favorita,* *"M'appari"* from *Martha,* *"Che gelida manina"* from *La Bohème,* and *"Salut demeure"* from *Faust.* Not

---

* The description, again, is Bernard Shaw's.

much of an orchestra could be grouped around the recording horn; and it was often necessary to rearrange the composer's instrumentation so as to bring the accompaniment within the limited compass of the acoustic recording process. A special violin with an attached horn had to be employed (the so-called Stroh violin, a shrewish-sounding instrument) which focused tones directly on the recording horn. Cellists and

CARUSO RECORDING FOR VICTOR—
A Self-Caricature

wind instrumentalists were obliged to stand on high chairs or stools to be "heard" at all by the unresponsive mechanism. It was like making music in a sardine can. But the results, though far from the sound of a "live" orchestra, were more evocative of opera-house atmosphere than the former piano-accompanied recordings. In addition to being orchestrally accompanied, the Caruso recordings of February 1906 were made with an improved technique—more forward-sounding and mellifluous than anything previously attempted. At the time, they were touted as "unquestionably the most wonderful specimens of recording which the Victor Company has ever issued . . . a little louder in volume than the 1905 records, but perfectly smooth, and so natural that it seems to be Caruso himself singing to you instead of a machine." The earlier discs by Caruso soon became collectors' items, but those from 1906 on have remained common phonographic staples. Thousands of them exist in original single-face Red Seal pressings, and they are still valuable properties in the current Victor catalogue.*

In March 1906 Victor recorded its first Red Seal duet—"*Solenne in quest' ora*," from *La Forza del Destino*, sung by Caruso and Scotti. For years it was the best seller in the Red Seal list. One of the reasons for its popularity had nothing to do with the extraordinary interpretative quality of the recording itself. There was a remarkable similarity between the low register of Caruso's voice and Scotti's natural baritone timbre; and in the opening measures of this duet, record listeners found it impossible to distinguish between the two singers. Was it Caruso who sang the first phrase, or Scotti? It became a question of national interest. Eventually, Victor decided the controversy by printing on the blank side of Record 89001 the musical notation of these opening measures so that all could know who was singing what.

Clearly, the Red Seal Record was a musical force to be reckoned with. But whatever might be said of the phonograph's increasing importance as a medium of music, it could not be described as a handsome instrument. The whirling turntable, the metal tone arm, the huge flared horns (they grew bigger every year) were attributes of a device that could be called efficient but hardly graceful. Many a fussy American housewife simply refused to have one in the house. To conquer her objections, Eldridge Johnson had set a crew of engineers and mechanics to work designing a phonograph that would be accepted, like the piano, as a fine piece of

* During his lifetime Caruso received approximately $2,000,000 in royalties from his Victor recordings. Since his death the tenor's estate has received an equivalent sum from the same source. When RCA Victor re-released a series of Caruso records in 1951, they sold nearly a million of them.

furniture. The prototype was already developed in the late spring of 1906, and in September of that decisive year initial shipments went out to dealers. The new instrument was a four-foot high console, made of "piano-finished" mahogany, with the horn pointed downward and entirely enclosed in the cabinet, and with a lid that kept the turntable and tone arm out of sight. It was called the Victrola, retailed for a very fancy price ($200), and immediately created the sensation that its sponsors had predicted. By November the Victor Company had to admit that it could supply only a small percentage of the orders for Victrolas that were spilling into Camden. Single telegraphic orders for as many as two hundred instruments were received from dealers within days of the Victrola's unveiling. They could not possibly be filled. Preparations were under way for quadrupling the production of Victrolas. Meanwhile the public would have to get in line and wait.

America had, indeed, accepted the talking machine without reserve. To some observers it was an infatuation fraught with worrisome consequences. One of these was, paradoxically, that habitué of the recording studio, John Philip Sousa, who fired an anti-phonograph broadside in the form of an article—"The Menace of Mechanical Music"—published in *Appleton's Magazine*. "Sweeping across the country," Sousa thundered, "with the speed of a transient fashion in slang or Panama hats, political war cries or popular novels, comes now the mechanical device to sing for us a song or play for us a piano, in substitute for human skill, intelligence, and soul. Only by harking back to the day of the roller skate or the bicycle craze, when sports of admitted utility ran to extravagance and virtual madness, can we find a parallel to the way in which these ingenious instruments have invaded the land." Sousa foresaw "a marked deterioration in American music and musical taste, an interruption in the musical development of the country, and a host of other injuries to music in its artistic manifestations, by virtue—or rather by vice—of the multiplication of the various music-reproducing machines." He admitted that "their mechanism has been steadily and marvelously improved"; but though "the ingenuity of a phonograph's mechanism may incite the inventive genius to its improvement, I could not imagine that a performance by it would ever inspire embryotic [*sic*] Mendelssohns, Beethovens, Mozarts, and Wagners to the acquirement of technical skill, or to the grasp of human possibilities in the art. . . . Under such conditions the tide of amateurism cannot but recede, until there will be left only the mechanical device and the professional executant. Singing will no longer be a fine accomplishment; vocal exercises will be out of vogue! Then what of the national throat? Will it not weaken? What of the national chest? Will it not shrink?"

Sousa's indictment of "canned music" provoked a storm of debate pro and con the phonograph. One of its defenders was Henry T. Finck, a prolific author and the music critic of the New York *Evening Post* from 1881 to 1924. He cited United States Census Bureau figures indicating an increase of fifty-seven per cent in the value of pianos produced in 1905 over the output in 1900. Surely, he argued, this did not betoken an ebb in the tide of amateurism. And as for a decline in taste, "it is a little difficult to see what there is to blunt in the musical sense of a nation which makes a hero of Sousa, paying him $50,000 for a mediocre march not worth $50." Indeed, Finck maintained that he "would rather hear Sousa's band in one of these superior phonographs than in the concert hall, because the record makes it less noisy while at the same time preserving the peculiar quality or tone color of every instrument and soloist as well as every detail of expression." Were there artistic nuances that the phonograph record was unable to transmit? Yes, Finck granted, but what of it? "I feel," he wrote, "in regard to phonographs as I do in regard to mountain railways in Switzerland. Being able to climb mountains easily, I have little use for them; but I am glad that they make the glories of the Alps accessible to thousands who could never know them without the aid of the railways. And the highest peaks still remain sacred to the professional climbers."

Sousa's jeremiad did nothing to interrupt the phonograph's inexorable invasion of the American home. In 1906, when his fulminations were uttered, the phonograph was already impregnable. A few die-hards might view it with dismay, just as certain malcontents were to deride television in the mid-1950s, but they were perverse souls divorced from the majority. In this prosperous and receptive atmosphere Red Seal Records throve magnificently. Across the land, in towns where opera companies had never set foot, a growing clientele for standard arias and ensembles was to be found patronizing Victor's ten thousand authorized dealers. It would be hard to say how much of this trade derived from a genuine desire for good music. There was, aesthetic satisfaction aside, a redolent snob appeal attached to Red Seal Records. They were expensive, and expensive in an autocratically stratified way. Red Seal artists were ranked, monetarily speaking, according to their eminence. Thus, "The Last Rose of Summer" could be heard on four twelve-inch Red Seal discs, single-sided of course, priced variously from $5.00 to $1.50, depending on whether it was Patti, Tetrazzini, Sembrich, or Alice Nielsen who sang. Quantity as well as quality entered into the calculations. Caruso's twelve-inch solo records sold for $3.00; but when he sang duets with other Red Seal artists, the price went up to $4.00 (excepting only his one duet with Melba, "O soave fanciulla" from La Bohème, which sold for $5.00). When Victor brought out its first recording of the Quartet from Rigoletto in March 1907 (with Caruso, Scotti, Bessie Abbott, and Louise Homer), it charged $6.00 for four singers—and four minutes of music. A year later, when the *Lucia* Sextet was added to the catalogue, the buyer had to part with $7.00 for the warblings *en masse* of Sembrich, Caruso, Scotti, Journet, Severina, and Daddi. Since a dollar bill, *circa* 1910, would buy a seven-course dinner at a first-class restaurant, it can be appreciated that the *Lucia* Sextet at $7.00 represented considerably more than a casual purchase made by the head of the family on his way home to dinner.* A collection of Red Seal Records established one as a person of both taste and property. Along with the leather-bound sets of Dickens, Thackeray, and Oliver Wendell Holmes, Victor Red Seals became a customary adjunct of the refined American parlor, to be displayed with becoming pride to impressionable guests and relations.

Whatever the underlying impetus, there resulted a priceless catalogue of operatic mementos diffused throughout the country to a large and avid public. The center of celebrity operatic recording had shifted increasingly from Europe to the United States. Caruso, Melba, Plançon, Calvé, Destinn, Farrar, Ruffo, and McCormack, all of whom had begun their recording careers in Europe, transferred their allegiance to the uniquely endowed Victor Talking Machine Company. European collectors were not thereby deprived—for the allied Gramophone Company made pressings on its own label from Victor matrices—but the initiative had passed to America and the developing repertoire reflected the musical scene in New York.

By 1912 the Red Seal catalogue contained some six hundred different recordings. To the untutored listener it presented an embarrassment of riches, tantalizing and at the

---

* The Victor people were well aware that $7.00 was an exorbitant price for a single-sided four-minute record, but they knew also that a $7.00 record had great publicity value. In an aside to the trade, Victor confided: "Do not underestimate the value of the Sextet as an advertising medium. This feature of the record is very much more valuable to the average dealer than the actual profit he may make on its sales. Not all of your customers can afford to purchase a $7.00 record, but the mere announcement of it will bring them to your store as a magnet attracts steel."

same time frustrating in its diversity. As a guide to this strange world of musical literature the Victor Company published *The Victor Book of the Opera,* a 375-page volume in its first edition (1912), printed on excellent paper and unstintingly illustrated, which was sold for seventy-five cents. It gave the stories of seventy operas (written, by Samuel H. Rous, with enviable clarity and concision), translated the major arias, and listed—at the appropriate places in the synopses—the various Victor recordings available. In its early editions *The Victor Book* proclaimed the virtues of the records thus encountered; and when an aria was recorded in several interpretations, the author bestowed his encomiums with the utmost finesse. For example, in the 1912 edition there were six versions listed of the *Lucia* "Mad Scene," sung by Luisa Tetrazzini, Marcella Sembrich, Nellie Melba, Maria Galvany, Graziella Pareto, and Marie Michailowa, ranging in price from $3.00 to $1.00, which the impartial Mr. Rous evaluated thus:

> Donizetti's scene seems especially set apart for the display of such a coloratura as Melba possesses, and she sings this florid music with such brilliancy and graceful fluency that the listener is dazzled. Her runs, trills, and staccato notes glitter and scintillate, and compel a new admiration for the wonderful vocal mechanism over which she has such absolute command.
>
> The role of the unhappy Lucy is also admirably fitted to Tetrazzini's peculiar talents, and as the heroine of Donizetti's lovely opera she has made quite the greatest success of her career. When she reaches this florid and difficult "Mad Scene," the listeners are absolutely electrified, and such a torrent of enthusiasm bursts forth that the diva is usually compelled to repeat a portion of the aria.
>
> Mme. Sembrich's rendition proves that the compass of her voice is all but phenomenal, and she sings the difficult music with delightful flexibility and with an intonation which is faultless.
>
> Other renditions of this well-known scene are given by

Mme. Galvany and Mme. Pareto, the famous Italian prima donnas, and by Michailowa, the famous Russian singer. Although none of these artists [the three just mentioned] has yet visited America, their beautiful voices are heard in thousands of homes in which the Victor is a welcome entertainer.

Revised periodically to catch up with changing tastes in opera and with the changing complexion of Victor's operatic catalogue, *The Victor Book of the Opera* remained a steady seller for decades and helped substantially to make Americans operatically literate.

During the years prior to America's entry in World War I the pattern for the Victor Talking Machine Company was onward and upward. Its assets of $2,724,016 in 1902 had jumped to $33,235,378 by 1917, and the four-story Camden factory which seemed like such a gamble when it was erected had been dwarfed by acres of newer and larger Victor buildings sprawling along the eastern bank of the Delaware River. Eldridge Johnson, whether he liked it or not, had become a tycoon; and several of the men whose careers dated back to the founding of the company were millionaires, or well on their way to that happy status.

And what of the competition? Thanks to the patent pool of 1902, Victor had only one serious rival in a country of vast buying potential; and that rival—though strongly ensconced —bulked far less formidably than might have been the case. Columbia had been thrown off balance from the very start. By scuttling its Grand Opera series so hastily, Columbia had relinquished its prior claim to the celebrity record field and had left Victor free to snatch up the Metropolitan's most illustrious stars and capitalize on the precious publicity that went with them. Columbia also made some early headway in another direction, and with equally still-born results. In August 1904, it announced the issuance of double-sided ten-inch discs, to sell for $1.50. Although the recorded contents were nothing special, standard semiclassical pieces played by the Columbia Band, the double-sided principle was well worth exploiting—as Odeon was demonstrating in Europe with unequivocal success. But the threat of a lawsuit from Odeon caused Columbia to abandon its double-sized records almost as soon as they were issued.

Next, Columbia concluded an *entente cordiale* with Guglielmo Marconi, the inventor of wireless telegraphy. To celebrate his joining the company as Consulting Physicist, Columbia imported the thirty-two-year-old Italian and his wife for a whirlwind tour of New York and Bridgeport. The Marconis docked on Saturday, the eighth of September 1906. On Monday they motored to the Bridgeport plant in company with Edward D. Easton and Mrs. Easton. That evening, back in New York, Columbia sponsored an expensive banquet at the Waldorf-Astoria in honor of its illustrious Consulting Physicist. On into the night the banquet hall resounded to speeches prophesying the incalculable boons that were to result from this collaboration. The next day, Signor Marconi and his wife boarded the *Caronia* and sailed back to Europe. There ensued a long silence. At last, a year later, the collaboration yielded some fruit. In October 1907, the Columbia Company introduced the Marconi Velvet-Tone Record, a flexible and unbreakable disc with "so velvety a surface that the annoyance of the usual scratching sound is entirely eliminated." To prove its authenticity, the advertisements showed a photograph of Marconi in the act of bending one of his pliable Velvet-Tone Records. This distinguished sanction notwithstanding, the Velvet-Tones were an abysmal failure. Within a matter of months Columbia had resumed full production of the tried-and-tested shellac discs. And nothing further was heard from its Consulting Physicist.

Memories of this disappointment were still fresh when Columbia made another bid for the phonograph owner's attention by plunging once again into the manufacture of celebrity records. For four unhappy years, Edward D. Easton and his *confrères* in Bridgeport had observed with growing dismay the institutional and commercial benefits that were accruing to the Victor Talking Machine Company from its thriving catalogue of Red Seal Records. Murmuring *mea culpa* for the forsaken Columbia Grand Opera series, they set out to woo the muse again. To say that Columbia had entirely disregarded grand opera after its ill-timed withdrawal of 1903 would be to oversimplify the case. There had been in the interim some passing shies at the formation of an operatic catalogue. Thus, in 1905 and 1906, Columbia had issued a number of standard arias and duets performed by two lesser lights of the Metropolitan Opera, the soprano Gina Ciaparelli and the baritone Taurino Parvis, as well as some selections sung by Romeo Berti, "a comparatively new singer with a phenomenal voice such as Caruso and many other celebrated tenors possessed when they were young and their voices were fresh in their prime." So read the advertising copy. But, woefully, Berti's singing on records served only to emphasize the widely appreciated virtues of Caruso's Red Seals.

Yet if Columbia were to match Victor's celebrities with celebrities of its own, where could they be found? The wily Calvin Child, Victor's director of artists and repertoire, had committed practically every singer of note at the Metropolitan Opera to a Red Seal contract. Melba, Sembrich, Eames, Gadski, Farrar, Calvé, Schumann-Heink, Homer, Caruso, Scotti, Journet—these were the stalwarts of the Metropolitan in 1907, and they were all Victor artists. In desperation Columbia turned to Europe and negotiated with the Fonotipia and Odeon firms for the rights to issue their operatic recordings in America. Overnight, as a result, Columbia acquired a constellation of indubitable luminaries. The sopranos Lilli Lehmann and Giannina Russ, the tenors Alessandro Bonci and Giovanni Zenatello, the baritone Mario

Sammarco, and the basso Adamo Didur were among the artists that Columbia fell heir to, several of whom were just then being introduced to America as members of Oscar Hammerstein's opera troupe based in the Manhattan Opera House—a rival to the Metropolitan. The first release of thirty-three records was placed on sale in March 1908, priced at $2.00 and $3.00 according to size, and for the first time in four years Victor faced domestic competition in the field of high-class musical discs.

That competition was intensified in the autumn of 1908, following Columbia's decision to issue its entire repertoire on double-sided records. The slogan for Columbia Double-Discs, "Two records at a single price," was not quite accurate, at least as regards the Fonotipia series, where prices were raised to $2.50 and $3.50. Even so, a pinchpenny opera-lover was sure to find the Columbia catalogue worth his attention, for though Victor quickly succumbed to competition and converted its own low-priced lines to double-sided status, it haughtily maintained the Red Seal Records in single-sided splendor. Thus, two arias by Caruso continued to cost a total of $6.00, whereas two by Bonci could be purchased for $3.50. But Victor was not producing the Red Seal repertoire for bargain hunters, and indeed it was not until 1923 that it bowed to the inevitable and issued Red Seals in economical double-sided form.

Ill fortune continued to dog Columbia's attempts to pull astride of Victor. Complaints were raised that the technique employed by Fonotipia did not meet American standards. To anyone who has played Fonotipia recordings on modern equipment such aspersions seem incredible, for the Italian discs have a thrilling immediacy of sound in no wise inferior to the smoother, more rounded tonal quality heard in Victor recordings of the same period. But partly because this forwardness and vibrancy appealed less to the American taste of 1910, partly because these Fonotipia characteristics which we so prize today were far less effectively reproduced on the acoustic phonographs of pre-World-War-I vintage, sales fell off badly and Columbia found itself saddled with a white elephant. The expedient of taking over a ready-made catalogue of European recordings and mass-producing them in America had failed.

Consequently, in 1910 the management at Columbia broke off its Fonotipia-Odeon alliance and adopted instead the policy of recording operatic stars in America for the American taste. Thanks to the activity of Oscar Hammerstein and to the flourishing opera troupes in Chicago and Boston, there was an abundance of first-rate singers in America—and not all of them were under contract to Victor. Columbia managed to snare the sopranos Mary Garden and Lina Cavalieri, whose names lent a glamorous embellishment to advertisements even though these ladies were far more effective on stage than as disembodied vocalists on phonograph records. Some erstwhile Fonotipia-Odeon artists—notably the soprano Emmy Destinn, the tenors Bonci and Zenatello—were persuaded to join with Columbia and record in New York, as were also such renegades from the Victor list as Leo Slezak, tenor, and Alice Nielsen, soprano. But Columbia's greatest coup in the celebrity field was its exclusive contract with the world-famous American soprano Lillian Nordica. Her connection with the company resulted from her friendship with Hermann Klein, an estimable British critic and vocal expert who had been working with Columbia on a projected "Phono Vocal Method" that would utilize textbooks and accompanying phonograph records for self-instruction in the art of singing. In the original plans Nordica was to sing the soprano exercises and some operatic arias; but when Columbia eventually issued the "Phono Vocal Method," it was without the participation of Nordica. She had been dissatisfied with her attempted exercise records and had bowed out of the project. Her interest in recording had been piqued, however, and a few years later—in 1911—Columbia was able to announce a series of special Nordica discs, which were issued, Red Seal fashion, in single-sided form only. Unfortunately, Nordica's records are among the poorest examples of acoustic recording to come down to us, being little more than a travesty of a spectacular voice. And very much the same must unfortunately be said of the recordings by Olive Fremstad, another exclusive Columbia artist whose discs appeared at about the same time.

By the outbreak of World War I, Columbia displayed a respectable collection of vocal literature. Yet at best it was a secondary role that this company continued to play. In its business affairs it followed a line of action characterized by a Columbia executive as the "me too" policy. Victor was the leader—in artists, in repertoire, in advertising, and in sales. Columbia tagged along in the wake of Victor's initiative and picked up the leavings (which were plentiful). But there was one exception to this general rule that was to prove of much consequence to the industry. It concerned the design of phonographs.

In the instrument business, as elsewhere, Columbia was content mainly to follow the leader; and the leader concentrated exclusively on its popular Victrolas, which were made in a wide range of models—table or console—to suit all tastes and incomes. But one thing each and every Victrola had in common, no matter what the model or price: they all looked like phonographs. It was in this regard that Columbia went beyond the "me too" framework. For in addition to a full assortment of imitation Victrolas (called Grafonolas), Columbia featured a line of phonographs designed to resemble ordinary parlor furniture and to be as unphonograph-looking as possible. The most ambitious example in 1911 was the $200 "Regent" model, a hulking monstrosity on Chippendale legs that doubled as a table and a phonograph. Columbia billed it as "the perfect union of utility and entertainment

... neither approached in any other instrument nor ever attempted. It is a complete library or living-room table for everyday use in exactly the same degree that it is a complete musical instrument of unexampled versatility and matchless tonal qualities." As a table it presented "an unbroken expanse of clear mahogany measuring 29 by 46 inches." A drawer on the right contained the turntable and tone arm, while "extending to the other end of the table [was] the tone chamber through which tone waves poured in magnified volume out of a grille."

Down at Camden such freakish inventions were viewed with lordly disdain. In an announcement to the trade, Victor made its position perfectly clear: "The Victrola is not a piece of furniture. It is a musical instrument which transcends every other. It was designed and built to meet its own requirements and not to *imitate anything,* for that would be bad art, bad mechanics, and bad judgment." But this was far from being the last word on the subject, as Victor would learn to its discomfort.

11 DECLINE AND FALL OF THE CYLINDER

WHILE VICTOR WAS COURTING THE PUBLIC WITH CARUSO and grand opera, Edison was holding forth with Arthur Collins and "coon songs"—and at the same time fighting a long, valiant delaying action against an ever more formidable adversary. Rasping indignation at the new form of competition was already evident in a "letter to the editor" that appeared in the November 1901 issue of Edison's house organ *The Phonogram*:

> I have noticed in the magazines for this month a very clever advertisement of a talking machine in which a little fox terrier is sitting in front of a horn with his ears cocked up very knowingly, "listening to his master's voice."
>
> Now, as a lover of the Phonograph, I do not understand this picture: perhaps you can explain it to me. I have always understood that the Gram-o-phone, the machine he is listening to, would not make records, and if you wanted to have a record made you had to go to a specially equipped laboratory, at the Company's headquarters. Since this is the case, I wonder how "his master's voice" happened to get on the record. All of the flat records I have ever heard have such a hissing, sissing, scratching sound, caused by the needle, that it is a wonder that a dog, or even a man, could distinguish a voice.
>
> Yours very truly,
HENRY G. BROWNING

But strictures like this did not impede the rise of the flat disc or brake the decline of the cylinder in relation to its "hissing, sissing" opponent. Edison's phonograph was headed

158

for the junk heap, but it took a long, long time getting there and on the way provided entertainment for millions of Americans.

Actually, the cylinder was on a downgrade only in comparison to the disc; taken by itself at the turn of the century, it was still an expanding and profitable business property—and would continue so for at least another decade. There was certainly no cause for alarm in the closing months of 1901, when the finishing touches were put on a long-overdue process for mass-producing duplicate wax cylinders from a master mold. Both Edison and Columbia claimed priority for inventing the "gold-molded" record, and both companies lost no time in proclaiming its superiorities of hardness and uniformity. As these records were molded under pressure (instead of being individually engraved by a stylus), a much harder wax composition could be used, with attendant gain in loudness and articulation. And as all copies of a given recording were molded from the same master, there was a consistent quality in the finished product such as cylinder buyers had never known before. "Flaws and imperfections," the Edison advertisements guaranteed, "are a thing of the past."

By March 1902, the hard-wax cylinders were issuing in full spate from the factories, and each month brought a fresh batch of titles recorded in the Columbia and Edison studios. Columbia's policy at first was to issue disc and cylinder versions of the same recording simultaneously. But there were some significant exceptions to this rule—such as the Grand Opera series of 1903, which appeared in disc form only. Already a distinction had been drawn between the disc public and the cylinder public: discs were meant for the Main Street parlor, cylinders for the shack on the other side of the tracks. Surely, the Edison issues of this period were aimed at something less than a sophisticated clientele. Consider the best sellers (as tabulated in the *Edison Phonograph Monthly*) from the April 1903 release. First place went to "I Wonder Why Bill Bailey Don't Come Home," a "coon song" sung by Arthur Collins with orchestral accompaniment; then came "Pretty Peggy" played on the bells by Edward F. Rubsam, a comic waltz song ("When the Winter Time Comes 'Round"), performed by Collins and Byron G. Harlan, and the *Alagazam* March played on the xylophone by J. Frank Hopkins with orchestral accompaniment. Such fare was not for cultured city folk but for the vast "cracker barrel trade" in rural areas and small towns. The day when Bettini could sell cylinders to William K. Vanderbilt at $6.00 apiece had passed. The cylinder had been relegated to the less privileged classes, and it was priced accordingly. In 1905 Edison cylinders sold for thirty-five cents and Columbia cylinders for twenty-five, whereas Victor's cheapest ten-inch discs sold for a dollar.

Edison knew what he was doing. He understood this market and he understood the music he was offering. His inexpensive phonographs and cylinders appealed to a large, faithful public; and during the first decade of the century the Edison plant in West Orange, New Jersey, was hard-ridden to keep up with the demand, even on a two-shift schedule. Indeed, in May 1906, the company had to apologize for being two and a half million records behind in filling orders; to catch up, Edison canceled the regular June release of new issues. Typical of the customers who kept Edison so well supplied with orders was a farmer in Michigan who wrote to *The Phonogram*, in September 1905, to express just what the Edison phonograph meant to him and his family:

> We have a Home Phonograph [Edison's $20 model] and we may, in view of the following, be excused for this one luxury. I am today out in the cornfield, cutting corn. The sun kisses the gray corn tassels and the ears tickle my ribs as I work. Across the lane my boy follows a wheat drill over the soft earth in his bare feet. The crows are flying toward

the nearest wood and the robins are gathering for their journey south. The air is still and it makes a fellow sweat. But
I know when the yellow corn is cribbed, and the storm is
howling, and the great white billows lay along our roads
and fences, while a big mound buries our mail box at the
front gate, and we can't get to town (we are a family of
eleven), and when the windows are covered with thick frost,
we will listen to "Blue Danube" and thank Edison for his
phonograph.

This letter may have been composed by an imaginative copy
writer in the Edison publicity department; but even if its
authorship is open to question, the letter admirably describes
the *ambiance* in which Edison products flourished.

Not content with cultivating this market, Edison decided
in 1906 to break into the higher reaches of the record business. He announced a series of Grand Opera Cylinders and
opened a studio on the seventeenth floor of the Knicker-
bocker Building, Fifth Avenue and Sixteenth Street, in which
to record this new repertoire. In an aside to its dealers, the
Edison company confided:

> In the past much has been said in criticism of the phono-
> graph [meaning the Edison phonograph] because no high-
> class records by grand opera singers could be had for it. . . .
> Now that the want has been supplied, dealers should lose
> no time in going after this high-class trade.

For the layman, Edison's publicists had concocted another
story:

> Hitherto, Mr. Edison has refused to permit Edison Rec-
> ords to be made by Grand Opera singers, preferring to wait
> until he could so improve his methods of recording, that the
> voices of great artists could be reproduced with all their
> characteristic sweetness, power, and purity of tone. These
> improvements having been effected, the artists cooperated
> with enthusiasm, with the result that the first ten Edison
> Grand Opera Records . . . are a distinct advance over any-
> thing of the kind heretofore attempted.

Edison lured some highly capable artists to his studio. His register in 1906 included four eminent members of the Metropolitan's Wagnerian wing: the tenors Alois Burgstaller, Andreas Dippel, and Heinrich Knote, and the baritone Anton van Rooy (whose first cylinder, the *"Chanson du Toreador"* from *Carmen,* was a portent of the weird miscasting that was to disfigure the Edison catalogue). Other Metropolitan singers in the early Edison Grand Opera lists were the sopranos Bessie Abbott and Marie Rappold, the tenor Florencio Constantino, and the baritone Antonio Scotti. These cylinders sold for only seventy-five cents each, "in accordance with Mr. Edison's desire to make his Phonograph the musical instrument of the people." But the Edison public did not gobble them up, and in December 1906 the company was forced to admonish its dealers: "We cannot help feeling that the trade in general are not paying the attention to them [the Grand Opera Records] that their high quality deserves." Operatic issues became fewer and fewer. By the summer of 1908 the focus of attention had shifted to another kind of celebrity. Edison had secured a series of cylinders from the Republican and Democratic nominees for President, William Howard Taft and William Jennings Bryan; and to its dealers the company crowed: "No matter how the November elections may result we shall have records by the new President. This makes history. It indicates progress."

One explanation for the neglect of Edison's operatic records by the "high-class trade" could be found in the uncomfortably short duration of standard wax cylinders. They played for a maximum of two minutes, which meant that almost all arias had to be abbreviated. Twelve-inch discs with a playing time of four minutes offered substantially more satisfaction to the serious music-lover. Indeed, the limitations of the two-minute cylinder were beginning to affect Edison's business as a whole. It was not only unmusical to pare a composition down to its vitals, but it was annoying to have to change cylinders every two minutes—especially as discs needed to be changed only half as often. Edison and his assistants at the experimental laboratory in West Orange wrestled with the problem and brought forth the Amberol Record, which was placed on sale in October 1908. The Amberols were grooved two hundred lines to the inch instead of the previous one hundred lines to the inch and thus played twice as long as the old two-minute cylinders. They were also molded from a considerably tougher material, for the grooves were twice as narrow and hence more fragile. Secret ingredients supposedly went into the Amberol material, and the crucial chemical element was said to be known only to Mr. Edison himself. Needless to say, Edison's devoted copy writers made the most of this situation. They described how at a certain stage in the manufacture of Amberol material Mr. Edison would emerge from his private laboratory carrying a small paper bag filled with this critical secret ingredient, whereupon he would walk to the vat of molten wax, dump the contents of the bag therein, and wait until he had seen it thoroughly amalgamated with the other ingredients. "Every effort to discover the identity of that mysterious and potent chemical by analysis," readers were told, "has met with dismal failure."

The four-minute Amberol Record inspired Edison to renew his solicitation of the culture-conscious record buyer. In November 1909, he launched a series of Grand Opera Amberols priced variously from $1.00 to $2.00 according to the eminence of the performer. At the same time he began manufacturing a handsome, de luxe phonograph with an enclosed horn. It was called the Edison Amberola and retailed for $200. For a while Grand Opera Amberols appeared regularly in Edison's monthly listings. Two Metropolitan Opera tenors were prominently featured, the Austrian-born Leo Slezak and the Kentucky-born Riccardo Martin, while the soprano representation in the Grand Opera Amberol series included Blanche Arral (whose recording career began with Bettini), Lucrezia Bori, and Selma Kurz.

With this kind of talent allied to the "cracker barrel" perennials, the Edison line was deemed to be irresistible. This was the theme elaborated in a short sermon on the text "Two Strings to Your Bow" which was addressed to Edison dealers in the *Edison Phonograph Monthly* for February 1910:

> Now that you've got Slezak and the Amberola to take care of one class of your customers, and all the other styles of Phonographs and all the other Records, both Standard and Amberol, to take care of the other classes, you're equipped to take out all the profit there is in the business. . . .
>
> That's what we mean when we say, "two strings to your bow."
>
> Because while the Amberola class is resting and the Grand Opera lovers are saving up to buy more Records, the good old "ragtime-coon songs-Sousa-Herbert-monologues-sentimental ballads" crowd will still be on the job buying Phonographs of the other styles, and Standard and Amberol Records, until there's frost on the sun.

For these lesser folk in 1910 there were heart-warming ballads by Ada Jones, monologues by Murry K. Hill, hymns by the Edison Mixed Quartette, and hot ragtime numbers by a young singer named Sophie Tucker (described in an Edison brochure as "a 'coon shouter' who is considered to be the foremost exponent of that type of song before the public"). And it was this kind of delectation that continued to keep the cylinder business alive, for the carriage trade still did not take kindly to the Edison cylinder—even though it played operatic arias for four minutes, and even though the Edison Amberola was constructed of the finest mahogany.

In June 1911, with a hundred and fifteen operatic Amberols issued, Edison gave up. There was just no public for Slezak cylinders at $2.00 each. Thereafter, Edison cylinder customers who yearned for good music were forced to content themselves with a new series of Concert Records, selling at seventy-five cents, that offered English ballads and operatic arias in English translations and utilized such singers as the soprano Anna Case, the contralto Christine Miller, and the tenor Orville Harrold.

The Columbia Phonograph Company, Edison's only large competitor, never attempted to interest the cylinder public in grand opera. Let Edison pursue the chimera of culture; Columbia was content to give good value: "clear, original, loud" cylinders at twenty-five cents each. The introduction of Edison Amberols, however, called for a competing gimmick, and Columbia countered with the Indestructible Cylinder Record selling for thirty-five cents. It was a celluloid-like cylinder, based on the patents of a Chicago inventor named Thomas B. Lambert, which had previously been manufactured by the Indestructible Phonograph Record Company of Albany, New York. In October 1908, Columbia took over the entire output of this factory and began tooting the attributes of the Indestructible Cylinders, which "won't break no matter how roughly they are used and won't wear out no matter how long they are played." A year later Columbia brought out a Four-Minute Indestructible Cylinder Record at fifty cents. But destruction haunted even the Indestructible Cylinder. More and more, the cylinder business was being relegated to the backwoods. Columbia's excessively noisy Indestructible Records were certainly not the appropriate device to gain new adherents to the cylinder phonograph. By the end of 1910 sales were sliding off dangerously. Finally, in July 1912, Columbia dealers were apprised of "The Finish of the Cylinder Record." The day of the cylinder machine was over, Columbia announced; thenceforth the company would devote all its efforts to the disc business.

Was Edison also going to abandon his "favorite invention" and renounce the cylinder repertoire that he had been amassing for so long? Rumors flew thick and fast, and Edison was forced to deny publicly that he contemplated discontinuing the manufacture of cylinder phonographs and records. As a matter of fact, Edison was about to make one last attempt to convert the heathen to a proper appreciation of the cylinder. The instrument of his persuasion was the Blue Amberol Record, an unbreakable plastic cylinder that could be played "3,000 times without wear." It made its debut in October 1912 and represented a marked improvement over the previous waxlike Amberols, which—for all the blarney about a secret ingredient—had proved highly susceptible to abrasion. Moreover, unlike Columbia's Indestructible Records, the Blue Amberols were relatively noiseless; and when played with an Edison Diamond Reproducer, they outperformed any other medium of reproduced music then available. Heard today, with electrical amplification, the Edison Blue Amberols reveal a standard of sound reproduction far above the general level achieved by pre-World-War-I recording technique.

Their superiority can be explained in several ways. To begin with, the surface speed of a cylinder was constant from beginning to end; hence it was free from the "inner groove" distortion that was, and is, a constant problem with flat discs (whose surface speed slows progressively from outer to inner grooves). Secondly, the hill-and-dale cut employed by Edison (the stylus bobbing up and down in the groove) was better adapted to the acoustic recording process than the lateral cut employed by Victor and its competitors (the stylus undulating back and forth in the groove). A recording engineer working with lateral-cut equipment had always to guard against a sudden loud tone that would blast its way right through the wall of the record groove. Singers were carefully instructed to back away from the horn when they emitted a ringing *fortissimo*—a practice which kept the grooves intact but clouded the impact of the reproduction.

The hill-and-dale engineer was less fettered. On his equipment a trumpeting climax merely engraved a deeper valley in the bottom of the groove; there was no danger of cutting through the delicate groove wall itself. In marshaling reasons for the Blue Amberols' superiority, one could point also to the advantages of Edison's smooth plastic over the fairly gritty shellac compound then used for discs, as well as to the benefits of Edison's precision-ground diamond styli in comparison to the mass-produced steel needles with which lateral-cut discs were played. But in setting forth all these objective explanations, there is a risk of neglecting what may have been the most important element: the sheer talent for making good recordings shared by Edison and his associates. Edison credited his success as a recorder to his deafness. "Being deaf," he wrote in 1925, "my knowledge of sounds had been developed till it was extensive, and I knew that I was not and no one else was getting overtones. Others working in the same field did not realize this imperfection, because they were not deaf." Whether one accepts this reasoning or not, the fact remains that the ears in Edison's recording studios were attuned with extraordinary sensitivity to the elements of good sound reproduction.

Unfortunately, the Blue Amberol Record was given little chance to prove its musical capabilities. A short flurry of operatic issues descended on the market in 1913, including a series by the tenor Alessandro Bonci, a newcomer to the Edison catalogue. But nothing now could induce the music-conscious public to install a cylinder phonograph in the front parlor, not even the acoustically superior Blue Amberol Record. The day of the cylinder machine was indeed over, as Columbia had announced a year before. Edison himself confirmed its demise in October 1913 when he unveiled his own Disc Phonograph, which played special Edison discs recorded by the hill-and-dale process. But though he capitulated to the public preference for flat discs, the old man did not forsake his faithful adherents of the cylinder. There were well over a million cylinder phonographs extant in 1913, and Edison continued to supply them with fifty-cent Blue Amberols. The market dwindled as the years went by; yet there was always a hard core of buyers, especially in the deep South, for whom Edison doggedly kept on manufacturing merchandise until he quit the record business altogether in November 1929.

The saga of Edison's Disc Phonograph must be reserved for a later chapter. But before dismissing the cylinder, it would be well to chronicle its fortunes in Europe. What Thomas A. Edison was to the New World, Emile Pathé was to the Old. During the early years of the century, Pathé's large factory near Paris was in full production manufacturing cylinders for every country in Europe. In size, Pathé was second only to the Gramophone Company among European phonographic enterprises; according to a 1904 advertisement, the company employed 3,200 workers, averaged a daily production of 1,000 phonographs and 50,000 cylinders (surely something of an overstatement!), and maintained branch offices in London, Milan, and Moscow. Some 12,000 different recordings were listed in Pathé's various catalogues of 1904, and a good proportion of them were aimed at a musically sophisticated public. French artists and French repertoire, of course, predominated. Felia Litvinne was represented on Pathé cylinders in arias from *Faust, Sapho,* and *Les Troyens,* and there were many lesser-known sopranos from the Opéra and Opéra-Comique—among them Jane Merey, Marguerite Carré, Marie Thiery, and Mary Boyer. Pathé had also recorded a young lady from Aberdeen, Scotland, named Mary Garden, who had just created the role of Mélisande in Debussy's controversial opera. Among the men there were such veterans from the nineteenth century as the tenors Albert Alvarez and Ernest van Dyck, the baritone Jean Baptiste Faure (whose song *"Les Rameaux"* is a concert staple), and the baritone Jean Lassalle, together with two tenors popular with the French opera public, Gustarello Affre and Albert Vaguet. Pathé cylinders were made in two sizes: the Standard, which sold for approximately twenty-five cents and the larger and louder Salon, which sold for approximately forty cents. To play them, Pathé manufactured a line of phonographs ranging in price from $4.50 to $35.

Meanwhile, in London the first flat-disc apparatus employing hill-and-dale recording had made its appearance in the spring of 1904. It was the invention of William Michaelis (brother of Alfred) and was called the Neophone. From his headquarters in Finsbury Square, Michaelis engaged in a full-scale campaign to convert the European public to hill-and-dale discs. Neophone records were made of a plastic material laminated to a cardboard base; they were exceptionally light, exceptionally cheap (the nine-inch disc sold for six-pence, the twelve-inch for a shilling), and exceptionally scratchy. For the convenience of those who already owned a regular gramophone, the Neophone Company manufactured the Repro-Neo adapter, which could be inserted on the small end of the tone arm and allowed a gramophone owner the option of playing either lateral or hill-and-dale records. For phonograph initiates there were complete Neophone instruments at various prices from twenty-one shillings to £20.

For a while, Neophone also manufactured a special series of single-sided twenty-inch discs that played from eight to ten minutes and offered uninterrupted versions of the *Light Cavalry, Poet and Peasant,* and *Bohemian Girl* Overtures. Alas, William Michaelis was ahead of his time with these long-playing orchestral records. From a tonal standpoint they left much to be desired, and Neophone customers saw little reason to pay ten shillings sixpence for a twenty-inch record when a twelve-inch record could be bought for a shilling. In 1906 the mammoth platters were dropped from the catalogue. Somewhat more successful was Neophone's Grand

Opera series offering performances by three of Covent Garden's lesser singers—the soprano Emma Trentini, the tenor Dante Zucchi, and the basso Paolo Wullmann—but these records, too, suffered from gratingly noisy surfaces. Before long, the public concluded that Neophone merchandise was no bargain at any price; in 1908 the company foundered.

Pathé had also adopted the hill-and-dale disc and—unlike Neophone—had made of it a successful commercial property. When the Pathé disc was first introduced, in October 1906, it was announced that the new product would supplement, rather than displace, the Pathé cylinder. But it was not long before Pathé Frères gave up pushing cylinders to concentrate exclusively on furthering the fortunes of the disc. Pathé discs were hard to resist. In 1908 double-sided eleven-inch Pathé records sold for the equivalent of a dollar and featured artists of quality—Emma Albani, Celestina Boninsegna, Maria Galvany, Louise Kirkby-Lunn, Albert Alvarez, Mario Ancona, and Enrico Caruso (whose early recordings for the Anglo-Italian Commerce Company had been inherited by Pathé). Shorter discs, also double-sided, sold for as little as forty cents. No wonder the British advertisements described Monsieur Pathé as "the man who broke the price of disc records" and "who supplies NEW TUNES for the millions at NINEPENCE each." Pathé discs could be played on a gramophone with the aid of an inexpensive Pathé adapter or on Pathé's own apparatus, the Pathéphone, which—like the discs—was of French manufacture and came in a variety of styles ranging in price from $8.00 to $200. By 1911, according to a Pathé bulletin, the annual production of Pathéphones had attained a retail value of over $2,000,000. Russell Hunting, the ex-actor from Boston who had originated the "Casey" dialogues back in 1890, was put in charge of Pathé's recording activity. From his headquarters in Paris, Hunting supervised a network of studios stretching from Shanghai across Europe to New York. An imposing catalogue was built up; but except in France, where Pathé Frères enjoyed a near-monopoly, the hill-and-dale disc always ran second to the lateral-cut gramophone record.

In Europe, as in America, the cylinder trade was left almost entirely in the hands of Edison. Edison recording studios and factories were established in England and on the Continent, and an ambitious recording program was pressed forward under the direction of a young American named Bill Hayes. But the decline of the cylinder in Europe was more precipitate than in America. In 1909 Edison was obliged to shut down his European plants. Thenceforth, though he still recorded in Europe, cylinders were exported from the factory in West Orange, New Jersey. After the outbreak of World War I, Edison's European recording program was brought to a halt. It was never resumed.

12 *THE ORCHESTRA CAME LAST*

A DISGRUNTLED RECORD COLLECTOR IN OHIO SAT DOWN AT his desk on August 5, 1913, and addressed a letter to the *Talking Machine News* of London. It concerned orchestral recordings. Americans with a taste for orchestral music, he complained, had no choice but to order their records from abroad. Not that the imports were better played or better recorded than domestic discs, "but they afford classical and standard selections either not recorded at all in this country or given in incomplete or fragmentary form." As a self-styled "enthusiast for disc music of the highest order," this correspondent was indeed in a predicament. He belonged to a minority for whom the American record companies evinced almost no concern. To judge from the 1913 Victor catalogue, the phonograph owner in America was a man of limited tastes but voracious appetite who could digest great quantities of vocal music—especially if it came from a much-performed opera—and nothing else. In its pages were to be found five different recordings of *"Una voce poco fa"* and *"Vissi d'arte,"* seven of *"Caro nome,"* and eight of the "Toreador Song."

But what if one's musical predilections extended beyond this abundant but confining largess? What if one longed to hear from the phonograph some instrumental music by Beethoven? Well, a collector with such inclinations could turn to the heading "Beethoven" in Victor's 1913 catalogue, and

172

there he would find the *Leonore Overture No. 3* played by the Victor Concert Orchestra (on three sides, and thus substantially complete); truncated versions of the Adagio from the Fourth Symphony and the Andante from the Fifth performed by the same group; a movement from the *Emperor* Concerto, abbreviated to one record side; another version of *Leonore No. 3* rent as well as rendered by Pryor's Band (since it was cut down to one fourth its normal length); and the first movement of the *Moonlight* Sonata as interpreted by Vessella's Italian Band. That was all.

Beethoven, as a matter of fact, came off comparatively well in the Victor catalogue of this period. Haydn was represented only by an abbreviated *Surprise* Symphony; and from the vast instrumental output of Mozart, the Victor Company saw fit to extract merely the first movement (or such of it as would fit on a single twelve-inch record side) from the Concerto for Harp and Flute, played by Ada Sassoli and John Lemmone with piano accompaniment, plus a Gavotte and a Menuett (neither of them identified further) in performances by the violinists Mischa Elman and Maud Powell. Johann Sebastian Bach could be sampled in two snippets: the *Air for G String* played by Victor Herbert's Orchestra and Mischa Elman, and a *Gavotte in E major* as arranged and performed by Fritz Kreisler.

The American Columbia catalogue was similarly bereft of symphonic substance: a few easily digestible instrumental *morceaux* and stray movements (always in abridged form) from the most popular symphonies were scattered amidst a plenitude of operatic arias.

In Europe, as the Ohioan had written, the enthusiast for orchestral music was better off. In part this was due to economic causes. Although European record companies had been the instigators of celebrity operatic issues, their leadership in this field was short-lived. The royalties offered by the

Victor Talking Machine Company (and later by Columbia) were unparalleled, and one by one the celebrated vocalists of the era transferred their phonographic allegiance to America. Thus, in a certain sense, the record industry in Europe was obliged, purely by force of economic circumstances, to explore a new area of recorded repertoire. But these considerations only partially explain the drift to orchestral recording that gathered momentum in Europe from 1910 on. Just as the pioneering operatic issues of a decade earlier had stemmed from the European record buyer's demand for something better than "coon songs" and quadrilles, sentimental ballads and Sousa marches, so now did the orchestral issues derive from a desire for something more ambitious than vocal sweetmeats.

This climate of opinion can be detected in the writings of Max Chop (1862–1929), German composer, journalist, and author, who contributed a weekly record review column to *Die Phonographische Zeitschrift* from 1906 to 1914. Early in 1909, Chop addressed himself to a survey of the recorded repertoire then available, with a view to determining how well the phonograph was serving the well-rounded music lover. The first thing to be noted, he wrote, was "the predominance of vocal selections over instrumental ones. One need only study the lists of new releases to recognize at once the preponderance of singing." This had been the case for years, he observed; almost every singer of reputation had made recordings, and as a result the vocal repertoire was more than amply represented. Chop continued:

> Compared to the plethora of vocal selections, instrumental works occupy a relatively small part of the repertoire. There are plenty of so-called "orchestral recordings," but with a one-sided emphasis: brass bands. The symphony orchestra is only rarely in evidence; yet it is, after all, the only instrumental body to be considered for really valuable literature and high artistic quality. The range of repertoire in

this field also remains narrow. First of all, there are marches, dances, medleys, abbreviated overtures, and little salon pieces of rather questionable merit—all of it rather mediocre entertainment music. Next to this we find a growing repertoire of "hits." I will not deny the hit's right to existence. As a child of the times, begotten of the shallow and the trivial, toward which a wide segment of the popular taste is oriented, it has a right to live. . . . But it certainly need not spread itself as widely as it does. . . . Let us have more Lortzing and less Lincke, more Mendelssohn and less Rudolf Waldmann. And what about serious music? The release of the entire *Third Leonore Overture* on four sides a few months ago seemed like Redemption itself. . . . But how rarely does this happen! And if it does, in transcription for brass band! Why do we not have any of the preludes to Wagner's music-dramas? Where are movements from the symphonies of our immortal masters? After all, the musical literature is bountiful indeed!

Elsewhere in this article the critic complained of the "arbitrary changes in orchestration" that were so often perpetrated on the unwitting record listener:

The original orchestration should be employed as far as the characteristics of the recording diaphragm and the sound box permit. It is true that double basses and cellos must be discarded *a priori* and replaced by the lower woodwinds and brasses. This is but yielding to necessity; and though it entails some coarsening of the melodic line, the total sound pattern is not too much altered. On the other hand, arbitrary replacement of the higher strings (violins) by high-pitched winds (flutes, clarinets, trumpets) is definitely objectionable. . . . Such transcriptions are entirely unmusical. They prove either that the company making such recordings lacks artistic understanding or that it places economic considerations above the musical. Such policies may perhaps bring an initial profit, but they will surely embarrass their perpetrators in the end, when a gradually awakening public begins to recognize the artistic impossibility of such instrumental manipulations. That serious critics are repelled goes without saying.

A few months later Chop could report that:

> a beginning has at last been made in presenting our orches-
> tral literature not only through well-disciplined brass bands
> but also through groups employing symphonic instrumenta-
> tion. . . . I recently heard some recordings of the Prelude
> and *Liebestod* from *Tristan* and the Intermezzo from *Caval-
> leria* played by large instrumental groups with symphonic
> orchestration and recorded almost to perfection. These are
> rare occurrences! Yet what a fertile field we have here in
> which to plant the seeds of the future!

Such was the *Zeitgeist* that led to the efflorescence of orchestral recording in Europe. But before describing the first
harvests from the fertile field to which Max Chop referred,
it would be well to examine the state of Europe's record industry as it existed *circa* 1910. The Gramophone Company,
which retained its pre-eminence in the industry, had developed in many respects since the early days of William Barry
Owen. Instead of depending on Eldridge Johnson for gramophone instruments, it was now making its own equipment
in an expansive new factory that had been built in an industrial town on the outskirts of London—Hayes, Middlesex.
The original plant in Hanover, which had once manufactured the entire output of Gramophone Company records,
was now taxed to capacity merely in meeting the demands of
the German market, while other branch factories had been
erected in Riga (for Russia), Aussig (for the Austro-Hun-
garian Empire), Ivry (for France), Barcelona (for Spain), and
Calcutta (for India), with the main plant at Hayes accounting for the English market and the export trade. The appearance of the discs themselves had changed, for the original
"recording angel" trademark on the label was now subordi-
nated to Barraud's dog and the legend "His Master's Voice."
Abbreviated to HMV, it became the name by which—among
English-speaking people, at any rate—the records were popu-
larly known. Despite the retirement of William Barry Owen,

the company's affairs were still largely under American influence: Owen's place as managing director had been taken by New York-born Alfred Clark, who continued to head the affairs of the company until shortly before his death in 1950, while the Gaisberg brothers from Washington, D. C., remained in charge of recording.

In Germany a new phonographic colossus was being formed by the Carl Lindström Company, which in a few short years had become a prominent manufacturer of talking machines on the Continent. In quick succession Lindström acquired the controlling stock of several independent German record companies—Odeon, Beka, and Favorite, to name the largest—as well as that of Fonotipia in Italy. By dint of these amalgamations and German manufacturing efficiency, Lindström provided effective competition to the Gramophone Company in the period before World War I. Pathé was receding in importance; its near-monopoly of the French market remained unbroken, but elsewhere the vertical-cut disc which this company continued to espouse had failed to keep pace with the lateral-cut gramophone record. Columbia, on the other hand, was growing in importance—especially in England. For years the British branch of Columbia had struggled along under an unimaginative management that saw fit to do little else than purvey English pressings of Columbia recordings made in America. In 1909, however, the London branch was taken over by Louis Sterling, a young expatriate from New York's Lower East Side who had previously managed an English cylinder company in partnership with Russell Hunting. Sterling (later Sir Louis Sterling) possessed an unquestioned genius for the record business; in 1910, as he began to revivify Columbia's affairs in England, it was just beginning to assert itself.

England, supposedly "the most unmusical nation in Europe," behaved in characteristically paradoxical fashion to emerge as the world's leading source of orchestral recordings (a distinction she was to maintain until 1939); and it was the English branch of the German-owned Odeon Company which, in April 1909, came forth with the first large-scale orchestral recording. Tchaikovsky's *Nutcracker* Suite was the music thus honored, in a performance by the London Palace Orchestra under the direction of Hermann Finck. The four double-sided English Odeon discs sold for sixteen shillings, including a special album to hold the records. Neither the orchestra (a forty-member music-hall ensemble) nor its conductor were of imposing musical stature, but they succeeded in breaking the old formula of overtures, medleys, and salon pieces and setting a new one that called for works from the standard orchestral repertoire in reasonably intact versions. According to a reporter from *The Sound Wave,* a British magazine for talking-machine fans, the *Nutcracker* recording sessions "occupied the orchestra for three whole days" and cost the Odeon Company "upwards of £800" (surely an inflated figure). This same publication averred that "no finer records of orchestral combinations have ever been placed on sale" and that "the tone of the strings (of which the Palace Theatre Orchestra is principally composed) is little short of perfection." Needless to say, Odeon's advertisements indulged in like hyperbole. They spoke of a tonal quality "pure in the extreme and of an ineffable sweetness," of an interpretation in which "all of the composer's most delicate effects of light and shade are handled in the daintiest possible manner." And with a fitting sense of historical perspective, Odeon's copy writer averred that "there is no person of musical perception, however prejudiced, who, having heard these records, will fail to become a convert to the musical possibilities of the Talking Machine."

A year later, Odeon's English branch came out with another four-record album by the same orchestra and conductor, this one devoted to Mendelssohn's incidental music to *A Midsummer Night's Dream.* "A veritable recording triumph," the advertisements said, and continued: "The makers believe that this series surpasses, if possible, their previous efforts in this direction. The tone of this new series is pure in the extreme and of an ineffable sweetness, and all the composer's most delicate effects of light and shade are handled in the daintiest possible manner."

Meanwhile, the Gramophone Company had climbed onto the orchestral band wagon. Landon Ronald, the accompanist-composer and musical ambassador of the Gramophone Company since 1901, was now cast in the role for which he was most congenially suited, that of conductor. His orchestra was the New Symphony Orchestra, an ensemble which really was new, having been formed in 1907 by a wealthy young musician named Thomas Beecham. Actually, in their debut on discs (January 1910) Ronald and the New Symphony were merely billed as "accompanists" to a twenty-six-year-old pianist from Germany, Wilhelm Backhaus, in the first recording ever made of a concerto (or part thereof). On two single-faced HMV record sides, the opening movement of Grieg's Piano Concerto had to be abbreviated by one half; but what remained moved *The Sound Wave*'s critic to applaud "bursts of eloquent magnificence which mere words fail to describe" and to register his amazement "at the success which has attended the first attempt to record a concerted work."

Critical scorn had not yet been heaped on abbreviated masterpieces, and such recordings managed to hold their own as creditable items of phonographic commerce. Undoubtedly the most popular of these "classics in cameo" was the *Unfinished* Symphony of Schubert in a recording by the Court Symphony Orchestra, which its sponsor—the English branch of Columbia—identified as "The Finest Orchestral Record Ever Issued." It sold in the thousands. Columbia's advertisements prated of "a wealth of melody that forms one of the most sublime examples of musical utterance in the history of symphonic writings," and the reviews lauded the reproduction "wherein the abounding delicatesses of instrumental treatment are rendered with most gratifying fidelity." But neither copy writer nor critic alluded to the disconcerting fact that a double-sided twelve-inch record could at best accommodate barely a third of Schubert's twenty-five-minute work.

Here is how things were managed for an orchestral recording session in Columbia's London studio, *circa* 1911, as described by Herbert C. Ridout, advertising manager of the English company, in a series of reminiscences published by *The Gramophone* in 1940:

> In the recording room . . . there were a number of small platforms of varying heights, each large enough to hold a chair and a music stand. The piano, always an upright, had its back removed. The Stroh violins were nearest the horn. Muted strings were never mentioned. The French horns, having to direct the bells of their instruments towards the recording horn, would turn their backs on it and were provided with mirrors in which they could watch the conductor. The tuba was positioned right back away from the horn and his bell turned away from it; he also watched in a mirror. The big drum never entered a recording room. . . .
>
> The horns projected into the recording-machine room through a partition. Here, where the operators worked, was a shrine of mystery. Nobody was allowed to pass into it. . . . Yet there was not much to be seen. A turntable mounted on a heavy steel base, controlled by a gravity weight, a floating arm with its recording diaphragm. A small bench, usually strewn with spare diaphragms, and a heating cupboard where the wax blanks were slightly warmed to soften the recording surface. Through a sliding glass panel in the partition the recorder could communicate with artists and conductor.

By the end of 1911 the Gramophone Company, impelled perhaps by Columbia's success with the *Unfinished*, had plunged into a bold program of orchestral recording. In

November of that year, three HMV records by Landon Ronald and the New Symphony were issued: the Scherzo from Mendelssohn's *Midsummer Night's Dream,* the *Marriage of Figaro* Overture, and Sibelius' *Finlandia* (in a cut version). *The Sound Wave* hailed them as "three orchestral reproductions which transcend any of their [the Gramophone Company's] previous triumphs in this direction." The Mendelssohn Scherzo seemed to be especially deserving of praise:

> The effect produced upon the listener is simply indescribable. Not only does the orchestra give a performance which is in every way worthy the delicate charm of its subject, but they are accorded a reproduction which faithfully reflects every inflection of tone, from the lightest to the heaviest passages. Again one cannot fail to note the really wonderful orchestral ensemble, the natural tone of the strings, the beauty of the flute, and the exquisite artistry with which the crescendos are worked up. Of a truth a superb performance and a wonder-compelling record.

More wonders from the same source were in store for 1912 with issues of Beethoven's *Leonore Overture No. 3* (on three sides), Grieg's *Peer Gynt* Suite (on four sides), and Schubert's *Unfinished* (on four sides), and for 1913 with issues of the Theme and Variations from Tchaikovsky's Suite No. 3 (on three sides), Grieg's *Lyric* Suite (on four sides), the Prelude to *Die Meistersinger* (on two sides), and the *Tannhäuser* Overture (on two sides). Almost all of these were abbreviated to greater or lesser extent.

In Germany the Beka Company had been promoting a series of orchestral records since 1911 played by the so-called Meister Orchestra ("the first orchestra formed specially for the purpose of playing for recording"), but the repertoire it espoused was not very adventurous, consisting principally of opera overtures. The same could be said for the orchestral records issued by the Gramophone Company's German branch—a series of overtures and brief instrumental trifles performed by the Grammophon Streich-Orchester under Bruno Seidler-Winkler. Indeed, it was not until 1913, with the release of two complete Beethoven symphonies on the Odeon label, that Germany began to challenge England in the area of orchestral literature. These Beethoven recordings, the first complete symphonies ever issued, were performed by the Odeon Streich-Orchester under an anonymous conductor, the Fifth Symphony taking eight sides and the Sixth taking ten. If we can believe the review by Max Chop, who listened to the discs, score in hand, not a single measure was deleted and there was not a deviation from the original instrumentation beyond what was absolutely necessary. "Only in a few passages," he wrote, "have the lower strings (violas, cellos, and double basses) been replaced or reinforced by bassoons—which simply cannot be helped in view of the incompatibility of these instruments with the recording diaphragm. Otherwise all has been retained. What we hear is not a Beethoven trimmed and clipped for the occasion, but genuine Beethoven in his regular symphonic vestments, played by a regular symphony orchestra. This I hold to be a great artistic achievement worthy of unreserved admiration." And though Chop recognized "minor unevennesses and variations in tonal quality," he insisted that these factors were in "ridiculous disproportion to the good and the extraordinary." "I must dwell on this point," he declared, "for what has been accomplished is significant as a principle, and this departure entails many logical consequences and opens many new perspectives."

One of these "logical consequences" was the appearance shortly thereafter of another complete Beethoven Fifth—the record industry, then as now, being nothing if not imitative. The competition in this case came from the Gramophone Company, which countered with a Fifth Symphony interpreted by the Berlin Philharmonic Orchestra under Arthur Nikisch. It was issued in Germany, February 1914, on four double-sided records and sold for thirty-eight marks (about $9.00 at the time); in England it was published in single-sided form and was issued piecemeal over a period of several months, the last record appearing in August 1914. Nikisch's involvement with the phonograph was comparable to that of Tamagno or Patti a decade before. As the first conductor of high eminence to work before the recording horn,* Nikisch bequeathed a distinguished endorsement of the phonograph as a medium for symphonic music. And that is about all he did bequeath. Nikisch was one of the first virtuoso conductors, a musician whose interpretations were held in the highest respect, and his recording of the Beethoven Fifth ought to be a historical document of the utmost importance. Unfortunately, it is nothing of the kind. No less an authority than Arturo Toscanini has pronounced it utterly unreliable as an index of Nikisch's abilities. Peter Hugh Reed, who played the records for Toscanini in 1943, reported that in Toscanini's estimation they are "not only poor in sound, they are downright misrepresentations of his [Nikisch's] artistry. . . . The tempi in the Fifth Symphony, as well as in the other works [Nikisch also recorded several overtures], are at variance with those of Nikisch's concert-hall presentations; and in the case of the Fifth Symphony the tempi are downright wrong. Nor do the phrasing and spirit of the performances correspond to [Toscanini's] memories of what Nikisch accomplished in his life." * * If Nikisch himself realized the phonograph's limitations, he did not admit to them. He was quoted in 1915 as having uttered the following: "I was delighted with . . . this wonderful instrument. The reproduction of vocal or instrumental music is absolutely [true] to nature from an artistic standpoint, and the sensation it produces is simply overpowering."

---

* Neither Landon Ronald nor Felix Weingartner, who conducted a few insignificant recordings for American Columbia in 1913, could be considered in the same class at the time.
* * *American Music Lover,* June 1943, pp. 229-30.

Clearly the ears of 1914 were less critical than ours. How else explain the exuberant praise lavished on these pre-World-War-I orchestral issues, recordings that seem to us laughable travesties of music? A Schubert *Unfinished* that played a total of eight minutes, a Fifth Symphony in which a world-famous conductor made do with six violins and two violas and dispensed altogether with timpani and double basses, a recording process that allowed no pianissimos and no fortes, that was deaf to subtleties of articulation, and that transmitted only the barest approximations of instrumental timbre—all this impels us in the age of "high fidelity" to expressions of disdain or, if we are charitably inclined, to tolerant mirth. But we might remember that every generation heralds the latest advance in recording as perfection itself, and that for most people deficiencies in reproduced sound become disturbing only in comparison with an improvement. How fortunate that this is so! Had the phonograph public of 1914 listened to their orchestral recordings with 1977 ears, the discs would have languished on the dealers' shelves, an unwanted and unsalable commodity. Happily, they were heard with 1914 ears; the muted rumblings presided over by Messrs. Finck, Ronald, and Nikisch afforded keen musical gratification to the willing listener; and the way was thus paved for an accumulating orchestral literature in years to come.

As for solo instrumental music, the phonograph offered much glitter and little substance. The glitter came from the reputations of several celebrated virtuosos who had been put under contract to make records, especially by the Gramophone Company. The 1913 HMV catalogue listed violin records by Mischa Elman, Josef Joachim, Fritz Kreisler, Jan Kubelik, Pablo de Sarasate, and Joska (later Joseph) Szigeti, but these worthies recorded only tidbits and trifles. "A considerable number of outstanding [violin] performances are

available," Max Chop informed the reader of 1909, "sometimes even by first-rate artists. But the bagatelle and pot-
boiler dominate even in this field where there is such ample
literature from Bach, Beethoven, Mendelssohn, and Brahms
to Bruch, Saint-Saëns, and Tchaikovsky." The piano was
treated somewhat better. In 1903 the French pianist Raoul
Pugno had recorded some Chopin and Liszt in the Gramophone Company's Paris studio, and in the same year and
place Edvard Grieg committed to wax some of his own piano
miniatures. More Chopin came from Vladimir de Pachmann
in some 1907 HMV issues, and in 1909 young Backhaus actually recorded a composition by Bach—the Prelude and
Fugue in C-sharp major from Book I of *The Well-Tempered
Clavier*. Another young pianist, Mark Hambourg, addressed
himself to the Beethoven *Moonlight* Sonata in 1910 (on two
single-sided HMV discs, hence drastically cut), and in the
following year Ignace Jan Paderewski recorded for the HMV
label some short works by Chopin. In Germany the pianist-
composer Eugen d'Albert was active recording similar literature for Odeon. But not one pianist, be he ever so eminent,
was allowed to play an extended piece of music before the
recording horn. One, or at most two, record sides seemed
to be the limit of a phonograph listener's attention—or so, at
least, the companies seemed to assume. Mr. John Symes, of
Walthamstow, who wrote to *The Sound Wave* in 1910 to ask
why "some classical music has been conspicuous by its absence on all makes of records," was a voice arguing in the
wilderness:

> Take the fifty-odd sonatas of Mozart; surely these would
> provide classical music enough for anyone, but there is none
> of it to be found on any record. Also the works of Bee-
> thoven, Schubert, Haydn, and many others—we cannot hear
> them at any price. . . . Surely a suite of Schumann's would
> be appreciated. . . . We have been living on crumbs and
> scraps long enough; now let us have some full meals.

But many more crumbs and scraps would be thrown at the record buyer before the phonograph offered a complete sonata by Mozart or a complete suite by Schumann.

If the pre-World-War-I phonograph owner wanted to gorge himself, there was only one way in which he could get a really full meal, and that—logically enough—was in the area of vocal recording, where the instrument was acoustically at its best. Recordings of "complete" operas, from overture to finale (more or less), were a phonographic staple by 1914. The first attempts, by the Gramophone Company in Italy, dated back to 1903. These—it is only fair to say—had little to recommend them musically, being not only riddled with excisions but performed by casts that kept changing from record to record. In the "complete" *Trovatore,* for instance, issued in 1906, sixteen singers were employed to perform music that Verdi had written for five principals. Evidently the eighteen sides allotted to *Trovatore* were recorded sporadically over a long period of time without any thought of attempting a sustained musical performance. Of these early Italian opera recordings by HMV the most interesting, and most unified, was the nearly complete *Pagliacci* made in Milan under the personal direction of its composer, Leoncavallo, a phonographic document which its sponsors claimed would settle "any question arising in the future concerning the composer's intentions."

The German branch of the Gramophone Company soon followed suit with a complete *Fledermaus* in 1907 and a complete *Faust* in 1908. These were a decided improvement. Not only were the casts unified throughout each recording, they were also of admirable competence. The *Faust* featured Emmy Destinn (Marguerite), Karl Jörn (Faust), and Paul Knüpfer (Mephistopheles)—which was as good a cast as could be assembled in Germany at the time. Destinn and Jörn also took part in a complete *Carmen* (sung, like the *Faust,* in German) which was issued in time for the 1908 Christmas trade.

Such recordings could not have sold on a spectacular scale (the *Carmen* cost a hundred marks, or $24, for eighteen records and an album), but they were popular enough to encourage competition from Odeon, which issued in quick succession *Cavalleria* (with Frieda Hempel as Lola), *Pagliacci,* and Act II of *Tannhäuser.*

More ambitious still were the opera sets produced by Pathé Frères utilizing the chorus, orchestra, and leading artists of the Opéra-Comique. In the years before World War I, nine operas were recorded by the Paris company, including *Roméo et Juliette* (with Yvonne Gall, Gustarello Affre, and Marcel Journet), *Faust,* and *Carmen.* They were issued on double-sided fourteen-inch discs, which—like all Pathé products—were recorded by the hill-and-dale process. Pathé even manufactured a phonograph with twin turntables, the Duplex Pathéphone, and coupled the sides in special sequence so that one could play through an entire act without interruption.

Unfortunately, the fever to record complete operas remained localized in Europe. Victor did not succumb. And thus we can only speculate on what might have been had the impresarios in Camden seen fit to pass on to posterity an entire *Madama Butterfly* with Caruso, Scotti, and Farrar, a *Traviata* with Melba and McCormack, or an *Orfeo* with Homer, Gluck, and Gadski.

13 *JAZZ IN CHIPPENDALE*

A FEVER OF QUITE ANOTHER SORT HAD ATTACKED AMERICAN record companies and their customers. Overnight the country had gone dance crazy. Under the heading "New Reflections on the Dancing Mania," *Current Opinion* declared in October 1913 that:

> people who have not danced before in twenty years have been dancing, during the past summer, afternoons as well as evenings. Up-to-date restaurants provide a dancing floor so that patrons may lose no time while the waiter is changing the plates. Cabaret artists are disappearing except as interludes while people recover their breaths for the following number. One wishes either to dance or to watch and to criticize those who dance.

Though the country was in discouraging economic doldrums and an onerous income tax law had just been passed, the New York *Evening Post* could single out dancing teachers as "the one class of citizens who regard the currency bill and income tax without trembling, and assert that there are no hard times."

Victor and Columbia promptly took advantage of the countrywide disposition to shuffle about on a dance floor. Tangos, One-Steps, Hesitation Waltzes, Bostons, and Turkey Trots came spewing forth from the record presses. Columbia placed its recording program "under the personal direction of the greatest authority in this country on modern dancing —G. Hepburn Wilson, M.B., *who dances while the band*

makes the record." A photograph accompanying this statement showed the aforesaid Mr. Wilson and his partner dancing in a recording studio with a fifteen-piece band huddled
behind them. This *modus operandi* had been adopted, Columbia assured prospective customers, so that each and every
recording would be in authentic dance tempo, and expensive
double-truck advertisements were taken in the *Saturday Evening Post* to spread the word about Columbia's dance-tested
records. Victor replied by engaging Vernon and Irene Castle,
the nation's ultimate arbiters of ballroom dancing, to supervise the making of all Victor dance records. To *The Victor
Book of the Opera* was now added another Camden publication illustrating in minute detail various modern dances as
performed by the Castles.

The dance mania stimulated the record business as nothing else ever had. Early in 1914 the American trade magazine *Talking Machine World* made a coast-to-coast survey of
the effect of dance records on the record business. The reports were uniformly extravagant. A representative in St.
Louis wrote that "dance music records have proven a great
business builder, as St. Louis has been, in common with the
rest of the country, 'dippy' over the new dances, and the sale
of a dozen records of this kind to a single customer or to a
stranger has not been unusual." Despite depressed business
conditions in the country as a whole, the talking-machine industry in 1914 prospered handsomely. Victor's assets jumped
from $13,940,203 in 1913 to $21,682,055 by 1915.

And Victor now was only one among many. More and
more people were beginning to make money out of the phonograph. One by one the basic patents were expiring, and
with them expired also the strangle hold that Victor and
Columbia had managed to impose on the lateral-cut talking-
machine business in America ever since the patent pool of
1902. The first large competitor to emerge was Sonora,
which introduced a line of table models and consoles in Oc-

tober 1914. They were "Clear as a Bell" and had the distinction of being able to play both lateral-cut and vertical-cut discs. A month later the Aeolian Company unveiled its Vocalion phonographs. They embodied a tone-controlling device called the "Graduola," which was nothing more than a shutter mechanism in the narrow part of the horn operated by remote control. It succeeded mainly in muffling further the already compressed tonal spectrum of acoustic recording and reproduction; but Aeolian, prosperous piano manufacturers with plenty of money to spend, made the most of it in advertising the Vocalion: "By a touch you can emphasize those delicate tonal qualities that are lost in ordinary reproductions; you can reduce harshness of tone or other faults in a record to a minimum, and you can impart a light and shade to the music that the record alone could never give." A third major competitor was the Brunswick-Balke-Collender Company of Dubuque, Iowa, from whence the nation's billiard parlors and bowling alleys had derived equipment for many years. Brunswick phonographs were placed on sale in 1916 and, like the Sonora and the Vocalion, were equipped to play both lateral- and vertical-cut records.

Dozens of smaller firms, in addition to the three mentioned above, swarmed into the fast-expanding talking-machine market. In 1912 there had been only three manufacturers in the business—Victor, Columbia, and Edison. In 1914 six new companies invaded the field; 1915 saw eighteen more newcomers; and in 1916 there were forty-six. Eldridge Johnson's dream of a phonograph in every American home was fast approaching reality—though not all of the instruments were to come from Camden, New Jersey. The dance craze had started the spectacular climb of the phonograph economy, and it was accelerated by a general upturn in business conditions when the country as a whole began to prosper from the effects of a great war in Europe. According to United States

Census figures, the value of the country's phonograph production increased from $27,116,000 in 1914 to $158,668,000 in 1919.

Salesmanship centered on cabinetry and styling. With the rising tide of prosperity in 1915 came a demand for high-priced phonographs. Victor's Victrola and Edison's Amberola consoles, which at $200 had represented the acme of prewar phonographic elegance, were now left far behind. They seemed quite *déclassé* compared to Sonora's "Supreme," an expensively veneered Victrola-type instrument that sold for $1,000. And they looked painfully gauche and utilitarian compared to the ornate Vocalion "Art Models," which ranged in price from $375 to $2,000. "Period design" became the new battle cry of the talking-machine industry, the manufacturers being abetted in their efforts by the glossy home-decoration magazines. In an article on "The Phonograph as a Decorative Element in the Home," *Country Life* deplored the fact that:

> this instrument . . . should have been so neglected in respect to its "outward and visible signs of inward and spiritual grace". . . . It is only now that purchasers as well as makers are beginning to realize that they are not dealing in an article of the caliber of a furnace or a laundry tub. Heretofore, both classes have taken the attitude of devout worshippers at the shrine of mechanical production. Now these same people are awakening to the inconsistency, and are dictating as to what it shall wear as a case. . . . Today the phonograph is encased with an eye to decorativeness and fittingness in the room scheme. . . . For inspiration, the designers have naturally turned to the period styles of their artistic forebears. Not only because so many people who want a phonograph will put it into a period setting, but also because the beauty of these products of recognized cabinet-makers is unquestioned.

The anonymous writer who laid down these principles in *Country Life* expressed a view that almost the entire indus-

try was to adopt: phonographs should look as little like phonographs as possible.

Columbia, which had pioneered in this area with its
tablelike "Regent" model before the war (see Chapter 10),
was quick to capitalize on the new trend. Its catalogue of
period phonographs ran the gamut from massive Gothic
chests to dainty Hepplewhite tables with large flat tops, half
of which remained permanently shut "so that a vase of flowers or a book rack may be placed on it and need not be removed when you wish to operate the Grafonola." Among
Columbia's gems was the "Donatello," a gawky piece of furniture five feet high and two feet wide on which were painted
four panels ("with their coloring toned down as if by the
passage of three centuries") showing symbolic figures repre-
senting Intelligence, Justice, Temperance, and Peace. For
this reproduction of "fifteenth-century Italian art at its im-
perishable best" Columbia demanded a mere $535. If you
were really in a spending mood, Columbia suggested the
"Queen Anne No. 5" at $1,075, which with its Chinese Chip-
pendale lacquer finish offered "a superb example of the exquisite work of the patient Oriental."

Even Victor succumbed to the national craving for curli-
cued carvings by grafting ornamental flourishes onto its
standard models and billing them as "Louis XVI Victrolas."
But Eldridge Johnson insisted that they remain basically
phonographs. There were no tables or cupboards or chests
in the Victor line of instruments; if you had a Victrola, you
were not encouraged to put a vase of flowers on top of it.

The great wartime phonograph boom came along just in
time to accelerate the fortunes of Edison's new Disc Phonograph. It had been officially unveiled in October 1913, when
the cylinder was failing fast as a viable article of commerce;
and it was publicized with all the *élan* that Edison's ingenious advertising department could muster. The combination
of vertical-cut recording, individually ground diamond styli,

and Edison's usual high standard of construction acted to make these instruments superior acoustically to any competing talking machine. Edison was not reticent about revealing this fact, and to drive it home he inaugurated his famous Edison Tone-Test Recitals. The purpose of these *soirées* was to prove that "the Edison Diamond Disc's re-creation of music cannot be distinguished from the original." A hall would be rented by the Edison organization, and on the appointed night an Edison artist (Maggie Teyte was one such) would appear in conjunction with an Edison Phonograph. There ensued a series of comparisons, with appropriate commentary by an Edison representative. Miss Teyte would sing "Believe Me If All Those Endearing Young Charms" in person, then she would be heard to sing it via the phonograph; the test was supposed to prove to everyone's satisfaction "that there was no difference between Miss Teyte's voice and the New Edison RE-CREATION of it." Apparently it convinced a lot of people, for Tone Tests featuring various Edison artists were held throughout the country to the accompaniment of steadily rising sales of Edison merchandise.

The Edison Disc Phonographs were not cheap. Ordinary console models sold for $200, while the period cabinets went for $800 and up. Such prices were in line with Edison's belief that the Disc Phonograph should make its chief appeal to "people of cultured and elegant tastes." Once again he set out to capture the market for high-class music. In 1913 he was quoted by *Cosmopolitan* as saying:

> Music is in the same backward state today that electricity was forty years ago. I am going to develop it. I hope to complete the task within three years. I shall also make the phonograph the greatest musical instrument in the world.

Highly paid singers were put under contract: Emmy Destinn, Frieda Hempel, Margaret Matzenauer, Claudia Muzio, Elisabeth Schumann, Maggie Teyte, Giovanni Martinelli, Jacques Urlus, and Giovanni Zenatello. But Edison was incapable of utilizing this talent to anyone's satisfaction but his own. He was continually interfering with the choice of repertoire and would stubbornly refuse to issue recordings that bore the approval both of his own recording directors and the artists themselves. His head teemed with half-baked notions about music. He preferred "melody" and "heart songs" to "the opera type." He had no use for accompaniments. "Every accompanist," he said, "tends to spoil the song. Accompanists should only be heard between the parts." His favorite song was "I'll Take You Home Again, Kathleen." All this resulted in a chaotically organized catalogue in which certain areas of music were totally ignored and where miscasting of accomplished musical artists was painfully apparent.

Nowhere in the talking-machine industry, to be quite fair about it, were there signs of real musical discrimination. Victor continued to enlarge the Red Seal catalogue: the Caruso repertoire grew in scope every year; Alma Gluck, Schumann-Heink, and John McCormack turned out dozens of best-selling songs; * and newcomers like Galli-Curci and Titta Ruffo served to compensate for the retirement of Eames and Plançon. But it was a tired formula that Victor was following. Opera arias and concert songs of the "I Hear You Calling Me" variety were already in towering oversupply, and yet still they emerged in billowing abundance to an audience that never seemed to have enough. The public that greedily bought Chippendale phonographs at inflated prices helped boost record sales to unprecedented heights in the lush period from 1914 to 1919. Americans had gone on a phonograph binge; since they were in a mood to spend money willy-nilly, record makers did not feel impelled to venture beyond the formula.

And yet these years in America cannot be written off as a

---

* Gluck's recording of "Carry Me Back to Old Virginny" was the first Red Seal disc to sell over a million copies.

total musical loss. The dance craze that started the boom was to provide a nucleus of historic recordings. In Victor's supplement of May 1917 there appeared a record billed as "the very latest thing in the development of music." It consisted of a blues and a one-step played by the Original Dixieland "Jass" Band, a group of five white musicians who had recently journeyed northward from New Orleans to reap the rewards of success in Reisenweber's Restaurant in New York. Like the Negro musicians of New Orleans from whom they had learned their art, these players improvised collectively on ragtime and dance themes in the style later described as *le jazz hot*. Their records were the first of thousands in this style, and they document the infancy of a musical form that was to reverberate around the world.

14 *SYMPHONIES FROM EUROPE*

In Britain, too, World War I had brought happy days to the phonograph industry, but there war-born prosperity was channeled into a more productive direction than thousand-dollar instruments immured in medieval chests. These years saw the decline in Europe of the venerable celebrity vocal record and the coincident ascendance of orchestral and instrumental repertoire. The shape of things to come was already apparent in the autumn of 1915, when British magazines began to carry full-page advertisements showing portraits of Mr. Thomas Beecham and Sir Henry J. Wood and offering details of their latest records. Never before in the history of the phonograph had conductors been awarded star billing in this fashion, nor had there ever been such sales effort expended in the direction of Mozart, Tchaikovsky, Stravinsky, or Elgar. The tenors and sopranos had had their innings; now the field was being cleared for new idols and new music.

The prime force behind these developments came from the English branch of Columbia, which was then picking up speed in its meteoric rise from obscurity. Shortly after the war began, this company stumbled onto a gold mine. The first of the amazingly successful war revues, Albert de Courville's *Business as Usual,* had just opened at the London Hippodrome, and Columbia hit upon the happy notion of recording the show's songs by the original cast. This set of records sold so well that Columbia promptly signed up the

196

principals of every successful revue in London—and there were a lot of them in those halcyon days of the music hall. Irving Berlin's ragtime revue *Watch Your Step, The Bing Boys* starring George Robey, and *Cheep* featuring a young comedienne named Beatrice Lillie figured among the many revues that Columbia recorded in this period. To soldiers on leave, the records were a perfect memento of an enchanted evening in London; and they helped push sales into the tens of thousands. Ever since, original-cast recordings have been a staple of the record industry.

With profits accumulating in the bank, Columbia started to invest money in a refurbished classical catalogue. Louis Sterling, general manager of the English Columbia branch, had to reckon with the Victor-HMV dominance in the Red Seal repertoire. Any efforts in this direction would be wasted; there was no way to compete on even terms with Melba and Tetrazzini, McCormack and Caruso. But in the orchestral and instrumental field the surface had just been scratched, and it was into this area that Sterling moved with all the resources of his growing company. Contracts were signed in 1915 with young Thomas Beecham, whose musical efforts were just beginning to make their mark on English musical life, and with Sir Henry J. Wood, the bearded impresario and conductor of London's popular Queen's Hall "Prom" concerts. Beecham addressed himself in his first discs to repertoire in which he has been long familiar, the *Magic Flute* Overture and the dances from *Prince Igor;* Wood made his recorded debut in the Prelude to Act III of *Lohengrin,* the Scherzo movement from Tchaikovsky's Fourth Symphony, and orchestrations of Rachmaninoff's Prelude in C-sharp minor and Percy Grainger's *Shepherd's Hey.* There followed Beecham renditions of the second and third movements of Tchaikovsky's *Pathétique,* Stravinsky's *Firebird* Suite, and the *Oberon* Overture; while Wood was heard in Richard Strauss's *Till Eulenspiegel* (though the advertisements did not mention the German composer's name; this was October 1916), the Prelude and *Liebestod* from *Tristan,* the *Tannhäuser* Overture, and Tchaikovsky's *Capriccio Italien.*

The manner was more significant than the substance. In musical content these orchestral recordings were still primeval. Although the reproduction was somewhat improved over prewar standards, the sound of Beecham's Mozart on records as yet bore only an incidental resemblance to his performances at the Shaftesbury Theater. In addition, mutilations of the score were all too common: the *Firebird* Suite and *Till Eulenspiegel* were each abbreviated to fit onto a double-sided record, being thus reduced by half or more; the *Tannhäuser* Overture and *Capriccio Italien* likewise became compressed into the double-sided mold, and in one horrible instance Sir Henry went so far as to squeeze Dukas' *L'Apprenti sorcier* on one side of a record and Wagner's *Flying Dutchman* Overture on the other. But whatever their musical shortcomings, these issues were publicized as orchestral recordings never had been before. Columbia bought double-spreads to launch Record No. L-1067, *Till Eulenspiegel's Merry Pranks;* it was described as "The Apotheosis of Genius & Art in Orchestral Performance & Recording," and next to Sir Henry's picture was his testimonial: "In my opinion the greatest Orchestral Recording yet produced." The public took the hint. According to *The Sound Wave* in 1916:

> The orchestral records made by Sir Henry J. Wood have interested the whole of the gramophone public. Sales are, of course, the proof, and in this connection it is interesting to learn that these records have achieved a phenomenal popularity.

The Gramophone Company, taking note of this, reactivated its own program of orchestral recording. Landon Ronald returned to the studio, this time with the Royal Albert Hall Orchestra; and Sir Edward Elgar, Dame Ethel Smyth, and Sir Edward German were engaged to conduct their own works for the HMV label. Banner headlines in large advertisements proclaimed that "Britain's Leading Composers & Conductors testify to the Supremacy of 'His Master's Voice' Records." Elgar was quoted as being "quite satisfied that the records of my compositions are remarkably faithful reproductions of the originals," and Ethel Smyth expressed her delight with the recordings that had been made of excerpts from her opera *The Boatswain's Mate*. Not to be outdone in promoting the cause of British music, Columbia issued the Vaughan Williams song cycle *On Wenlock Edge* (five single-sided records in an album, performed by the tenor Gervase Elwes and the London String Quartet) and Sir Henry J. Wood's *Fantasia on English Sea Songs*. Both companies also saw fit to publish abridged recordings of the Elgar Violin Concerto, Columbia's with Albert Sammons as soloist and Wood conducting, HMV's with Marie Hall and the composer conducting.

Columbia also took a flyer in the direction of chamber music with a series of discs by the London String Quartet (Albert Sammons, Thomas W. Petre, H. Waldo Warner, and C. Warwick Evans). The prospect of recording a string quartet in full was yet too revolutionary to consider. Isolated movements, and usually abridged at that, were all that most phonograph listeners could be expected to digest. One of the first issues, in the summer of 1916, coupled a movement of Ravel's Quartet in F with a snatch (no other word will do) from Beethoven's Opus 131! Later that year came a fairly complete version of Mozart's Quartet in E-flat, K.428, on two double-sided records, which *The Sound Wave* praised as "one of the daintiest of string reproductions to which we have ever harkened." When two movements, grievously cut, of Brahm's Quartet in B-flat, Opus 67, were issued in April 1917, *The Sound Wave* commented that the records by the

London String Quartet "enjoy a popularity that is not merely new to record-world experience but is in itself a revelation of the marked degree of advance being shown in public taste. Who so recently as three years ago would have ventured to present to the record public a Brahms quartet?" Such popularity as they enjoyed, however, was only relative, for chamber music then—and for years to come—paid dividends in prestige rather than cash. Still, Columbia persevered in its policy and even went so far as to record Albert Sammons and the pianist William Murdoch in some of the sonata literature for violin and piano. Their first record, two abridged movements from the Grieg Sonata in C minor, was accurately hailed as "the first recording of a genuine duet for violin and piano, each part of equal importance, with each instrument played by an artist of equal rank."

In England and on the Continent orchestral records had "arrived" by the end of World War I. Acoustically they were good enough to afford at least moderate satisfaction to critical listeners; commercially they were easily on a par with the old-style celebrity vocals. But musically there was still much ground to be covered. There would be no pleasing the discriminating music-lover as long as Beethoven was pared down to fit the exigencies of a twelve-inch record.

Germany had set a precedent with its two recordings of the entire Beethoven Fifth issued just before the holocaust of 1914, and it was from Germany that the leadership came for propagandizing the virtues of uncut performances. In August 1919 announcements were made of a new series of Wagnerian orchestral recordings for Parlophone by the Charlottenburg Opera House Orchestra under Eduard Mörike. They were to be played, the Parlophone copy writers stressed, "according to the original score, without tampering or abridgments." Parlophone had originally been the trade name of a phonograph manufactured by the Salon-Kinematograph Company of Berlin. After the merger of this firm with the Carl Lindström group, the name was applied to a medium-priced line of popular and operatic records with small claim to anyone's attention. Lindström's decision to assign all important orchestral recordings to this label brought Parlophone out of obscurity. During the next few years its uncut recordings of symphonic literature were to enjoy international esteem.

The Wagner series was followed the next year by a Schubert *Unfinished* also conducted by Mörike. Then in 1921 came competition from another German firm, the Deutsche Grammophon Gesellschaft of Berlin and Hanover. Originally this had been the German branch of the British-owned Gramophone Company. For four and a half years of war, while ties with Britain were severed, it had operated as an independent company; and by complicated legal maneuvering after the Armistice, the branch had managed to secede entirely from the British parent company. Curiously, Deutsche Grammophon retained the "His Master's Voice" trademark for use in Germany and for many years kept its prewar matrices of "Red Seal Aufnahmen" by Caruso, Scotti, Melba, and company. In the early 1920s this company exported unauthorized bargain-price pressings of Red Seal recordings, marketing them in Europe on the Musica label and in the United States on the Opera Disc label. But this was patently *de trop* and soon was brought to a halt after litigation by Victor and the Gramophone Company. Thereafter, Deutsche Grammophon exported only its own German-made recordings. They too were to gain world recognition, under the export label Polydor. Following Parlophone's lead, Deutsche Grammophon-Polydor heralded its orchestral issues as *"Partiturgetreu—Ungekürzt"* ("Faithful to the score —Unabridged"); and like Parlophone, it concentrated on Wagner, featuring the Berlin State Opera Orchestra under

Leo Blech and the Berlin Philharmonic under Max von Schillings.

A sense of musical ethics had come to England too. When Columbia issued a truncated recording of the *Eroica* Symphony in 1922 on three double-sided discs (instead of the required six), it reaped scathing abuse for having dared to tamper with a masterpiece. The tide had turned. Abridgments became more and more of a rarity, and a company that sponsored them could no longer bank on the ignorance and indulgence of a benighted public. For the phonograph was now attracting a new kind of listener—the serious, intellectual connoisseur of the arts who collected records of symphonic and chamber music with the same gusto as the novels of Virginia Woolf or the poetry of Ezra Pound. He discovered his spokesman in a new magazine called *The Gramophone,* founded in 1923 by the novelist Compton Mackenzie "to encourage the recording companies to build up for generations to come a great library of good music." Several other magazines devoted to phonographic affairs had preceded *The Gramophone* both in Europe and America, but Mackenzie's was the first to be edited by record listeners for record listeners and the first to be primarily concerned with serious music.

The rationale of the cultivated enthusiast to whom *The Gramophone* appealed was summed up well in an article by Frank Swinnerton, "A Defence of the Gramophone," which appeared in the magazine's August 1923 issue. The potential audience of the gramophone was innumerable, Swinnerton believed, but most people had no inkling of the strides it had made in recent years.

> To them it is an infernal machine which makes all music sound as if it were being played by nursery soldiers. They decry it. They do so in ignorance; and they should all be good material for the gramophone companies. . . . Instruments and records have improved very much indeed within the past few years. That is a point which must not be forgotten. It is full of promise for the future.

He understood that the instrument was not yet perfect:

> It cannot yet render satisfactorily the full volume of an
> orchestra or the pure tone of the pianoforte. Always the
> orchestra has a tinny vibration—a dwarfing of the original;
> nearly always the piano has many notes—particularly loud
> notes—resembling the banjo. . . . And finally, what is to me
> the gravest defect of all (since I am little disturbed by details
> of the mechanism, so long as I love the music), the regulation
> size of the twelve-inch disc imposes restrictions upon the
> piece of music which is to be reproduced. Too often, far too
> often, the music has been ruthlessly cut. . . . These defects
> will almost certainly be diminished in the near future. They
> are already less than they were a few years ago. The com-
> parative noiselessness of the needles upon the records, the
> reduction of "crackle," the elimination of blare and bray,
> provided care is taken with needles, are all signs of incessant
> search for improvement. . . . Listening to a gramophone
> used to be an irksome business. Nowadays, however, it is
> possible to be altogether absorbed in a fine piece of music
> which is being performed by means of the gramophone—to
> be moved by it and absorbed in it as one would be in the
> concert hall.

Just as Swinnerton wrote the above, English record companies were beginning to flood the market with exactly the
kind of repertoire that would appeal to him and his fellow
readers of *The Gramophone*. The acoustic recording process
had reached its apogee. Although the records were still being made according to the basic principles evolved by Berliner and Johnson in the 1890s (the mechanical vibrations of
sound acting directly on a diaphragm-stylus device and cutting a lateral pattern in a wax disc), various refinements had
been developed over the years—in the sensitivity of the recording diaphragm, in the fineness of the wax, in the gal-
vanoplastic process of converting an original wax impression
into a metal matrix. A full symphony orchestra could now be
recorded without recourse to the substitution of tubas for
double basses or Stroh violins for unadorned strings. It is

true that the overtones which give music its sensuous flavor were largely missing. At its best, the acoustic recording process was limited to a range of 168–2,000 cycles * (as compared to a range of 20–20,000 cycles audible in the concert hall), and this did not augur well for an expansive or vivid kind of sound. But it was recognizable as the sound of an orchestra; it was music, not tooting; and it gave pleasure.

In its first issue, *The Gramophone* noted with approval "the first record which has been made of an orchestral piece by Bach"—the Brandenburg Concerto No. 3 performed by Eugene Goossens and the Royal Albert Hall Orchestra on two double-sided HMV discs. In September 1923 there appeared a five-record album containing an uncut recording of the Beethoven Seventh Symphony performed by the London Symphony Orchestra under Felix Weingartner, the first of many Beethoven interpretations which this conductor was to record for English Columbia; while the HMV list for that month featured the Tchaikovsky *Pathétique* played by Sir Landon Ronald and the Royal Albert Hall Orchestra, complete except for one repeat in the second movement. The same conductor and orchestra, with Isolde Menges as soloist, augmented the Beethoven literature later in the year with the Violin Concerto for HMV; and from Columbia came a freshet of British music—Gustav Holst's suite *The Planets* conducted by the composer, Delius' *Dance Rhapsody,* and Vaughan Williams' *London* Symphony. Contemporary music was not immune to the recording director's blue pencil: the Delius work was cut slightly, the Vaughan Williams

---

* That is, from E below middle C to three octaves above middle C. This does not mean that music beyond this range was entirely lost. As J. P. Maxfield explained: "A reproducing system which fails to reproduce all frequencies below, let us say, middle C will, nevertheless, reproduce the auditory sensation of a musical note whose fundamental is below this, even though the fundamental and one or two of its harmonics have been eliminated in the reproduction. While this elimination of the lower components in no way changes the apparent pitch of a note, it does change what is commonly called the 'character' or 'timbre' of the note. The 'metallic' quality of tone characteristic of the older type talking machine was largely brought about by the failure to reproduce these lower notes."

horrendously (the first movement hacked to pieces, the second and fourth omitted entirely).

By 1924 the trickle of orchestral issues in England had turned into a river. From Columbia that year there were complete recordings of Dvořák's *New World* Symphony (Hallé Orchestra under Sir Hamilton Harty), the Beethoven Eighth and Mozart E-flat symphonies (London Symphony under Weingartner), the César Franck Symphony (New Queen's Hall Orchestra under Sir Henry J. Wood), and the Mozart Violin Concerto in A (Arthur Catterall, violin, with Harty conducting). In the same period HMV offered the Beethoven Ninth * and the Tchaikovsky Fifth (Albert Coates conducting), the suite from Stravinsky's *Petrouchka* (Royal Albert Hall Orchestra—Goossens), the Brahms Second Symphony and the Liszt E-flat Concerto (Arthur de Greef, piano, Sir Landon Ronald conducting). In the early months of 1925 the river became a torrent, with recordings of Mozart's Violin Concerto in D (Fritz Kreisler, Ronald conducting) and *Jupiter* Symphony (Coates), Schumann's Piano Concerto (the first of three recordings for HMV by Alfred Cortot and Sir Landon Ronald), Strauss's *Tod und Verklärung,* and the Berlioz *Symphonie Fantastique.*

Chamber music was similarly well favored. After years of isolated movements and abridgments, Columbia had set still another trend by issuing a Mozart sonata (in A, K.526) without a single note missing, the participants being Hamilton Harty, piano, and Arthur Catterall, violin. Collectors with long memories still recall the impact these discs made when they were first issued. In its turn, HMV rushed forward in February 1924 with the first uncut recording of a quartet— the Brahms Quartet in C minor, Opus 51, No. 1, performed by the Catterall Quartet. "It is to be hoped," voiced *The Gramophone,* "that the public will respond to this overture

---

* Which massive work did not respond at all well to the acoustic recording process.

and show the manufacturers that they will back their enterprise; this alone will make complete recordings possible." While HMV rested temporarily on its laurels, Columbia quickly offered uncut recordings by the Lener Quartet of works by Mozart (C major, K.465), Haydn (D major, Opus 76, No. 5), and Beethoven (C-sharp minor, Opus 131). And in the realm of solo music there was such recondite matter to be sampled as seventeenth- and eighteenth-century harpsichord pieces played by Violet Gordon Woodhouse (on the instrument for which they were written) and Bach's *Chromatic Fantasy and Fugue* played by Harold Samuel (on the piano).

In Germany the recording studios were equally active. By May 1925 both Deutsche Grammophon-Polydor and Parlophone had issued all nine Beethoven symphonies, and such mammoth works as Bruckner's Seventh and Mahler's *Resurrection* symphonies had been undertaken for Deutsche Grammophon-Polydor by Oskar Fried and the Berlin State Opera Orchestra. Some of these were not as *Partiturgetreu* as the advertisements promised: Parlophone's Ninth Symphony, conducted by this company's "house conductor," Frieder Weissmann, deleted two chunks from the last movement and substituted tubas for double basses; and the Deutsche Grammophon-Polydor recording of Strauss's *Also Sprach Zarathustra* could hardly have been *Ungekürzt* on three double-sided discs. But on the whole, German record buyers were as well off as the English. In both countries the phonograph was at last able to offer a fairly representative and well-balanced sampling of musical literature in creditable performances and with tolerable recorded sound.

The promising future that Frank Swinnerton had envisaged seemed assured. Phonograph and record sales had maintained a steady climb, and the leading European companies were in sound financial condition. Bit by bit the acoustical recording process was being improved; meanwhile, an increasing number of works from the standard literature would be made available to the serious music-lover. The purchase of a new phonograph and an ample library of symphonic masterpieces seemed a prudent and worthy investment in view of the years of musical pleasure to come. And then, without forewarning, news from America brought European recording activity to a standstill and overnight made existing records as obsolete as the pinhole camera.

15 *THE FLATTENED VICTROLA*

The news that announced the closing of one era and the opening of another had been preceded in America by five perilous years. The phonograph had fallen on evil days —or at least comparatively evil days, considering how promisingly the postwar years had started out. In 1919 customers had fallen all over themselves buying phonographs and jamming into shops in a seller's market where demand far exceeded supply. That year nearly two hundred manufacturers in the United States were churning out more than two million phonographs—compared to eighteen manufacturers in 1914 and a production of five hundred thousand instruments. Many of these newcomers in the industry were filling the vacuum created by Victor's temporary defection, for the large Camden plant had been turned into an arsenal and was in full production manufacturing antisubmarine gear for the Navy and other matériel when war work suddenly ground to a halt in November 1918. Victor could not reconvert overnight, and it was a full year before deliveries of Victrolas reached full stride. In the interim Eldridge Johnson took space in hundreds of newspapers to reprint an official letter from Washington commending Victor on its valuable help in the war effort. It was signed by the Acting Secretary of the Navy, Franklin D. Roosevelt.

Newcomers appeared in the record field too that year. The patents that had given Victor and Columbia a monopoly in the manufacture of lateral-cut records had at last run out.

208

It was a lucrative business, or so it appeared, and the woods were soon full of competitors. As a matter of fact, some of them had been producing vertical-cut records for several years. Pathé had opened an American recording studio and pressing plant in 1914 (under the aegis of the ubiquitous Russell Hunting), an offshoot of Germany's Lindström group had launched the Okeh records in 1915, and the Aeolian Company had been issuing records on the Vocalion label since 1916. But the market for vertical-cut discs was tiny, and they were abandoned as soon as the Victor-Columbia patent constraints ceased to apply. In 1919 Okeh and Vocalion switched to lateral cut; Pathé followed in 1920 with its Actuelle record, the venerable French concern having finally recognized after a quarter century's devotion to the hill-and-dale system that lateral cut had come to stay. Brunswick made its debut as a record maker at the same time; so did a number of smaller firms whose business careers were mostly short-lived.

At the end of 1919 the industry's balance sheets were wonderful to behold. Columbia's net income before taxes exceeded $7,000,000, enabling the directors to declare a dividend of $3.32 a share. Victor wound up the year with assets totaling $37,860,694 (ten years earlier they had been a little less than $5,000,000) and with enough cash in the bank to pay out $9,000,000 in July 1920 for a fifty per cent interest in the overseas Gramophone Company. It hadn't been so many years since Eldridge R. Johnson was a struggling young manufacturer and the Gramophone Company his biggest and most affluent customer. Now he was able to buy a half interest in that world-wide enterprise without causing an inordinate drain on Victor's resources. Fifteen years later, Johnson's successors were to dispose of this holding for a little over $10,000,000.

From the trade papers in the phonograph industry the dawn of a new year elicited many rosy prognostications and

jubilant palaver about the sales records that would certainly
be set during 1920. Unfortunately, it did not work out that
way at all. By June the signs of hard times were already evident and the word "deflation" was on everybody's tongue;
however, this was always a slow season for the phonograph
business and things were bound to improve. They did not.
The Columbia Company, in anticipation of mammoth sales,
had ordered thousands of cabinets from twenty-one wood-
working factories scattered throughout the country; but instead of mammoth sales, there was a mammoth inventory.
To pay for them the firm was obliged to float a $7,500,000
bond issue payable in five years with an annual interest rate
of eight per cent. This marked the beginning of the end of
a company dating back to 1889. Edward D. Easton, Columbia's founder, might well have turned in his grave. He had
died in 1915, leaving his company with a surplus of $2,000,-
000 in undivided profits; however, it had passed into the
control of financiers who knew little about the phonograph
business, and ruin was in clear sight. By borrowing money,
Columbia managed to stave off extinction. Other firms with
lower credit ratings were not so fortunate. The edifice of
war-born phonograph manufacturers toppled into a pit of
bankruptcies and receiverships.

To the overproduction of 1920 was added the business depression of 1921. Columbia's ledgers looked grimmer than
ever. Gross sales, which had been $47,000,000 in 1920, dwin-
dled to $19,000,000 in 1921, and the red ink showed a net
loss of $4,370,611. Francis S. Whitten, Columbia's chairman
of the board, pleaded with its bondholders to accept a volun-
tary adjustment in interest payments. They did. But the
decline in Columbia stock from 65 to 15⅝ did not betoken
much faith on Wall Street in the company's prospects. In a
desperate bid to regain solvency, Columbia sold its prosper-
ing British branch to the European General Manager, Louis
Sterling, and a group of English capitalists with whom he

was associated. This occurred in December 1922. Three months later the busy Dictaphone branch was put up for sale; it brought in $1,000,000. But it was too late for even these transfusions to help. In October 1923 the company went into receivership following the filing of a petition in involuntary bankruptcy by three creditors. Columbia's books showed liabilities of $21,000,000 and assets of $19,000,000. As the retiring chairman of the board put it, "the news of the receivership was not unexpected."

For a time the people at Victor were able to view these developments with benign complacency. The company had started off the critical years with a backlog of unfilled orders amounting to millions of dollars, and it sailed smoothly on despite the feverish competition from Columbia and other rivals laden with bulging inventories By the end of the year Victor's total sales volume exceeded $50,000,000; in 1921 it climbed to $51,000,000. The company seemed impregnable. In the face of industry-wide overproduction and a national depression, it thrived as never before. But there were chinks in Victor's armor, and they began to show in 1922.

Actually, the company had been living for some time on its capital—on twenty years of intensive advertising, on the strength of the "Victrola" and "His Master's Voice" trademarks, on a reputation for quality merchandise built up over the years, on the aura of its Red Seal artists enveloping Victor merchandise with musical respectability. New ideas in Camden had become few and far between. The Victrola of 1921 looked almost identical with the original model of 1906. And the Red Seal catalogue was the same as ever. Caruso had died and Farrar and Melba were on the point of retiring, but their records continued to sell in quantity (Caruso records alone gave Victor a gross income of $2,500,000 per year in the early 1920s); and when new artists like Gigli and Galli-Curci and Ruffo were added to the roster, they repeated the same old formula that had always been so lucrative. There comes a time, however, when a formula outlives its appeal and when the tried and true way of conducting business falls afoul of public apathy. Victor's troubles began over cabinetry. The Victrola with the squat hinged lid was becoming *démodé*. Public fancy had switched to period cabinets with broad, flat tops. Although the expensively veneered models carrying a price tag of $1,000 had dropped from favor, their poor relations were much in evidence. The flat-top vogue had spread across the country, and in the $100–$200 price range were to be found great quantities of phonographs masking as eighteenth-century cabinets. Brunswick and Sonora had been exploiting the demand for this type of instrument with marked success, and from thousands of Victor dealers came pleadings for a flat-top Victrola. The public, they wailed, was no longer attracted by the old models—and behind these lamentations lay the threat that dealers might switch to more profitable lines if Victor did not mend its ways.

For years Eldridge Johnson had resisted the flat-top. His cherished Victrola was held to be *sui generis;* it did not need to imitate anything. In 1922, however, he appeared to have capitulated. That summer word was sent out to Victor's overstocked dealers of a change in policy. flat-top Victrolas, priced from $100 to $375, would be available from Camden in the fall. But they were flat-tops with a difference, for right in the middle of the cabinet was a familiar looking object—the raised Victrola lid covering the phonograph mechanism. Johnson just would not have the Victrola serving as a table. This instrument was promptly nicknamed "the humpback" in phonograph trade circles. Customers took a similarly derisive view of it, and Victor found its inventory of unsalable instruments growing steadily larger.

The record business, fortunately, remained in fairly good condition. In 1921, United States production of records had exceeded 100,000,000 (a fourfold increase over 1914); and though the figure had dropped to 92,000,000 in 1923, there was still no cause for alarm. This prosperity was largely attributable to jazz, a form of music by then in full flower, though the original improvisatory jazz played by small ensembles had been submerged by a more commercial variety to which the whole country was dancing in new, gaudy ballrooms. Its detractors were voluble and impassioned. In *The Ladies' Home Journal* for August 1921 the question was posed, "Does Jazz Put the Sin in Syncopation?" Mrs. Marx E. Oberndorfer, National Music Chairman, General Federation of Women's Clubs, answered vigorously in the affirmative. To her, jazz was "that expression of protest against law and order, that bolshevik element of license striving for expression in music." She recalled that "dancing to Mozart minuets, Strauss waltzes, and Sousa two-steps certainly never led to the corset check-room, which holds sway in hotels, clubs, and dance halls. Nor would the girl who wore corsets in those days have been dubbed 'old ironsides' and left a disconsolate wallflower in a corner of the ballroom. . . . Such music has become an influence for evil." According to Fenton T. Bott, a leading light in the American National Association of Masters of Dancing, jazz dancing was "a worse evil than the saloon used to be." "Those moaning saxophones," he exclaimed, "and the rest of the instruments with their broken, jerky rhythm make a purely sensual appeal. They call out the low and rowdy instinct. All of us dancing teachers know this to be a fact. . . . The music written for jazz is the very foundation and essence of salacious dancing. The words also are often very suggestive, thinly veiling immoral ideas." Despite such sentiments, the public did nothing to curb this pernicious music. Instead it went to the nearest record store, bought copies of the latest hits, rolled up the rugs, and danced. Record companies vied with each other to sign up popular bands. Victor featured Paul Whiteman and Fred Waring, Columbia had Ted Lewis and Fletcher Henderson, while Vincent Lopez could be heard on the Okeh label and Leo Reisman on Brunswick. Lesser record companies in the hinterland, such as Gennett (of Richmond, Indiana) and Paramount (of Port Washington, Wisconsin) and Sunshine (of Los Angeles), went after the so-called "race" market and recorded most of the accomplished Negro musicians from New Orleans, among them Kid Ory, King Oliver, Louis Armstrong, and Jelly Roll Morton.

Jazz enthusiasts were better off than the devotees of serious music. There had been no efflorescence of orchestral recording in America such as Europe was enjoying, though Victor had been pursuing a halfhearted policy in this direction since October 1917. At that time a few recordings were made by the Boston Symphony under its conductor, Karl Muck; only three of these were ever released: the Prelude to Act III of *Lohengrin*, "Marche Miniature" from Tchaikovsky's Suite No. 1, Opus 43, and the last movement of Tchaikovsky's Fourth Symphony. They elicited the following adulation from R. D. Darrell, a usually sober critic: "The tone of the woodwinds is so exquisite that one can only marvel. Precision, phrasing, and tone are equaled only by the balance and clarity. It is hard to avoid superlatives when describing these records. . . . There was never anything like them before, there can never be anything quite like them again." Such praise seems incredible when one hears these records today. Three years later Victor enticed Arturo Toscanini into the studio. The maestro and an orchestra of Italian musicians, with whom he was touring the United States, recorded a total of sixteen sides, including two movements from Mozart's E-flat Symphony, the last movement of Beethoven's Fifth, and such specialties of his as the *Don Pasquale* Overture and the Scherzo from Mendelssohn's *Midsummer Night's Dream* music. Toscanini detested the cramped conditions under which acoustic recordings were made, and he was rightfully impatient with the unsatisfactory results. Victor found a far more co-operative musician in the person of Leopold Stokow-ski, the young blond-haired conductor of the Philadelphia Orchestra. From its very first recording date (October 22, 1917) until 1940 the Philadelphia Orchestra reigned as Victor's prime musical property. At first it was heard only in short bonbons of the *Hungarian Dance No. 5,* Boccherini Minuet, or *Mignon* Gavotte variety * and in abridged versions (cut to fit on one twelve-inch side) of such standard orchestral war horses as Weber's *Invitation to the Dance,* Chabrier's *España,* and the Largo from Dvořák's *New World* Symphony. Finally, in 1924 and 1925, Victor took the plunge and issued two complete works by Stokowski and the Philadelphia Orchestra: Schubert's *Unfinished* and Stravinsky's *Firebird* Suite. All of these were waxed in Trinity Church, 114 North Fifth Street, Camden, which the Victor company had purchased as an orchestral recording studio. The remarkable acoustic properties of this structure accounted in large part for the superior sound quality of Victor's orchestral issues. Reporting to *The Gramophone* on the Stokowski-Philadelphia *Unfinished* Symphony, a young collector in New Jersey, C. G. Burke, commented that "for clarity and differentiation of instruments, smoothness of performance, balance of tone, and freedom from extraneous noises there is nothing to compare with it."

Victor's cautious orchestral recording program seemed revolutionary beside the domestic efforts of Columbia and Brunswick, its chief competitors. Columbia had been reorganized by its creditors, but this company—with its paucity of capital—could hardly be expected to venture where even Victor feared to tread. Some snippets and abridgments recorded by Josef Stransky and the New York Philharmonic and by Walter Damrosch and the New York Symphony were all that Columbia could offer from home sources. However, this company made up for domestic inactivity by issuing sev-

* Victor's classification for this repertoire was "Melodious Instrumental."

eral complete recordings produced by its ally in England; five symphonies and three quartets, each in a special album, appeared in the Columbia list for November 1924, and more followed at regular intervals. Brunswick's Cleveland Symphony recordings (conducted by Nikolai Sokoloff) were confined to their own "Melodious Instrumental" category. In total, then, the American record buyer in the winter of 1924–25 could choose from among three complete chamber works and seven complete orchestral works, of which only two had been recorded in his own country. Otherwise he had to content himself with semi-classics, abridgments, and a plethora of operatic arias. It does not become us to berate Victor and its competitors too vigorously for their continued concentration on vocal repertoire; there resulted some treasurable records by Rosa Ponselle, Elisabeth Rethberg, Sigrid Onegin, and other accomplished singers, without which we would be the poorer today. But at the time they were issued, the musically sophisticated record collector did not care at all about the preservation of accomplished vocalism for posterity. He saw them only as the continuation of a worn-out formula and wondered, with growing impatience, how long it would take the American record industry (Victor in particular) to rouse itself and follow Europe's lead in amassing a representative catalogue of orchestral and chamber music.

But nothing seemed to shake Victor from its torpor. Not even radio. For a new menace was now at hand, threatening to reduce the company even further from its position of former eminence. The radio boom got under way in 1922. There was not much to listen to, and radio sets were inordinately addicted to whistles and screeches; but Americans took to radio with gusto and cheerfully stayed up until long past midnight in hopes of "logging" a station hundreds of miles away. Minor phonograph manufacturers jumped onto the bandwagon in 1922 and began building combination phonograph-radios (that was still the order in which the words appeared). A year later one of the leaders in the phonograph industry, Sonora, followed suit with its combination Sonoradio; and in March 1924 the Brunswick company announced details of an arrangement with the Radio Corporation of America to install the popular Radiolas in Brunswick phonographs. RCA was in the forefront of a mushrooming industry; already in 1923 its net earnings were $26,394,790, almost a hundred per cent gain over 1922, while Victor in 1923 had barely managed to hold its own. People began to say that the phonograph was doomed. And still the colossus in Camden moved with cautious tread. Two months after the Brunswick-Radiola alliance had been announced, Victor let it be known that their autumn line would include console Victrolas with an empty compartment in which a customer could install any radio receiver of his own choosing. With unabashed condescension it was explained that in this way Victor could participate in "the best features of radio prosperity without becoming liable to the worst features of radio depression." When the consoles appeared some months later, the trade noted with satisfaction that Victor had finally produced a genuine flat-top: the famous Victrola lid had been flattened out at last.

But was this really to be Victor's answer to the encroachments of radio? The trade refused to believe it. Surely this was only a makeshift measure while the world's biggest phonograph factory tooled up for a full-scale assault on the growing radio market. But in October, Eldridge Johnson exploded all such rumors with these words of wisdom:

> The radio is not a Victor competitor nor a substitute for talking machines. If the radio ever gets straightened out in America the Victor company will be greatly benefited. The Victor company has no notion of becoming a dominating factor in radio. . . . Radio bears some relation to the talking machine but the contact comes chiefly through the combined talking machine and radio. However, the demand for this

combination will always be but a small fraction of either business.

In one sense he was right. The radio in 1924 was not a substitute for the phonograph. Broadcast entertainment remained more often than not on an amateurish level; musicians and actors were still chary of performing before a microphone. But Johnson had neglected to consider one vital circumstance. The radio receiver of 1924, for all the inadequacies of its amplifier and loud-speaker, gave a quality of sound reproduction that the phonograph could not even approach. Suddenly people came to realize that machine-made music need not sound tinny and muffled and scratchy. The radio might not give you Galli-Curci, but what you did hear sounded more like real music than anything the phonograph could offer.

Although Eldridge Johnson did not know it, the mechanical phonograph and acoustically recorded disc on which he had built a fortune were ready for the history books.

16 *RECORDING BECOMES ELECTRIC*

ELECTRICAL RECORDING HAD BEEN A MATTER OF SPECULATION
for a long time. After all, the twentieth century was supposed to be the Age of Electricity: railroads, iceboxes, and
irons had been electrified; and it was held to be only a matter
of time before every piece of equipment used by man would
respond to the call of the kilowatt. Actually, an electrome-
chanical recorder had been designed and patented as early as
1903; but without the condenser microphone and vacuum-
tube amplifier as adjuncts, its potentialities could not be
recognized. It was only during World War I that research in
wireless telephony, as radio was then called, brought forth
the first workable microphones and amplifiers. Thereafter,
the practical realization of electrical recording was open to
anyone who cared to work on it.

It is surprising how few people availed themselves of this
opportunity. A revolution in recording technique was just
around the corner, yet no one seemed in a hurry to get there.
Two British experimenters, Lionel Guest and H. O. Merriman, made the first publicized sortie in this virgin field.
They began tinkering with electrical recording in 1919, using a home-built laboratory in a London garage for their
work. On Armistice Day 1920, Messrs. Guest and Merriman
recorded the Unknown Warrior burial service in Westminster Abbey by an electrical process. It was the first recording
ever made from a remote pickup, the sound being relayed
over telephone lines from inside the Abbey to the recording

machine in a near-by building. Like most first attempts, it was rough at the edges, and the record had only limited circulation. But its significance was not lost on Britain's two leading record manufacturers, HMV and Columbia, who thereafter began conducting secret experiments (unbeknown to each other) on electrical recording. Neither company pushed this research with great vigor, however. Why upset the applecart when business was flourishing?

Victor, indeed, so relished the *status quo* that it did not even conduct experiments. In America the initiative was assumed by Bell Telephone Laboratories, the research division of American Telegraph & Telephone Company, where work on electrical recording was begun in the late fall of 1919 by a team of engineers under the general supervision of Joseph P. Maxfield. For the first time in its history the phonograph was subjected to thorough scientific scrutiny and discipline. Up to then it had been developed by trial and error, and in the process a large reservoir of empirical knowledge had been accumulated. But as Victor's chief engineer, S. T. Williams, later conceded: "A complete theory connecting the great series of disjointed facts was still lacking. Development along empirical lines had reached its utmost and the art of sound reproduction had come practically to a standstill in its progress." At the Bell Laboratories physics and mathematics were now applied to the problem of sound reproduction. Specifications for an electromagnetic recording head were drawn up (based on analogous telephone and microphone research) and translated into tangible equipment. Next, space was found for a recording laboratory in the Bell building at 463 West Street, New York City, where trial recordings were soon being made from a private telephone line that ran from the stage of the Capitol Theater, providing Maxfield and his associates with a variety of musical and spoken entertainment on which to exercise their equipment.

An improved acoustical phonograph to play electrical recordings was developed by these engineers at the same time. It derived from the conviction of Henry C. Harrison, chief "idea man" in this team of experts, that the electrical principles of matched impedance employed in telephone transmission could be translated into mechanical equivalents for sound transmission in the phonograph. Harrison remembered from his student days that the theory of electrical wave transmission had been explained in terms of analogous mechanical systems. Now he reversed the process and used the carefully worked-out telephone transmission theory to design a mechanical wave transmission system for the phonograph. "Energy," he argued, "obeys the same laws whether it be in the electrical or mechanical form. . . . By using a list of corresponding constants a known electrical equation may be readily converted to an analogous mechanical equation." Thus was born on the drawing board the exponential-horn phonograph, later known as the Orthophonic Victrola. Harrison's equations had shown that a definite relation existed between the length of the phonograph horn, the rate at which it tapered, and the size of its opening.* Such a horn, it was found, should be at least nine feet long to reproduce properly the range of sound engraved by the electrical recording process. The next problem, therefore, was to work out (again using electro-mechanical analogues) a method of folding the horn on itself so that it would fit into a cabinet of commercial size and at the same time be free of unwanted reflections and resonances. Early in 1924 the specifications had been completed and a prototype constructed.

At first glance it seems odd that a mechanical phonograph should have been developed to play the new electrical recordings, inasmuch as electrical amplification had already been developed (and indeed played a vital role in the elec-

* The so-called morning-glory horn, in vogue prior to the appearance of the enclosed Victrola in 1906, approximated the exponential horn developed by Bell Laboratories; but it was not nearly so efficient.

trical recording process). To be sure, the reproduction of records by electrical means was entirely possible. Bell Laboratories had built an all-electric phonograph employing an electromagnetic pickup, a vacuum-tube amplifier, and a loud-

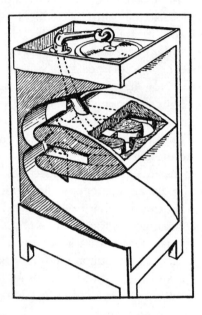

CROSS-SECTION OF EXPONENTIAL-HORN PHONOGRAPH

speaker; but it was expensive to produce and prone to distortion. An electrical phonograph must transform mechanical energy from the record grooves into electrical energy in order to amplify the sound; then the electrical energy has to be transformed back into mechanical energy by means of a loud-speaker. The equipment of 1924 did not do this job very efficiently. Hence, the Bell technicians decided on the cheaper and acoustically purer exponential-horn phonograph as preferable for home use.

So far, Bell Laboratories had worked in complete secrecy.

Now the time had come to demonstrate what had been accomplished. The new method of recording, in conjunction with the exponential-horn phonograph, had produced three striking improvements in the reproduction of sound. First, the frequency range had been extended by two and one-half octaves so that it now encompassed 100–5,000 cycles. Bass frequencies never heard before from phonograph records added body and weight to music; treble frequencies introduced a definition and detail previously missing (sibilants, for instance, could be heard for the first time). Second, the "atmosphere" surrounding music in the concert hall could now be simulated on records. Musicians were no longer forced to work in cramped quarters directly before a recording horn but could play in spacious studios with proper reverberation characteristics—for the electrically amplified microphone system of recording did not depend on sheer force of sound as had the old mechanical system. Third, records were louder and at the same time were free from blast.

Bell Laboratories, convinced that America's leading talking-machine company would welcome these improvements with quick appreciation, invited representatives from Victor early in 1924 to hear the new records and phonograph. Victor's men were not impressed and returned to Camden with an unenthusiastic report. Western Electric, the manufacturing and licensing company for A. T. & T. products, had offered Victor use of patent rights to electrical recording on a royalty basis. Victor did not turn them down; neither did it accept. The company merely dithered. To understand this extraordinary behavior two circumstances need to be remembered. One was the antipathy in Victor's high echelons to radio. Johnson's view of radio has already been noted. That sad estimate of radio's potentialities had permeated the whole Victor organization; and when a newcomer was added to Victor's inner circle, he was specifically warned not to mention radio in the sacred precincts of Camden.* Electrical recording smacked too much of radio; it employed microphones and vacuum tubes and other paraphernalia offensive to hardened phonograph sensibilities; it "didn't sound like a phonograph." The second circumstance was Johnson's own state of mind. In 1924 he had suffered a nervous breakdown and was unable to make any decisions regarding the Victor business. No one with real authority was left at the helm.

In October 1924 the vast Victor Talking Machine Company perilously resembled a rudderless ship headed straight for destruction. Sales had been lethargic all year, and for the first time in the company's history there was no appreciable upturn as pre-Christmas buying got under way. Johnson roused himself sufficiently to order an extra million dollars' worth of advertising, but it was money ill spent. Americans in 1924 could not be cajoled into buying Victrolas on the old scale. Victor's sales that year declined to $37,000,-000—and this despite an unprecedented outlay for advertising. Altogether, Victor's advertising budget in 1924 ran to $5,-000,000. Someone in Camden got to work with an adding machine and found that over one billion full-page Victor messages were printed every year in American newspapers and magazines. To businessmen this computation somehow seemed far less impressive than the balance sheet of the Radio Corporation of America, which showed net earnings for 1924 of $54,848,131—more than double its net earnings for 1923.

By December the urgency of drastic measures was painfully clear to Johnson and his associates. They swallowed hard and requested Bell Laboratories to put on another demonstration of electrical recording, this time for the entire technical and business staff in Camden. On January 27, 1925, Joseph P. Maxfield came to the Victor plant and made pre-

---

* This was told to me by Walter Clark (brother of the Gramophone Company's Alfred Clark), who joined Victor's councils in 1924 and was so admonished.

liminary arrangements. The full-dress demonstration took place early in February. This time electrical recording sounded far more attractive. Victor's complacency had vanished with the debacle of Christmas business in 1924. In March 1925, Victor signed on the dotted line.

But in the interim someone else had got into the act. The circumstances are worth recording. Bell Laboratories had been sending their electrically recorded wax masters to the Pathé factory in Brooklyn for processing into regular shellac pressings. Pathé's American business at that time was being managed by Frank Capps, who had been active in the phonograph industry ever since he perfected the pantographic method of duplicating cylinder recordings back in the 1890s. Capps was an old friend of Louis Sterling's, and on his own initiative he had some extra pressings made of the Bell Laboratories test records and mailed them off to Sterling in London. They arrived on December 24, 1924. Sterling took them home to play on Christmas Day. When he heard them, his heart sank. English Columbia had just gone to great expense recording, by the acoustic process, a tremendous number of symphonic works. The records sent by Capps showed that this investment would shortly be worthless. Sterling had foreseen the eventual coming of electrical recording; in fact, experiments had been proceeding for some time in Columbia's Clerkenwell Road laboratories. But he had not counted on its coming so soon, or from such a source.

On December 26, Louis Sterling boarded a ship for New York. Early in January he met with officials of Western Electric and learned that the now unaffiliated Columbia Phonograph Co., of New York, had been offered rights to electrical recording along with Victor. In fact, experimental Western Electric equipment had already been tried out in the Columbia studios. Unfortunately, the American Columbia company (from which Sterling's English company had separated itself in 1922) was in parlous financial condition, and the bankers who controlled its affairs boggled at the $50,000 that Western Electric was demanding in addition to a share in royalties. Since Western Electric insisted that rights to the electrical recording process could be assigned abroad only through an American affiliate, Sterling had only one course to follow: he bought a controlling interest in the American Columbia company for $2,500,000 (thanks to a loan from J. P. Morgan) and organized it as a branch of the English firm. Nothing then stood in the way of an agreement with Western Electric. Contracts were written, and Columbia actually managed to sign up for electrical recording a few weeks ahead of Victor.

The public at large remained ignorant of all these developments. Trade circles were apprised of electrical recording, but the news was supposed to travel no further. A premature announcement would merely undermine the sale of old records while creating a demand for a new product that was as yet unavailable. Between them, Victor and Columbia agreed to keep mum about electrical recording for at least a year. By then there would be enough repertoire recorded by the new process to warrant publicizing it fully.

At Camden the atmosphere shivered with daring plans. In May 1925 an entente was reached between Victor and RCA allowing for the incorporation of Radiolas into the new line of Victrolas coming that fall. Meanwhile production in the Camden factories had all but halted; almost the entire plant was in process of retooling for an entirely new kind of instrument. For along with electrical recording Victor had also bought manufacturing rights to the exponential-horn phonograph developed by Bell Laboratories. Victor dealers were alerted to expect something wonderful in the fall; at the same time they were urged to clear out stocks of old-style Victrolas at no matter what sacrifice. Then began the biggest advertising campaign in Victor history. The day of unveiling the new instrument, to be called the Orthophonic

Victrola, was set for November 2. It was dubbed Victor Day. A deluge of advertising informed America of the miracle that Victor dealers were preparing to demonstrate, "a musical instrument which in performance and in construction is unlike, and vastly superior to, anything the world has ever known." Old John Philip Sousa, who had given Victor its first important testimonial in 1901, obliged again with another terse comment. "Gentlemen," he was quoted as saying, "that's a band." At a banquet for the phonograph trade held in New York's old Waldorf-Astoria Hotel, electrical recordings and the Orthophonic Victrola were demonstrated by Walter Clark, the Victor executive who had led the fight for them within the company and who had taken charge of Victor's recording policy. Victor's dealers were hugely impressed with the new Victrola and the new records. Their enthusiasm infected the stock market, where Victor shares in mid-October climbed to 117; earlier in the year they had dropped as low as 65. Approximately $6,000,000 was spent by Victor that year in launching its new line of Victrolas. It represented a last-ditch gamble. Everything the company had was thrown into this effort; Victor's surplus at the end of 1925 was down to $122,998, where only a few years earlier it had been $23,000,000. But the gamble paid off. America flocked to the dealers on Victor Day and began buying Victrolas again. Within a week the Victor company had pocketed orders for $20,000,000 worth of instruments.

No sooner had Victor Day passed into history than Brunswick came forth with a gala unveiling of its own. In collaboration with the General Electric Company, Brunswick had built an all-electric phonograph which it deemed practical for use in the home. It was called the Panatrope and came in various models (with or without radio) for $350 and up. Together with this pioneering instrument, the first electrical record player to be placed on sale, Brunswick had a new system of electrical recording to offer, also developed by

General Electric. Instead of using a microphone, the Bruns-wick-GE method relied on light rays and a photoelectric cell. A powerful beam of light was reflected to the cell by a tiny crystal mirror so mounted as to respond to minute vibrations of sound waves; thus the movements of the mirror could be translated into electrical vibrations by the photoelectric cell and subsequently made to engrave a phonograph record. It sounds complicated and it was. Brunswick's "Light Ray" method of recording was not destined to last long.

So unfolded the events that revolutionized and reanimated the phonograph and record industry during the crucial year of 1925. Some of the immediate effects must now be considered.

17 *LARGESS FROM THE MICROPHONE*

Between 800 and 900 voices were united in a surge of sound at the Metropolitan Opera House on Tuesday evening, March 31 [1925], when fifteen glee clubs of the metropolitan district were massed in one huge chorus for the second joint concert arranged by the Associated Glee Clubs of America. Thirteen conductors participated, each leading the ensemble in one of the numbers of the program. A huge audience that completely filled the opera house applauded with lively enthusiasm, and to a certain extent heeded the printed request to join in the singing of the final number, *Adeste Fideles.*

THUS DID *Musical America* DESCRIBE A CONCERT THAT WAS to provide electrical recording with its first great success. High over the heads of choristers and audience in the Metropolitan Opera House hung a microphone that picked up the entire proceedings for relay to Columbia's newly installed electrical recording equipment. A twelve-inch record, Columbia 50013-D, was swiftly processed and demonstrated to the trade. On one side was "John Peel" sung by the 850 voices on the stage; on the other was *"Adeste Fideles"* sung by the assembled forces of 4,850 voices.* William C. Fuhri, Columbia's general sales manager, hailed it as "the most inspiring and thrilling effect ever produced on a phonograph record." The disc went on sale in June with an all-out pro-

---

* This was Columbia's own computation, and it seems rather inflated.

motion. Advertisements trumpeted customer reactions to 50013-D, such as the joy of the lady who exclaimed: "I thought I was tired of phonograph music—but that was because I had never really heard any." To its dealers Columbia gloried: "This one record alone is bringing back customers who haven't bought records in months." It was staggeringly loud and brilliant (as compared to anything made by the old method), it embodied a resonance and sense of "atmosphere" never before heard on a phonograph record, and it sold in the thousands. Although Columbia's *"Adeste Fideles"* was not the very first electrical recording to reach the public, it was the first one to dramatize the revolution in recording and the first to make a sharp impression on the average record buyer.

Chronological pride of place goes to Victor 19626, a ten-inch ordinary black label disc containing two numbers from the University of Pennsylvania's thirty-seventh annual production of the Mask and Wig Club. It was recorded in mid-March and rushed to Philadelphia record shops in April. For the country at large, Victor's first electricals became generally available in May, when a catchy fox trot entitled *Let It Rain, Let It Pour*—as played by Meyer Davis' Le Paradis Band—spread the gospel of electrical recording to the dance floor. Meanwhile, the first Red Seal electrical had been recorded on March 21 by the French pianist Alfred Cortot in Victor's Camden studio. This twelve-inch record (Victor 6502, containing Chopin's Impromptu in F-sharp major and Schubert's *"Litany"* as arranged by the pianist) reached the dealers in June. Its acoustic superiority, however, was nowhere near so apparent as that of Victor's first electrically recorded orchestral issue, Saint-Saëns' *Danse Macabre* in a performance by Stokowski and the Philadelphia Orchestra, which appeared in July. In this piece of orchestral acrobatics, with its clattering xylophone obbligato and dynamic percussive effects, the potentialities of electrical recording were heard to exciting effect. So were they in Tchaikovsky's stentorian *Marche Slave* (also conducted by Stokowski), which came out in October. Although none of these was advertised at the time as electrical, sharp-eared listeners could tell that a new dimension had been added to recorded sound, and Victor dealers were urged to play the new discs when demonstrating the Orthophonic Victrola on Victor Day and after.

By the end of 1925, Victor had issued a smattering of electrical Red Seals, enough to whet the musical appetite but not to satisfy it. They were all short pieces on single records; not a symphony or sonata or quartet was among them. To England again went the distinction of pioneering in the area of full-length works, for it was in the HMV release of December 1925 that the first electrically recorded symphony appeared —Tchaikovsky's Fourth Symphony, performed by Sir Landon Ronald and the Royal Albert Hall Orchestra. The two large British record companies had each acquired rights to the Western Electric recording system through their American affiliates. By mid-June *Let It Rain, Let It Pour* had begun making its way through England, to be followed in September by Columbia's 4,850-voice *"Adeste Fideles"* (which within a month was selling at the rate of two thousand discs a day). In England, as in America, an agreement had been made to avoid, temporarily, the phrase "electrical recording"; but British writers had got around this difficulty by using the circumlocution "new recording." Since news of the Bell Laboratories development had already been published in England, it did not take much imagination to equate "new recording" with electrical recording.

Surprisingly, the "new recording" in England received something less than unadulterated approbation. Compton Mackenzie in his editorials for *The Gramophone* led the chorus of detractors. In November 1925 he was writing:

The exaggeration of sibilants by the new method is abominable, and there is often a harshness which recalls some of the worst excesses of the past. The recording of massed strings is atrocious from an impressionistic standpoint. I don't want to hear symphonies with an American accent. I don't want blue-nose violins and Yankee clarinets. I don't want the piano to sound like a free-lunch counter. [What *does* a free-lunch counter sound like?]

Two months later he waxed even more indignant apropos the new Tchaikovsky Fourth:

There seems to me to be something almost deliberately defiant in choosing this particular work for a symphonic debut in the latest methods of recording. . . . The music itself is a jangle of shattered nerves, and even where there is any attempt to rid the music of the exasperation which sets us on edge the recording steps into the breach and sees that our nerves are not allowed any rest.

By this time *Gramophone* readers had taken up the refrain and were airing their views in the correspondence columns: "Mellowness and reality have given place to screaming . . . peculiar and unpleasant twang . . . the marvellous music is completely spoilt by the atrocious and squeaky tone . . . the din is ear-splitting, a continual humming roar pervading everything." As an antidote to those remarks, *The Gramophone* published some favorable comment by one of its regular technical writers, H. T. Barnett, in regard to Columbia's "*Adeste Fideles*":

It was given to me in great disgust by a friend on whose machine it sounded more like a complicated cat fight in a mustard mill than anything else I can imagine. I brought it home and put it on my own gramophone and the result overwhelmed me; it was just as if the doors of my machine were a window opening on to the great hall in which the concert was held. If it produces any less perfect result in your hands, blame your reproducing apparatus and not the record.

Barnett's view was seconded by a reader who ventured the suggestion that "some at least of the unpleasant noise described by your correspondents may perhaps be due to the way the records are played and not so much to the records themselves."

It is true that electrical recordings were not heard to best effect on old-fashioned acoustic talking machines. It is also true that the first attempts to record an orchestra with microphones resulted in overly strident reproduction. But aggravating these sources of displeasure was a pervading resistance to change. England was not the only place where such cavilings were heard. In America, too, the change-over from acoustical to electrical recording met with considerable obloquy. "At that time," wrote R. D. Darrell some years later, "the old process, then at its height, oftentimes put the crudities of the new to shame. One thought shrieking string tone and sour wood winds inseparable from the new method, and more than one verbal tear was cast over the passing of cool, dark beauty of the old at its best." But the die-hards began to change their tune in the spring of 1926. In March, English Columbia released a complete *Symphonie Fantastique* (Weingartner and the London Symphony), and HMV followed in April with the *Magic Fire Music* and *Siegfried's Rhine Journey* (Albert Coates conducting) in recordings that demonstrated more than anything yet published how superior the electrical process really was. They induced Mr. Mackenzie to revise his opinion and elicited commendation from an unexpected and authoritative source.

Ernest Newman, the respected critic of the London *Sunday Times*, had been listening to the new records. His reaction to what he heard is worth reprinting at some length:

> Until lately it was a little difficult to take even a good orchestral record quite seriously. . . . They were manifestly misrepresenting the original at many points, and so could hardly give complete pleasure to musicians who knew the

original; but they could still be useful to the student and lover of music whose opportunities for concert-going were limited and who could not get much pleasure or profit out of a score. All at once, however, as it seems, gramophone recording has taken an enormous step forward. . . .

Those who have heard these records for themselves will have probably felt, as I did at my first hearing of them, that at last it is possible for the musician to sit at home and get the thrill of the real thing as he knows it in the concert room. The records have their weaknesses, but they seem trifling in comparison with the great mass of their virtues. At last an orchestra really sounds like an orchestra; we get from these records what we rarely had before—the physical delight of passionate music in the concert room or opera house. We do not merely hear the melodies going this, that, or the other way in a sort of limbo of tonal abstractions; they come to us with the sensuous excitement of actuality.*

No one could have bestowed a more glowing accolade on the new method. Electrical recording had proved its worth.

Another eminent personage in the world of music had also been favorably impressed with the electrical process, none other than Arturo Toscanini. His interest was piqued in March 1926, when he conducted the first New York performance of Respighi's *Pines of Rome*. The third movement of this symphonic poem calls for a recording of a nightingale's song to be played against a murmuring accompaniment of strings and harp. To reproduce the nightingale record at sufficient volume, the New York Philharmonic had acquired a Brunswick Panatrope. According to William A. Brophy, director of Brunswick's recording laboratory, "the success which attended the performance of the instrument awakened in Mr. Toscanini the great possibilities which the Brunswick Panatrope had in influencing the future development of music. A visit to our laboratory gave Mr. Toscanini the opportunity of seeing and hearing a practical demonstration of the exclusive recording process now used by the

* *The Sunday Times,* July 11, 1926.

Brunswick Company. He was so impressed with the method and results of the process that he expressed a desire to make records." Toscanini's ardor cooled, however, when he actually got down to the business of recording. Only one twelve-inch record resulted from his association with Brunswick —the Nocturne and Scherzo from Mendelssohn's *Midsummer Night's Dream* music. It was reviewed in the first issue (October 1926) of *The Phonograph Monthly Review,* an American equivalent of *The Gramophone,* and praised as a noteworthy issue in which "composer, conductor, and reproduction [were] all at their best." Conductor did not seem to concur; and when Brunswick brought out further recordings of the New York Philharmonic, someone else led the orchestra.

By this time Victor had seen fit to publish a full-scale work recorded by the electrical process: Dvořák's *New World* Symphony played by the Philadelphia Orchestra under Stokowski and issued as album M-1 in a series that was to run well into four digits before the 78-rpm record met its demise. From the same source in 1927 and 1928 came a half dozen issues that set a world standard for reproduced sound: the Brahms First, Beethoven Seventh, and Franck D minor symphonies, Rimsky-Korsakoff's *Scheherazade,* Stravinsky's *Firebird* Suite, and—most arresting of all—the Stokowski transcription of Bach's Toccata and Fugue in D minor. This was electrical recording at its most powerful, luminous, and enveloping. Much of the credit goes to Victor's engineers, who adapted to the new process with remarkable success; but in all fairness it must be acknowledged that they had surpassingly good material to work with: an orchestra that could hardly be equaled in warmth and brilliance of tone, an acoustically perfect auditorium in which to record (after June 1926 most Philadelphia Orchestra recording sessions were held in the Academy of Music), and a conductor vitally interested in the problems and potentialities of reproduced sound. Stokowski was not content merely to conduct and leave all else to the engineers. Microphone placement, the seating arrangement of his orchestra, sound reflectors, monitoring panels—the entire paraphernalia of recording intrigued him. It has been said, indeed, that he became too intrigued and dabbled so persistently in the deep waters of electrical engineering that Victor had to appease his lust by providing him with a set of control dials next to the podium that were connected to absolutely nothing. This is a good story, but it is doubtful that anyone of Stokowski's intelligence would be fooled by such a ruse, doubtful too that his over-all contributions to the electrical aspects of recording were other than imaginative and helpful. Purists might boggle at Stokowski's interpretations, for the handsome blond conductor had learned how to project the full impress of his musical personality onto a record and the net effect was often criticized for being too flamboyant, too opulent, too eccentric; but considered solely as examples of beautiful sound, Stokowski's recordings dwelt in a class by themselves.

Victor's engineers produced far less startling results when they went afield to record the Chicago Symphony under Frederick Stock, the San Francisco Symphony under Alfred Hertz, and the Detroit Symphony under Ossip Gabrilowitsch. But with the first release of a recording by the Boston Symphony under Serge Koussevitzky (Stravinsky's *Petrouchka*, issued in January 1929) Victor could boast of another splendid orchestra and conductor with a phonographic potency akin to that of the famed Philadelphia-Stokowski combination. That year, also, Arturo Toscanini came back to the Victor fold after his ephemeral collaboration with Brunswick. With the New York Philharmonic-Symphony he recorded Haydn's *Clock* Symphony, Mozart's *Haffner* Symphony, and shorter pieces by Gluck, Mendelssohn, Dukas, Rossini, and Verdi (magical performances of the Preludes to the first and third acts of *La Traviata*). The Victor advertisements gabbled fatuously about his "fine Italian hand" and dilated on the delightful gaiety of "Papa" Haydn, whose "*Clock* Symphony is charming all through." However, for music lovers the world over these recordings, which mirrored so faithfully the delicacy and precision (though not the dynamic amplitude) of Toscanini's artistry, were able to survive any amount of uninformed chatter from Victor's copy writers. Unhappily, the Italian maestro was still dissatisfied with the sound of his recordings, and after these few issues he again retreated into phonographic silence.

In America the responsibility for recording serious music had gone by default almost exclusively to Victor. Brunswick had made a few shies at the orchestral repertoire (notably with the Cleveland Symphony under Nikolai Sokoloff), and the American branch of Columbia had flirted momentarily with Walter Damrosch's New York Symphony before that orchestra's merger with the Philharmonic; but by 1929 these companies had let domestic commitments lapse and were relying on European sources for their classical catalogues. Fortunately, the Deutsche Grammophon studios (from whence Brunswick's European recordings derived) and the Columbia studios in England and France and Italy were extraordinarily active, so that there was an abundance of material to draw upon.

Abroad the repertoire was accumulating at a breakneck pace, with Louis Sterling's mushrooming English Columbia leading the field. The hundredth anniversary of Beethoven's death gave Columbia an opportunity to splurge in a magnificent way. The centenary idea was broached by a young American, Frederick N. Sard, who first approached Columbia's American branch with his suggestions and was then sent on to headquarters in London. He proposed that Columbia organize a Beethoven Week to be celebrated on an international scale from March 20 to 26, 1927. Sterling and his associates fell in with the plan and pledged the spirited support of the company. Columbia had already issued, in October 1926, a new electrical recording of the Ninth Symphony conducted by Weingartner. Now the company embarked on recording the other eight symphonies and as much else of Beethoven's *oeuvre* as could be got on records before the March deadline. The First Symphony was entrusted to Sir George Henschel, the Second to Sir Thomas Beecham, the *Eroica* to Sir Henry J. Wood, the Fourth to Sir Hamilton Harty and his Hallé Orchestra, and the rest to Weingartner. All were ready by March, as were twelve of the sixteen quartets played by the Leners, three piano sonatas, and the *Archduke* Trio.

Columbia extracted all the publicity they could from this expensive and expansive venture. An International Musicians' Advisory Body had been organized that included most of the top-ranking conductors and instrumentalists in the world; * these names were proudly listed in advertisements proclaiming Beethoven Week. And to make the United States properly aware of what was in store, the English company hired a seventeen-year-old messenger from the District Messenger Service in London and dispatched him to New York on the *Aquitania* with £5,000 worth of record matrices in his care so that the American branch could issue its Beethoven albums on time. Free Beethoven lectures were subsidized, and programs for radio stations were mapped out "so that the message of Beethoven's life and work may be broadcast in the literal sense of the word." But these maneuvers for attention in the press in no wise detracted from the solid core of Columbia's achievement: the symphonies and quartets on records. One of these 1927 issues was still available a quarter century later in an LP reissue: the *Pastoral* Sym-

---

* Even Victor's Stokowski was among them!

phony recorded by Weingartner and the Royal Philharmonic Orchestra in London's Scala Theater. It serves as a good example of early electrical recording: somewhat deficient in bass and treble, robbed of the thunder of a true fortissimo, and marred by a never-ending background of scratch—but withal a genuine and absorbing musical experience.

No sooner was the Beethoven cornucopia emptied than Columbia began planning for an even more ambitious program to mark the centenary of Schubert's death, in November 1928. Again the guiding light was Frederick N. Sard. This time an International Composers' Contest was formulated in which $20,000 in prizes were offered—separate prizes of $1,000 for winners in each of ten zones plus a grand international prize of $10,000. Originally, the contest called for the completion of Schubert's *Unfinished* Symphony. This roused a howl of protest from musicians on both sides of the Atlantic who waxed indignant at the very thought of a contemporary composer presuming to graft a conclusion on to Schubert's masterpiece. In deference to these objections the rules of the contest were changed so as to require merely an original orchestral work conceived "as an apotheosis of the lyrical genius of Schubert." Juries of prominent musicians were organized in each zone to choose the local winners, and an International Grand Jury was picked to meet in Vienna in June 1928 to award the grand prize.* A three-movement symphony by a forty-year-old Swedish composer, Kurt Atterberg, won the $10,000. It turned out to be something of a mystery. The work was replete with reminiscences and drifted inconclusively from one musical style to another. After its first London performance, in mid-November, Er-

---

* It consisted of Franco Alfano, Alfred Bruneau, Walter Damrosch, Alexander Glazounov, Emil Mlynarski, Carl Nielsen, Adolfo Salazar, Franz Schalk, Max von Schillings, and Donald Francis Tovey—an imposing list of names. Glazounov had been allowed by the Soviet authorities to leave Russia for this occasion; he never returned.

nest Newman suggested that the borrowings might have been deliberate. He offered two possible explanations:

> Atterberg may have looked down the list of judges, and slyly made up his mind that he would put in a bit of something that would appeal to each of them in turn—a bit of *Scheherazade* for the Russian, Glazounov, a bit of *Cockaigne* for Mr. Tovey, a bit of the *New World* Symphony for Mr. Damrosch, a bit of *Petrouchka* for the modernist Alfano, a bit of Granados for Salazar. . . . But I wonder if there may not be another explanation. . . . Atterberg is not merely a composer. He is a musical critic. . . . Suppose he looked round with the cynical smile that, as all the world knows, all critics wear, and decided to pull the world's leg? The tribute paid to certain other works in this symphony is so obvious that it would indeed be a strange thing if the composer himself (who, I repeat, is also a critic) should be the one man in the world of music to be unaware of them. . . . And if my theory is correct, the laugh is Atterberg's today.

Newman's remarks were picked up by the news agencies and given world-wide distribution. Atterberg himself ventured an evasive answer when an interviewer asked him point-blank whether the composition had been a hoax. All this publicity, of course, did not harm the sale of Atterberg's symphony, which had been recorded for Columbia by Sir Thomas Beecham and the Royal Philharmonic Orchestra; and the general centennial hoop-la helped draw attention to the seventy Schubert works that were in the Columbia catalogue. Nevertheless, Columbia attempted no more anniversary celebrations.

While the Schubert developments were unfolding, Columbia had not neglected other musical areas. A recording expedition to Bayreuth in 1927 yielded some excerpts from *Parsifal* and *The Ring* conducted by Siegfried Wagner, Karl Muck, and Franz von Hoesslin. A year later Columbia's engineers returned to the Bayreuth Festspielhaus to record a sizable chunk of *Tristan* under the direction of Karl Elmendorff, with the soprano Nanny Larsen-Todsen and the tenor Gunnar Graarud; thirty-eight sides were employed, which sufficed for virtually all of Acts I and II but necessitated wholesale cuts in Act III. Not the least of its virtues was a booklet of musical commentary by Ernest Newman supplied with the set. Another ambitious Columbia venture of this period was the near-complete *Messiah* conducted by Beecham, issued in January 1928 soon after Beecham first startled musical conservatives in Britain with his unconventional performances of Handel's hallowed oratorio. "His racy tempos," wrote Gerald Abraham, "not only caused the hair to stand upright on some thousands of elderly heads; they did remind us that *Messiah* is a musical masterpiece and not a religious monument." The Columbia recording remained a phonographic classic and a touchstone of imaginative Handelian performance for two decades, until Beecham did it again with the benefit of improved recording techniques.

Meanwhile, the Gramophone Company had been offering some classics of its own on the HMV label. The world-renowned Casals-Cortot-Thibaud Trio had been enticed to the Hayes recording studio in 1926 for a session that resulted in the Schubert B-flat Trio, Opus 99. Before the collaboration of these three instrumentalists broke up during the 1930s, they also recorded for HMV trios by Beethoven, Haydn, Mendelssohn, and Schumann. Sir Edward Elgar conducted performances of all his major works for the recording microphone, Vladimir de Pachmann and Paderewski gave posterity recorded evidence of Chopin's music as it was played in his own century, and Bach's Mass in B minor was issued uncut on thirty-four sides in a performance directed by Albert Coates with Elisabeth Schumann and Friedrich Schorr among the soloists. In the month-to-month issuance of standard repertoire the two companies were keenly competitive. When HMV scored a hit with the Beethoven and Brahms violin concertos played by Fritz Kreisler, Columbia came up with equally desirable performances of the same works by Joseph Szigeti. Occasionally the two rivals would issue duplicate versions simultaneously, as happened in April 1928, when Schubert's long C major Symphony made its appearance on both lists, and in May 1929, when two complete recordings of Verdi's *Aïda* (both emanating from La Scala) were lavished on the British public.

The opera race had begun in 1928. Each company maintained a branch in Milan; and one by one the popular operas of Verdi, Puccini, Mascagni, Leoncavallo, Donizetti, and Rossini were recorded *in toto*—usually by both companies. A similar pattern was followed in France (though duplication was there not so rampant): there were two complete *Carmens,* two abridged recordings of *Pelléas,* and single versions of *Faust, Manon,* and other staples of the Opéra and Opéra-Comique. Despite this spirited competition, the level of performance in complete opera recordings *ante* 1930 did not often soar high. They were respectable interpretations with an occasional outstanding performance—Aureliano Pertile as Rhadames, for instance, or Marcel Journet as Mephistopheles, or Rosetta Pampanini as Mimi—but frequently they were marred by stolid singing and routine conducting. The correspondent who wrote to *The Gramophone* in 1929 suggesting a recorded *Cavalleria* with Ponselle, Martinelli, and De Luca—or a *Tosca* with Martinelli, Jeritza, and Scotti—was wasting his ink.

This digression into recorded opera serves to demonstrate the international scope of HMV's and Columbia's efforts. The two companies had studios and factories scattered throughout the Continent, and drew on them heavily for specialized repertoire. Columbia could call on the Madrid Symphony for Spanish music, the Straram and Brussels Conservatory orchestras for French music; HMV through its Ger-

man branch, Electrola,* leaned heavily on the Berlin State
Opera and Vienna Philharmonic orchestras, and in France
employed the Paris Conservatoire and Paris Symphony orchestras for the Berlioz-to-Ravel school of music. The Lindström companies—Parlophone and Odeon—were also busy in
every large European country; but though they worked dili-
gently to compile a respectable list of orchestral and instrumental records, their real strength lay in vocal repertoire:
the world is richer today for the songs and arias interpreted
by Lotte Lehmann, Conchita Supervía, Ninon Vallin, Meta
Seinemeyer, and Richard Tauber in the late 1920s for these
two labels. Although the Polydor catalogue had its quota of
vocal celebrities too (the lieder singer Heinrich Schlusnus in
particular), there the emphasis lay clearly with orchestral literature. With such conductors as Wilhelm Furtwängler,
Richard Strauss (in Mozart and Beethoven as well as his own
music), Hans Pfitzner, and Oskar Fried for the Mozart-to-
Strauss repertoire—and Albert Wolff and the Lamoureux
Orchestra for French music—Polydor records held a strong
lien on the attention of connoisseurs.

Needless to say, these secondary producers had secured
rights to the electrical process of recording. Record companies the world over had converted to the new methods.
Simply by introducing a microphone into the recording studio, Bell Laboratories had loosed a hurricane of activity such
as the phonograph had never seen. Symphonies, operas,
masses, and oratorios were inscribed wholesale on wax,
rushed to the factories, and showered on an avid public.
New stars in the phonographic firmament were quick to
make their mark: Stokowski, Beecham, Weingartner, Cortot,
and Szigeti became the idols of a new generation, and their
latest records were received as eagerly as Caruso's had been
two decades earlier. It was, in truth, a real revolution—and,

---

* Formed in 1926 to replace the renegade Deutsche Grammophon company in HMV's chain.

like all revolutions, it began with unbounded energy and crusading zeal. Such momentum, however, could not be sustained indefinitely. A reaction was sure to set in, and it started, justifiably enough, where the revolution had originated—in the United States.

18 *THE PHONOGRAPH IN*
TWILIGHT

FOR ELDRIDGE JOHNSON AND OTHER ORIGINAL STOCKHOLDERS in the Victor Talking Machine Company, Orthophonic recording (as the electrical process was termed) and the Orthophonic Victrola had engendered fortunate consequences. The assembly lines in Camden were once again working at capacity, and throughout the country dealers reported lively public interest in Victor's new products. The prosperity of the 1920s had hit full stride and spending money was plentiful. Victor's most expensive model, the Borgia II at $1,000, became such a fast seller that Camden fell weeks behind in delivery—Borgia II being a stately piece of furniture that housed an eight-tube superheterodyne Radiola and an Electrola, Victor's all-electric record player introduced in 1926 to compete with the Brunswick Panatrope. In September 1926 a Victor representative boasted that current production was the biggest in the company's history: earnings for the first nine months of the year had been almost $6,000,000, indicating a profit of about $8,000,000 for the year as a whole.

At this rosy juncture in Victor's affairs a gentleman from Wall Street came to Camden with an offer to buy the company outright. Johnson had been turning down prospective buyers for years, but this time he listened attentively. The near-debacle of 1924–25, his own fluctuating health, and perhaps a presentiment of troubles ahead inclined him to get out of the phonograph business while the getting was good. Two banking houses had combined to make the offer; one was Speyer & Co., the other was J. & W. Seligman & Co., the firm that had shown such dubious interest in Edison's Improved Phonograph back in 1888. They proposed to pay Johnson approximately $28,000,000 for his 245,000 shares of Victor stock and to pay another $12,000,000 for the remaining shares held by various individuals (Emile Berliner among them). Johnson did not delay long in arriving at a favorable decision. On December 7, 1926, the agreement was signed. It was exactly thirty years after Johnson made his debut in the talking-machine business by designing a practical motor for the Berliner Gramophone Company, and he had certainly earned an affluent retirement; but the drifting life of a leisured millionaire grew irksome to him, and before his death in 1945 he often expressed the view that he should never have sold Victor.

To all appearances, Seligman and Speyer had bought into a thriving industry. Victor's total sales in 1926 amounted to $48,000,000—only a shade below the 1921 peak of $51,000,-000. Even the American branch of Columbia had managed to operate in the black for the first time in several years. Victor's affairs under the new owners continued very much as before. Some of the old-timers in the company resigned along with Johnson, but the great majority of Victor executives and employees kept their jobs and maintained a continuity in the business. At the end of 1927, Victor's first year without Johnson, the company showed a net income of $7,269,523—down a bit from the 1926 figure, but not so much as to cause any alarm. Almost a million phonographs were manufactured that year and well over a hundred million records. It looked as though the optimists had been right when they predicted, during the early days of broadcasting, that radio and the phonograph could prosper side by side. Victor, Brunswick, and Columbia were all featuring radio-phonograph combinations, of course, but they remained primarily phonograph and record producers; the radios were manufactured elsewhere and merely introduced as an added attraction to the basic phonograph instrument.

The image of radio and phonograph striding together side by side was evoked by newspaper writers early in 1928, when negotiations for a proposed merger between RCA and Victor were first rumored. What was more natural, they asked, than for the leading radio and phonograph companies to link together in one great partnership? The coalition was hammered out at numerous conferences extending over a nine-month period, and an agreement was finally ratified on January 4, 1929, by directors of RCA, Seligman, and Speyer. Under its terms the Radio Corporation acquired all outstanding Victor stock, disbursing for each share of Victor common a cash payment of $5.00, one share of RCA $5.00 preferred stock, and one share of RCA common stock. Reports of the merger stressed that "the two great concerns will unite, not as a holding company and subsidiary, but as a joint new company." The last act of the Victor Talking Machine Company was to issue its annual fiscal report for 1928 showing net income of $7,324,019. Thereafter it sank into anonymity as the RCA Victor Division of the Radio Corporation of America, its separate accounts no longer a matter of published record.

No sooner had the ink dried on the agreement giving RCA control of Victor than plans were set in motion to begin the manufacture of radio sets in the Camden factory. This was a signpost pointing straight to the future, though few seemed to recognize it at the time. For despite the assurances about radio and phonograph joining together on equal terms, the management of RCA had no real interest in the talking machine. In absorbing Victor, the directors of RCA were interested essentially in an extensive plant and a well-organized system of distributors and dealers. The fact that the plant happened to be devoted to the manufacture of fine phono-graphs and a catalogue of world-famous recordings was only incidental. *That,* as Lady Bracknell would have said, could easily be altered. No precipitate steps were taken, of course. It was 1929, the economy was still booming, personal income stood at an all-time peak, and phonographs and records were much in demand. RCA would not turn good money away.

In October the stock market crashed, the national economy began to contract, and the phonograph and record business withered as if frozen in full bloom by a bitter Arctic frost. Everything went into a decline, but the phonograph went into a tail spin.

The first defection came from the man who had startled the world with the original talking machine fifty-two years before. On November 1, 1929, Thomas A. Edison, Inc., made it known that production of records and phonographs was to be discontinued; thenceforth the company would con-centrate on radios and dictating machines. Edison himself, then eighty-two, remained a shadowy figure in the back-ground; what part he played in the decision to abandon his "favorite invention" is not known. The announcement was made by an Edison vice-president, Arthur Walsh, who hinted that RCA Victor would soon follow suit and choke off the supply of Victrolas and records. The last years of the old Edison company had been a sad hodgepodge of misdirected effort. In 1925 electrical recording had delivered the final blow to Edison's vertical-cut cylinders and discs. At first the Edison publicists had tried to maintain that electrical record-ing figured in the mysterious Edison "secret process." "There is much talk these days about 'electrical recording' as though it had just been discovered," one of these pro-nouncements wheedled. "Let us stop and reflect. Hasn't it been pretty generally acknowledged that Mr. Thomas A. Edison knows *something* about electricity? He knows its ad-vantages—he knows its limitations. Isn't it reasonable to suppose that this 'Master of Electricity' knows how to employ it in every possible way?" Yes, it was reasonable; but despite the insinuations of Edison advertising copy, the records continued to be recorded mechanically. To offset this drawback, the Edison company launched a long-playing record in 1926 that would give up to twenty minutes of uninterrupted entertainment per side. "Imagine what this means to the Edison owner," vociferated the indefatigable copy writer. "Symphonies, entire—not piecemeal; acts from operas; recitals of artists; concerts by famous organizations; these are only a few of the bright stars in the almost limitless expanse of possibilities now unfolded." But no one at Thomas A. Edison, Inc., bothered to unfold the possibilities. Complete symphonies, entire operas were not to be found among the long-playing records issued. Instead there appeared a collection of dinner music played by the Hotel Commodore Ensemble and some operatic overtures and excerpts played by Sodero's Band and the American Symphony Orchestra. Not one Edison "Long Playing Record" contained a piece of music lasting longer than the standard four minutes. Worse still, the records were faint in volume and the diamond stylus was forever jumping out of the tiny grooves. Within a few months they disappeared from the market. Finally, a mere ten weeks before Edison shut down the phonograph business, an electrical *lateral-cut* Edison record was placed on sale. Axel B. Johnson, editor of *The Phonograph Monthly Review,* found the first issues "distinguished by remarkably clear and powerful recording, and also by a very successful eradication of surface noise. . . . I shall look forward to the first Edison symphonic recordings." They never came. Edison's flirtation with the once despised lateral-cut record was fleeting, to say the least.

The announcement of Edison's retreat from the phonograph business let loose a spate of pent-up resentment which record collectors had long been nurturing. In the correspondence pages of *The Phonograph Monthly Review* were to be found sentiments like these:

> Has Thomas A. Edison, Inc., proved to be a house of false alarms, a dispenser of disappointments, a mere "promising" business? What *is* its record but one of inadequacy and change, brief production and abandonment, promise of fine things and a "reneg"? . . . The explanation of the Edison incident is not far to seek. It is partly the lack of fighting spirit, of course, and partly the lack of business competence on the part of the company's officials. But the essential reason is deeper, the lack of true musical insight and sympathy. From the very first, Mr. Edison himself regarded the phonograph as merely a machine. He has never had any understanding of music: how could he hope to succeed in a musical venture?

Such complaints hit the mark only too accurately. But it would be a pity to take final leave of Edison on a note of pique. It is the young inventor of Menlo Park hurrying into New York to demonstrate his new tin-foil phonograph whom we should remember, not the octogenarian businessman of West Orange puttering in his outmoded laboratory and deserting his invention after years of bumbling mismanagement.

The retreat of Edison set in motion a general retrenchment and realignment in the phonograph business. In April 1930 the Brunswick-Balke-Collender Company delivered its fast-failing record and phonograph division into the more optimistic hands of Warner Brothers Pictures, which had been doing well with Vitaphone talkies and saw advantages in a subsidiary record line using Warner stars. Brunswick's recording studios and general headquarters were moved to New York, thus bringing to a close the short-lived participation of the Middle West in phonographic affairs led by Brunswick and abetted by such others as Gennett of Richmond, Indiana, and Paramount of Port Washington, Wisconsin. The transfer of locale and ownership also brought about a complete cessation of domestic additions to the Brunswick "Hall of Fame" catalogue. Even under the old management, Brunswick's monthly lists had been showing an increasing dependence on foreign sources for classical repertoire; but throughout 1929 and until May 1930 a leavening of records from the Chicago studio continued to appear, featuring the singers Elisabeth Rethberg, Mario Chamlee, and Michael Bohnen, the pianist Leopold Godowsky, the violinist Max Rosen, and the Minneapolis Symphony. Brunswick's new owners shut off even this trickle and thenceforth relied entirely on Deutsche Grammophon-Polydor for fresh additions to the classical catalogue. Another casualty was the Okeh Phonograph Corporation, American branch of the Carl Lindström chain, which had been purveying domestic repressings from the Parlophone and Odeon catalogues since the early 1920s. Although the Okeh label was maintained by Columbia for a secondary line of popular records, the company ceased to operate as an independent entity in 1930.

It was definitely a depressing year for the phonograph, and it substantiated the belief held by high executives of RCA that the phonograph belonged to the past and radio to the future. This lack of faith in recorded entertainment explains the parsimonious policies that were now decreed by RCA executives. Good money would no longer be wasted on an outdated commodity. The advertising budget was drastically pared (an abrupt change of course for a company that had become America's largest advertiser), and the company's plans for the future were re-evaluated and sharply curtailed. Contracts with Red Seal musicians were allowed to lapse, expensive orchestral recording sessions were deemed largely expendable, and the whole slowly woven fabric of Victor's involvement with music making in America was allowed to unravel. On September 19, 1930, humiliation was added to injury when RCA sponsored a ceremony in Camden dedicating the city as "Radio Center of the World." To all outward appearances the Victor plant had not changed perceptibly since the palmy days of Eldridge Johnson's reign, but within the walls a tremendous metamorphosis could be observed. Instead of Victrolas the assembly lines were now producing radios in all sizes and models, only a small percentage of which were equipped with record-playing mechanisms. And just to underline the passing of an era, RCA Victor issued in 1930 what were advertised as the very last Caruso recordings in the vault. "The book of Enrico Caruso's recording is closed forever," said the announcement accompanying the release of his three final efforts before the acoustic recording horn. "There will never be another new Caruso record released—for no more exist." * In the same breath RCA Victor suggested that listeners "hear them on the new Victor Radio-Electrola."

Despite these ominous events, the phonograph in America still showed a few faint signs of life, and various expedients were tried to coax it back into some semblance of its former vitality. Columbia noted the increase in radios (3,745,000 were manufactured in 1929) and attempted to crash this market with a portable record player that could be plugged into any radio set. It was called the Radiograph:

> All you do is to seat yourself in your favorite chair at any desired distance from the radio loudspeaker and play any record you want, as many times as you want, and at any volume you desire. The Radiograph is pint-sized in price and bulk, but its capacity to give pleasure and entertainment is unbounded.

This was a worthy idea, as later events were to prove, but the price was not pint-sized enough to put it over; Americans in the trough of the Depression could find better ways of spending $55.

RCA Victor's proposed restorative was a long-playing rec-

---

* Actually, a few more unpublished Caruso items were forthcoming after World War II.

ord, capable of reproducing "the longest movement of a symphony without interruption," which it demonstrated at the Savoy-Plaza Hotel for the first time on September 17, 1931. Rumors of it had been circulating since July, when the news had leaked of a Stokowski-Philadelphia Orchestra recording session in which the Beethoven Fifth Symphony was played straight through without the usual breaks every four minutes to mark the end of a record side. Reporters came away from the demonstration full of enthusiasm, and the public was primed for great things when the new records went on sale in November. Unfortunately, they never seemed quite so good again as they had that September afternoon in the Savoy-Plaza. Victor had put its best foot forward with the Beethoven Fifth, recorded especially for the long-playing record. Other discs that were offered at the same time had merely been dubbed from existing four-minute recordings, and they exhibited an undeniably secondhand sound. One critic complained:

> The recording is conspicuously lacking in color, brilliancy, and character; it is thin, flabby, faded, and lusterless; the music is all there, but it is pale and weak and lacks the life of the original. There is always an unmistakable feeling of emptiness, dullness, and artificiality. Indeed, despite the great advantages these records have in their long-playing feature, we would prefer to put up with the nuisance of frequent record-changing and listen to the standard discs.

If this sort of comment did not discourage a potential buyer, the financial outlay involved was certain to do so. Victor's engineers had achieved greater playing time (up to fourteen minutes per side) by doubling the number of grooves per inch and by slowing down the speed of the record to 33⅓ revolutions per minute (as compared to the standard 78 rpm).* This meant that a special turntable was required, and for

* The 33⅓-rpm speed had previously been employed for radio broadcast transcriptions and for the sound recordings synchronized with early talking pictures.

some inexplicable reason RCA Victor failed to produce an inexpensive player with which to convert radios and standard phonographs to the new slow-speed records. Instead, one had to buy an elaborate RCA Victor radio-phonograph, priced anywhere from $247.50 to $995, in order to get a two-speed turntable—a circumstance that provoked the uncharitable suspicion that the long-playing record was just a gimcrack devised to sell expensive radios. The records themselves were attractively priced; for example, Haydn's *Clock* Symphony conducted by Toscanini sold for $4.50 in long-playing form, whereas the album of standard records fetched $8.00. But even this economy proved to be a mirage. The records were pressed in a flexible composition called Vitrolac (required because of the finer grooving), and this material ill withstood repeated subjection to the heavy magnetic pickups then in use; long-playing records were not long-lasting.

Under more favorable circumstances Victor's long-playing record might have surmounted these handicaps. The idea, which promised to expand the scope of phonograph listening, was excellent. The execution, though faltering, could have been improved: by withdrawing "dubbed" records in favor of those specially recorded for the long-playing process; by manufacturing an efficient two-speed turntable in quantity and selling it at a rock-bottom price; by using a more durable record material; by refinements in recording and reproducing equipment for greater tonal response. But in 1931 the encouragement to proceed simply did not exist. The tide of adversity continued to run against the phonograph. RCA Victor had attempted to explode a dud; when it refused to go off, the company quickly buried it instead of attempting to discover what was wrong.

As this sickly venture limped along in the winter of 1931–32 the American phonograph and record business entered into its most doleful phase. Companies that once had occupied a respectable position in the business community were sold for whatever they would bring. Warner Brothers had seen the folly of their flyer in the record field and for a nominal sum had turned over the Brunswick catalogue and trademark to the American Record Company, producers of bargain-priced discs sold by Woolworth's and similar chain stores. At the same time (December 1931) the Columbia Graphophone Company Ltd., of London, divested itself of its tottering American branch, which then passed inauspiciously into the control of the Grigsby-Grunow Company, manufacturers of Majestic radios and refrigerators. There remained only an obituary to be written, and this was provided in September 1932 by *The American Mercury* in an article by Dane York entitled "The Rise and Fall of the Phonograph."

Rigor mortis had all but set in. A total of six million records were sold in the United States during 1932, *approximately six per cent of the total record sales in 1927.* Is it any wonder that people spoke slightingly of the phonograph record in circles where profits and production carried weight? All business had suffered grievously, it is true, but not to this calamitous extent. What had happened to the phonograph? Why had record sales dropped from 104,000,000 discs in 1927 to 6,000,000 in 1932, and the production of phonographs from 987,000 instruments to 40,000? A definitive answer can never be given. Radio broadcasting undoubtedly figured as the major cause. Entertainment on the air had reached high professional caliber and it was free—an irresistible attraction in a period of unemployment and diminishing wages. The latest hit tunes were to be heard in abundance from broadcasting stations. No longer was it necessary to buy the new dance records; they were being played *ad nauseum* over the air waves. But radio alone could not have brought the phonograph to such a sorry plight, nor could the indifference and apathy of RCA, nor the inflated prices at which most records and equipment continued to be quoted.

These were surely contributory. But there was in addition
something else, something intangible: a sudden disenchantment on a country-wide scale with phonographs, needles, records, and the whole concept of "canned music." The malaise
broke out in 1929 and spread devastatingly to every city and
state in America. Albums of Red Seal Records, displayed so
proudly by a former generation, were unceremoniously relegated to the attic or sold by the pound to a junk dealer; so
were the expensive Victrolas on which they had been played.
The talking machine in the parlor, an American institution
of redolent memory, had passed from the scene. There was
little reason to believe that it would ever come back.

19 *PROCEEDS FROM A MERGER*

THOSE FEW RECORD COLLECTORS IN AMERICA WHO DID KEEP faith with the despised phonograph during the lean years of the Thirties were obliged to rely increasingly on foreign sources for their musical pleasure. Brunswick and Columbia were using their studios for nothing except dance music; Victor contented itself with occasional recordings by the prestige-building Philadelphia Orchestra under Stokowski and otherwise gave classical repertoire a wide berth. Sales simply did not warrant investing money in costly recording sessions: even a popular symphonic album usually sold less than five hundred sets a year, which was hardly enough to foot the bill incurred in hiring a full orchestra for the time-consuming business of making records. Instead, Victor and Columbia imported matrices from their associates in Europe, pressed up small editions for sale in home territory, and threw them on the market with minimal advertising and promotion. It was a cheap and effortless way to meet the demands of a tiny class market. At the same time, a few specialty record dealers—notably The Gramophone Shop and New York Band Instrument Company—supplied this same market with imported pressings of the English, French, German, and Italian recordings that were not chosen for domestic issue on the Victor or Columbia labels. Customers for such imported merchandise were few in number; but those who did patronize The Gramophone Shop and its rivals were invariably enthusiastic, and often affluent, buyers. They held the phonograph's last line of defense in America during the dim days of the Depression when the country as a whole had written it off as beyond saving.

Fortunately for these stalwarts, Europe was still producing a steady supply of recorded music, despite economic conditions akin to those in the United States. On that side of the Atlantic, too, phonographic commerce had taken a wild spurt in the late 1920s, followed by a swift decline as the great Depression made itself felt. Combined net profits of the two major English manufacturers—HMV and Columbia—for the twelve months ending June 30, 1930, were £1,422,-090; but a year later they had dropped to £160,893. This abrupt diminution in profits provided the background for negotiations that led to the merger of the two long-time rivals. British businessmen were well conditioned in favor of combine arrangements, and the formation of Electric & Musical Industries Ltd. in March 1931 followed a normal and accepted pattern. Indeed, the consolidation of European phonograph interests was really half-completed when the E.M.I. merger took place, for the English Columbia company had already purchased control of the world-wide Carl Lindström chain (in 1925) and Pathé Frères (in 1928). Thus, the merger of Columbia and HMV centralized most of Europe's production under one over-all management; only Deutsche Grammophon-Polydor and a few small independents were left to provide competition. Outwardly the various member companies of E.M.I. carried on as before, with their own labels and their own artists; and they maintained the formal procedures, at least, of their erstwhile rivalry. But there ensued behind the scenes a determined effort toward consolidation and standardization. During the Depression such measures were extraordinarily helpful in maintaining profits at an acceptable level, but the lack of competition bred sluggish habits that were to cost E.M.I. dearly later on.

At its lowest ebb, however, the record business in Europe never reached the depths that were plumbed in America; and though the merger of leading manufacturers into one efficiently directed combine contributed in large degree to Europe's better fortunes, it was by no means the only factor. For one thing, competition from radio was far less intense: broadcasting had not been developed into the potent mass medium that it had become in America, nor had radio sets been manufactured in such inundating quantities. For another, a faith in the future of recorded music characterized the entire European industry, from the high officers of E.M.I. down, whereas defeatism was all too apparent in the United States. But, again, the pivotal reason for the phonograph's continued health in Europe must be sought in the area of intangibles. The wholesale disenchantment that swept Victrolas out of the American parlor never crossed the Atlantic. Europeans—and especially the English—remained loyal to the phonograph, music lovers continued to listen to records with satisfaction, and the phonograph instrument was still considered an ornament to the home. General economic adversity had made it difficult for most collectors to buy records and equipment on the old scale—but the desire for them persisted, and so did sales at a lesser tempo.

This durable kind of support for the phonograph was nowhere better evidenced than in the emergence of the "Society" projects, which had been suggested by a young employee at HMV, Walter Legge, as a means of adding off-the-beaten-track music to the catalogue. Legge's idea was to form different societies for the purpose of recording the more recondite works of various composers and to obtain enough subscriptions in advance to defray the cost of the undertakings. Attention was first directed, in the autumn of 1931, to the songs of Hugo Wolf. An album of six HMV records to be sung by Elena Gerhardt was proposed as the first of a series; texts of the songs in German and English together with annotations by Ernest Newman were also to be furnished. For this project the Gramophone Company required subscriptions of thirty shillings each from five hundred people. If the Hugo Wolf Society were to prove successful, it was hinted that a similar Society devoted to Beethoven's complete piano works would also be formed. The Wolf quota was filled by December, thanks in part to 111 subscriptions emanating from Japan, and in April 1932 the Gerhardt album was issued; today Volume I of the Hugo Wolf Society is worth at least ten times what it cost the original subscribers.

Once the healthiness of this scheme had been demonstrated, Walter Legge was given a free hand to set up other Society projects. His second venture, the Beethoven Sonata Society, which was to record every major Beethoven piano work in performances by Artur Schnabel, met with an extraordinary response. The first volume of seven records, containing the Opus 78, 90, and 111 sonatas, appeared in June 1932. Three years and three volumes later, HMV reported that £80,000 had been spent on these records by customers throughout the world (of which England alone had accounted for £24,000). Schnabel completed the fifteen-volume series in 1939, and it stands as an enduring memorial to his compelling and penetrating musicianship. Fortunately, the original plan of limiting Society editions to the original subscribers was soon abandoned; Society sets were added to the regular catalogue, and today many of them (including the Schnabel-Beethoven recordings) have been reissued in long-playing form. In 1933, the Society idea spread to France, where it yielded such valuables as Bach's *Goldberg* Variations played on the harpsichord by Wanda Landowska, and subsequent issues by this same artist devoted to harpsichord works of Couperin and Domenico Scarlatti; they contributed measurably to a reawakening of interest in the instrument throughout the world. Before World War II brought the Society program to a halt, the recorded litera-ture had been expanded by it to include Albert Schweitzer's performances of Bach's organ music, the *Forty-Eight Prel-udes and Fugues* performed on the piano by Edwin Fischer, Bach's unaccompanied cello suites in the seminal interpreta-tions of Pablo Casals, twenty-nine Haydn quartets played by the Pro Arte String Quartet of Belgium, Beethoven's ten vio-lin sonatas in performances by Fritz Kreisler and Franz Rupp, Sir Thomas Beecham's authoritative readings of the large orchestral works of Frederick Delius, several Sibelius symphonies and tone poems, and—most ambitious of all—the incomparable Glyndebourne Opera performances of Mozart's *Nozze di Figaro, Così fan tutte,* and *Don Giovanni* con-ducted by Fritz Busch, together with an equally finished re-cording of *Die Zauberflöte* made in Berlin under Beecham's direction. The phonograph had come a long way since the days when Vessella's Italian Band had blooped out a brassy travesty of the *Moonlight* Sonata.

The Society issues by their very scope deserve first men-tion, but it would be misleading to suggest that they were the only significant additions to phonograph repertoire ema-nating from Europe during the 1930s. In regular month-to-month releases E.M.I.'s various branches in England and on the Continent favored the discriminating record collector with a continuing stream of musical classics: from Vienna came Beethoven symphonies conducted by Weingartner and a reasonably complete *Der Rosenkavalier* with Lotte Leh-mann, Elisabeth Schumann, and Richard Mayr; from Paris came Monteverdi madrigals directed by Nadia Boulanger, Schumann's *Dichterliebe* sung by Charles Panzéra with Cor-tot accompanying, and Bach's *Italian* Concerto played by Landowska; from Barcelona came a series of choral perform-ances by the remarkable Orfeó Catalá, and from the Abbey of St. Pierre de Solesmes authoritative recordings of Gregorian chant; from London came the Beethoven piano concertos played by Schnabel, the Chopin mazurkas played by Rubinstein, and a series of symphonic recordings by the London Philharmonic under Beecham that set a world standard for polished and imaginative orchestral execution.

Although the powerful E.M.I. combine dominated the European scene, it did not entirely monopolize the attentions of serious collectors. A small French firm, Anthologie Sonore, formed in 1933 for the express purpose of recording repertoire from the Middle Ages to the eighteenth century that had fallen into unmerited obscurity, maintained a reputation for scholarship and musicality that endeared its discs to students and connoisseurs on both sides of the Atlantic. Telefunken, a new German record company with headquarters in Berlin, astounded listeners with the superior tonal qualities of its products; Telefunken's orchestral recordings of the Berlin Philharmonic and its operatic recordings made in the Bayreuth Festspielhaus during the 1936 Festival embodied a sense of presence and a vibrant warmth of sound second to none. Undoubtedly the most influential newcomer was the Decca Record Company, of London, which pioneered in the field of low-priced discs. Decca as a trade name dated back to World War I, when it denoted a portable phonograph much favored by British soldiers. The record company was formed in 1929. One of its earliest issues, in December of that year, consisted of some Handel concerti grossi conducted by Ernest Ansermet. This Swiss musician, who was later to bring Decca its greatest triumphs, made little impression on record collectors then, and he was dropped in favor of the British conductors Basil Cameron and Julian Clifford. At three shillings sixpence each, their records were something of a bargain in price (HMV Red Labels sold for six shillings sixpence) but were otherwise undistinguished. For several years thereafter Decca concentrated on its popular catalogue and relied on repressing Polydor masters, to which it had acquired English rights, for its classical issues. Then in 1935 the company returned to orchestral recording with a flourish by launching a new series at a price of two shillings sixpence per twelve-inch disc.* By December 1935 the Decca Record Company was able to advertise recordings by the Queen's Hall Orchestra under Sir Henry J. Wood, the London Symphony under Sir Hamilton Harty, the Boyd Neel String Orchestra, and the Griller Quartet at this bargain rate. Sir Henry, with his penchant for delighting over his own records, declared that they "are not only faithful reproductions of my interpretations, but there is a subtle balance of parts, a melodic interest, a true orchestral color, and a grip of essential detail that really give me an intense artistic satisfaction." Others were not so easily satisfied by Decca's cheap classics. They were vilified as being "rackety, harsh, and overamplified," and dealers complained that the two-shilling-sixpence record would sound the death knell of the industry. Apparently there were certain qualms entertained by the Decca Company too, for it was not long before the preponderance of Decca issues carried a five-shilling price tag.

By 1936, when the first comprehensive encyclopedia of recorded music was compiled by R. D. Darrell, European sources had provided collectors with ten piano concertos and seven symphonies of Mozart; nine symphonies by Haydn and twenty of his quartets; song cycles of Schubert, Schumann, Fauré, and Debussy; a sampling at least of Palestrina and Victoria, Rameau and Couperin, Monteverdi and Vivaldi; to say nothing of the standard (and nonstandard) works of Bach, Beethoven, Chopin, Tchaikovsky, and Wagner. With production of this order and at this level, it is no wonder that England alone exported more records at the height of

---

* About sixty cents at the 1935 rate of exchange.

the Depression than were manufactured *in toto* in the United States. To employ a favorite phrase of the times, America had become a "have-not nation"—at least so far as recorded music was concerned. Leadership in phonographic affairs was coming from across the ocean.

20 *THE ROAD BACK*

By January 1933 the record business in America was practically extinct. You did not buy luxuries when banks were foundering on all sides; you saved whatever hard cash you had for groceries. Under such circumstances the record industry (what was left of it) could not possibly continue. Phonograph records would either have to die a natural death and be decently buried or they would have to show some distinct signs of improvement. Miraculously, they began to recover. A new administration in Washington had managed to inject a stimulant into the badly shaken United States economy; the hypodermic even reached the lowly phonograph record. In October the Brunswick company was emboldened to report a rising demand for phonograph records in all sections of the country. RCA Victor's 1933 record sales were purported to show a hundred per cent increase over 1932. That hardly connoted a booming business, since doubling the 1932 sales figure still brought a grand total of only five million records—or less than one tenth of Victor record sales in 1927. Nevertheless, it was a hopeful sign for an industry that had been clutching at straws for three dismal years.

Early in 1934 the RCA Victor Company was sufficiently encouraged by the upturn in business to begin advertising its phonograph records in radio trade magazines. Dealers were exhorted to take another look at the once despised disc. It was, RCA had to admit, alive after all. "We'll grant you," said one of RCA's advertisements, "that back when the depression was hitting bottom, phonograph records were perhaps a dead item. 'Them days are gone forever.' . . . It's time we told the world what's happening in the record business—that sales of phonograph records jumped up 100 per cent last year—and that they're still going up." This was a new tune for RCA to take, and it was owing in large degree to the influence of Edward Wallerstein, who had just been put in charge of Victor's record business after having served a fourteen-year apprenticeship with Brunswick. The period of boom and bust had not soured Wallerstein on the phonograph. Quite the contrary, he was more than ever convinced of its basic appeal, and his enthusiasm began to reanimate the entire Victor Record Division. But enthusiasm alone could not hurdle one large obstacle: the menacing dearth of workable phonographs on which to play records. Since 1930 the manufacture of phonographs in America had all but ceased. Those that survived were obsolete—and usually in the attic. On the other hand, twenty million American homes had one or more radio sets to which a record player could easily be hooked up. They presented a dazzling potential market, and in September 1934 the RCA Victor sales department began to capture it with a potent little attachment called the Duo Jr. It consisted of an electrically powered turntable (not a very steady one) and a magnetic pickup (far too heavy for the good of any record) mounted in a tiny wood box. Despite its limitations, the Duo Jr. reproduced records tolerably well when attached to a radio set of adequate size and power. Moreover, though it carried a list price of $16.50, it was practically given away with the purchase of a certain number of Victor records. The miscalculation of Columbia with its $55 Radiograph attachment had been duly noted. RCA's Duo Jr. was not only made as inexpensively as possible but was sold at cost. Its low price helped to overcome the national resistance to phonographs and converted tens of thousands of Americans into record collectors. This writer was one of them.

At the very time when RCA Victor introduced its little player, a bold new record company made a significant debut. Its guiding genius was Jack Kapp, another ex-employee of Brunswick with an unshaken faith in the phonograph record, and its financial backer was E. R. Lewis, a canny London stockbroker who had taken over the management of the English Decca Company. The new American company was also called Decca. Its *raison d'être* lay in the conviction, shared by Kapp and Lewis, that good phonograph records did not need to be expensive. Ever since World War I, the big three—Victor, Columbia, and Brunswick—had been charging seventy-five cents for their bread-and-butter staple, the ten-inch dance record. In the prosperous days of the 1920s this did not seem unreasonable; but in the 1930s, with coffee selling for twenty cents a pound, seventy-five cents was plainly too much to spend for a couple of evanescent dance tunes. Others besides Kapp had seen the necessity for cheap records. Several brands were already on the market at cut-rate prices: Victor and Columbia had introduced subsidiary lines (Bluebird and Okeh, respectively) to sell at thirty-five cents, and the American Record Company was putting out, in addition to the high-priced Brunswick records, a string of labels (Melotone, Perfect, Vocalion) selling for a quarter. But none of these offered "name" artists, and the quality of performance was often as substandard as the price. Jack Kapp's gambit was to offer the biggest personalities in popular music at thirty-five cents a record. He persuaded most of the Brunswick "seventy-five-cent artists" to sign up with Decca, and in his first advertisements was able to announce exclusive contracts with Bing Crosby, the Dorsey Brothers, Guy Lombardo, Glen Gray, Fletcher Henderson, the Mills Brothers, and Arthur Tracy (the "Street Singer"). The notion of advertising records on a large scale was in itself fairly revolutionary in 1934. Newspaper readers must have blinked with amazement in December of that year when they came across a five-column streamer, "Decca Scoops Music World," headlining an advertisement that boasted:

> Here they are—your favorite stars of radio, screen, and stage—in their greatest performances of instrument and voice! *Not* obsolete records, cut in price to meet a market, but the latest, newest smash hits—exclusively DECCA. Hear them *when* you want—as *often* as you want—right in your own home.*

With Wallerstein at RCA Victor and Kapp at Decca providing imaginative direction to the record business, the future of the phonograph looked better than it had in many years. Nevertheless, no one in 1934 could have been sanguine about its ability to recapture the profits of the 1920s. The low esteem in which this business was still held was effectively underlined by a transaction consummated in 1934 between the receivers of the Grigsby-Grunow Company and the American Record Company. Grigsby-Grunow had gone broke and its subsidiary, the Columbia Phonograph Company, was again up for sale. American Record Company bought it—the plant in Bridgeport, the entire catalogue of discs built up slowly over three decades, the trademark, the affiliation with Columbia in Europe, everything—for $70,500. Nine years earlier Louis Sterling had paid $2,500,000 for the same property.

Discerning record collectors first became aware of the upward swing in phonographic affairs when RCA Victor began evincing some interest again in its Red Seal catalogue. In the space of four years Victor had practically jettisoned its hard-won eminence in the field of recorded music. Exclusive contracts with the Boston Symphony and New York Phil-

---

* Kapp could never stimulate an interest in classical music; and though he embarked on a few ventures into this territory, the results could not be termed memorable. Only after his death in 1949, at the age of forty-seven, did American Decca address itself at all vigorously to the classical repertoire.

harmonic-Symphony and with Victor's large list of singers and instrumentalists had been allowed to go by default. There remained only the Philadelphia Orchestra, and even this had been pared down for recording sessions to sixty players in an effort to economize. Early in 1934 Victor began to mend its fences. A team of engineers was sent out to record the Minneapolis Symphony under its young and extremely competent conductor, Eugene Ormandy. This too was something of a penny-pinching operation, since RCA acquired an extensive group of recordings for practically nothing by virtue of this orchestra's contract with the musicians' union, which provided that its players could be employed without any extra compensation for purposes of recording. The outcome, nevertheless, was a series of skillfully performed and recorded albums, including several phonographic firsts (Kodály's *Háry János* Suite, Bruckner's Seventh Symphony, and Schoenberg's *Verklärte Nacht*) as well as many pieces from the well-trodden repertoire. A year later, records by the Boston Symphony reappeared on the Victor lists. To publicize this return to the fold, RCA Victor bought time on the NBC radio network and broadcast part of an actual recording session in Symphony Hall, Boston. Charles O'Connell, Victor's recording director at this period, told the radio listeners what was going on; and the orchestra played sections from Richard Strauss's *Also Sprach Zarathustra* as well as from symphonies by Beethoven, Mendelssohn, and Sibelius.

The release in May 1935 of the *Also Sprach Zarathustra* records, containing "the greatest crescendo ever recorded," gave added impetus to a new phenomenon that was helping to revive the phonograph. It was known as "high fidelity." Just who coined this magic phrase has never quite been determined. An English electrical engineer, Harold A. Hartley, is the strongest contender; he claims to have invented the phrase "about the end of 1926" to describe the improved

reproduction then offered by first-class radios and gramophones. If this be so, "high fidelity" lay fallow for some
time. Not until late 1933 or early 1934 did the phrase come
into general use, but then it was exploited with a vengeance.
Actually, the tonal spectrum of records had been substantially expanded: the frequency response of a 1929 recording
ran from 50–6,000 cycles, while that of a 1934 recording ran
from 30–8,000 cycles. Naturally, record companies were not
remiss in trumpeting these advances with appropriate ro-
domontade— "The surging and excitement of a first-class orchestra have been captured for the first time." "As great an
advance in electrical recording as electrical recording was
over the old mechanical process," et cetera, et cetera. Would
record buyers never tire of hearing that absolute perfection
in phonograph reproduction had finally been achieved? They
had been hearing the same sort of claims for thirty years
and would be hearing them still thirty years later. The
idea of high fidelity, of the ultimate in recorded perfection,
of reproduced music indistinguishable from actuality—this
idée fixe threads its chimerical way throughout the history
of the phonograph. Unfortunately for most of those who
succumbed to its blandishments in the 1930s, the increased
fidelity of records did not necessarily bring increased fidelity
from the loud-speaker. Although recording engineers were
able to engrave a wider gamut of sound onto discs, the vast
majority of reproducers could not do justice to their efforts.
No tonal advantages would derive from a high fidelity recording of 30–8,000 cycles if the equipment on which it was
played could handle only 100–5,000 cycles—the very most
that could be expected from an inexpensive record player
attached to an ordinary radio. But the concept of high fidelity was literally in the air: Station W2XR (later WQXR)
in New York began "high fidelity broadcasting" in 1934, and
several radio manufacturers were advertising equipment specially designed for "high quality reception of the new 'high

fidelity' stations." In all this there was much more gimmick than gain; but the notion of high fidelity sound achieved wide currency, and it helped to sell records.

With the reappearance of Toscanini before Victor recording microphones in 1936, the evidence became unmistakable that the phonograph was on its way back. It was an important event, appropriately publicized. For years record collectors had despaired of ever hearing further recorded interpretations by the magnetic Italian maestro. Toscanini's dissatisfaction with the start-and-stop method of making records was well known, and he had been heard to mutter, "Never again" at the end of his last recording session in November 1929. RCA Victor had once tried to charm him back by recording the Beethoven Fifth Symphony at one of his regular concerts in Carnegie Hall, March 4, 1931. Employing two recording machines and switching from one to the other every four minutes, the engineers had been able to get the entire work on wax without losing a note. Toscanini knew nothing of this until RCA Victor surprised him with test pressings of the recording. When he heard them, he found them impossibly bad and insisted on the masters being destroyed forthwith. By 1936 Toscanini had mellowed. Just before retiring from the New York Philharmonic-Symphony —and presumably taking leave of America for the last time— he agreed to record a Beethoven work (the Seventh Symphony), some Wagnerian excerpts, Brahms's *Variations on a Theme by Haydn,* and two Rossini overtures. Technically they were among the best recordings ever issued; musically they were incomparable. RCA risked a few thousand dollars on some expensive advertisements and waited to see what would happen. The response was immensely gratifying. In no time at all the Wagner album, five records for $10,* had sold 2,500 copies in New York City alone. It provoked radio

* Through thick and thin, Victor had maintained its $2.00 price for Red Seal Records by top-ranking artists.

trade magazines into writing editorials on "The Return of the Record." By December business was so much improved that RCA Victor felt inspired to divulge some statistics: sales for the month had amounted to 1,222,000 records, of which 300,000 were Red Seals.

Of the 900,000 popular records figuring in the above total, a good proportion were consumed by a tubby, gaudily colored machine that would blare out your favorite song with the deposit of a nickel. It was called the jukebox. To the teen-agers of 1936—who invested millions of nickels to hear the "King of Swing," Benny Goodman, give forth with "One O'clock Jump"—the jukebox appeared to be a boon of surpassing modernity. Their grandparents, who had gone through the same phase—with wax cylinders and ear tubes—in the 1890s, knew better. Coin phonographs in one form or another had been around for a long time, but like everything else to do with recorded music they had gone into a serious decline during the early years of the Depression. They came out of retirement with the end of Prohibition and—as jukeboxes—proliferated in bars, drugstores, and diners. By 1939 there were 225,000 of them, and it took 13,000,000 discs a year to nourish them. For record companies the jukebox served the double function of buyer and seller. Millions of records were purchased solely because they had been heard and enjoyed the night before on a jukebox. It became possible once again to talk of record best sellers. In 1936 a record of "The Music Goes Round and Round" sold more than 100,000 copies. Nothing like that had happened since Al Jolson's "Sonny Boy" back in the 1920s. By 1939 the ceiling had been raised to 300,000 with Victor's "Beer Barrel Polka" and Decca's "A-tisket, A-tasket." The Decca policy of "top tunes and top artists for 35¢" had paid off. In 1939, on its fifth anniversary, it had grown into the second-ranking company in the industry with an annual production of 19,-000,000 records.

Just as jukeboxes sold swing, radio was selling the classics. During the mid-Thirties the air was saturated with live music as never before (or since). In addition to the Metropolitan Opera and New York Philharmonic broadcasts, there were such other laudable programs as the Ford Sunday Evening Hour, the General Motors Symphony, and the Radio City Music Hall concerts conducted by Erno Rapee. Delivery boys could be heard whistling Ravel and Tchaikovsky. Deems Taylor, an articulate and engaging dispenser of musical knowledge, became a national celebrity. Musical classics were even deemed susceptible of selling newspapers. In 1938 the New York *Post* launched a circulation drive that used phonograph records as the bait. Ten albums of standard symphonic works, specially recorded by RCA Victor for this purpose with unidentified musicians, were offered for twenty-four coupons and $1.93 each. The idea quickly spread to other cities, and during the winter of 1938–39 these so-called Music Appreciation albums sold in excess of 300,000. They were amazing bargains—but that alone could not explain success of this order. Years of symphony broadcasts had begun to show their effect: Americans were evincing a growing disposition to absorb Bach, Beethoven, and Brahms in stout quantities. Radio, which once had laid the phonograph low, was now bringing it millions of new customers.

Of the 33,000,000 records sold in 1938, seventy-five per cent at least were accounted for by RCA and Decca. The American Record Company, which controlled Columbia, Brunswick, and some minor labels, ran a poor third with what was left—about 7,000,000 records. The old Columbia policy still obtained of drawing almost exclusively on European sources for what *Variety* liked to call "longhair music." A few New York recording sessions had yielded some Columbia discs by Walter Gieseking, the Roth Quartet, and the CBS Symphony under Howard Barlow; but these were scattered sparsely among the importations from abroad, and none of Columbia's records—whether domestic or foreign in origin—was being merchandised with any flair. A moribund and lackluster company, Columbia drifted inconclusively waiting for someone to rescue it. That person turned out to be Edward Wallerstein, an RCA Victor executive prepared to quit his job in favor of revitalizing Columbia. All he needed was somebody to buy the old company, and in 1938 he found a backer in the person of William S. Paley, president of the Columbia Broadcasting System. A check for $700,000 enabled CBS to purchase control of the entire American Record Company enterprise. Although the price had risen considerably since 1934, it was still a bargain.

With the weight of CBS prestige and resources behind him, Wallerstein set out to rebuild the Columbia catalogue. Benny Goodman, Duke Ellington, Count Basie, and many other idols of the Swing Era were put under contract. For the serious music lover, whom Wallerstein considered the mainstay of the record business, Columbia began signing up orchestras all over America: the Cleveland Orchestra under Artur Rodzinski, the Minneapolis Symphony under Dimitri Mitropoulos, the Chicago Symphony under Frederick Stock, and the All-American Youth Orchestra under Leopold Stokowski (whose name had seemed almost inseparably linked with Victor's for over two decades). In March 1940 the first of Columbia's new recordings by American orchestras were placed on sale. Like Victor's Red Seal issues, the discs were priced at $2.00 each. *Scheherazade* conducted by Rodzinski cost $10, so did the Beethoven *Pastoral* conducted by Mitropoulos, each consisting of five records. Collecting records in the spring of 1940 was still an expensive hobby—but it would not remain so for long.

On August 6, without any advance warning, Columbia reduced the price of every twelve-inch record in the catalogue to $1.00. Overnight the cost of Rodzinski's *Scheherazade* dropped to $5.50 (the extra fifty cents being charged for the album, which was no longer thrown in free). This wholesale devaluation had been part of Wallerstein's original plan for reviving Columbia, but he had held off implementing it for almost two years until a good start, at least, was made in rebuilding the catalogue. A double-spread advertisement in *Life*, followed by announcements in other magazines and the leading daily papers, left no one in doubt about what had happened. The reaction was immediate and decisive: record collectors flocked into the stores and bought Columbia merchandise to the exclusion of practically all else. RCA Victor had no recourse but to reply in kind. On August 21, just fifteen days later, the price of all twelve-inch Victor Red Seal Records came down also to $1.00 each. Old-timers at Camden, who remembered the days when a single-sided Red Seal retailed for as much as $7.00, shook their heads and inveighed against the evils of price-cutting. They had no cause for alarm. Wallerstein's hunch that Americans would buy classical music in quantity if only the price was right proved to be entirely justified. Following the price cut, sales of classical records in the United States were said to have increased fifteen hundred per cent.

For the first time in decades the American record business was being enlivened by intense competition, especially in the hallowed domain of classical music. Ever since 1903, when Columbia came a cropper with its pioneering series of Grand Opera discs, Victor had roamed through this territory without any serious opposition. But after 1940 the colossus of Camden no longer had the field to itself, and competition from the revitalized Columbia company grew ever more dangerous. To the already imposing number of American orchestras on the Columbia list was now added the venerable New York Philharmonic-Symphony, which made its debut on the Columbia label in September 1940. Victor was left with the Philadelphia Orchestra and its new conductor, Eugene Ormandy, the Boston Symphony under Koussevitzky, and the young NBC Symphony under Toscanini. These were musical properties of no mean order. But could they rival the orchestral line-up of Columbia? The high councils at Victor decreed that added recruits would help, and emissaries were dispatched to conclude contracts with the San Francisco Symphony (Monteux), the Cincinnati Symphony (Eugene Goossens), the Indianapolis Symphony (Sevitzky), the Rochester Philharmonic (Iturbi), and the National Symphony (Hans Kindler). By the winter of 1941 there was hardly a major orchestra in the United States that had not been impressed either by Columbia or Victor into making records. Without the rivalry of the two companies, this scramble for home-grown music might never have reached such proportions; but orchestral recording in America would surely have increased in any case, for the chief source of supply on which Victor and Columbia had been relying since 1925 could no longer be tapped. Whatever was happening in the recording studios of Germany and France and Italy, the results were not available across the blockaded Atlantic; and England was far too preoccupied with German bombers and submarines to bother with exporting quantities of recorded music to the United States of America.

Price cuts, jukeboxes, and intensive promotion by three highly competitive companies served to swell and quicken the phonograph's return to public favor. When the figures were compiled for 1941, the industry rubbed its eyes with amazement and found that 127,000,000 discs had been sold that year. Production of radio-phonographs was also in a splendidly healthy state. Under normal circumstances, nothing would have impeded the rise of record and phonograph sales to a total volume exceeding anything that the industry had ever known. But the times were anything but normal. On December 7, 1941, the United States found itself at war. Importations of raw materials from Asia were among the first casualties, and the basic ingredient of phonograph records—shellac—came principally from India. In April 1942 an order from the War Production Board cut the nonmilitary use of shellac by seventy per cent. At about the same time, the nation's manufacturers of electrical goods turned out their last radios and radio-phonographs for civilian consumption and converted to war production. The phonograph, which was just on the threshold of its greatest triumphs, had to dig in for the duration.

21   *A WAR AND ITS AFTERMATH*

FOUR MONTHS AFTER THE GOVERNMENT ORDER RESTRICTING the use of shellac, a complete cessation of all recording activity descended on the United States. This was also due to a war: not the global conflict in which seventy million men in uniform were involved, but a private war between James Caesar Petrillo, president of the American Federation of Musicians, and the phonograph record. Mr. Petrillo had revived the old chant about the menace of mechanical music. Unlike that earlier malcontent, John Philip Sousa, Petrillo felt no apprehension over phonograph music in the home. As befitted a strong-willed labor leader, he aimed his jeremiads rather at the kind of recorded entertainment that had thrown musicians out of work. The nation's jukeboxes (400,000 of them by 1942) and broadcasting stations were assuredly depending on phonograph records to the detriment of those who made live music. Petrillo remembered the days when thousands of restaurants and dance halls had employed their own small ensembles, when every radio station had hired its own studio orchestra. Many of his 140,000 union members could recall those departed days too; and when their representatives gathered in Dallas in June 1942 for the annual AFM convention, there was no mistaking the militant climate of opinion.

In a speech to the convention, Petrillo set forth his proposed plan of battle: union musicians would be allowed to make no more recordings after a specified date except for

278

the war effort and for use in the home. This was tantamount
to saying that recording would cease altogether, as record
companies could not possibly control their products after
shipment from the factory. The bleak prospect of a recording ban hovered over the industry. Yet no one took it too
seriously. Petrillo had threatened before, and little had happened. This time, however, he meant what he said. An
order went out to every local in the country instructing
union members to refuse all recording engagements after
July 31, 1942. The edict, which applied equally to Leopold
Stokowski and Benny Goodman, to the drummer in Tommy
Dorsey's band and the tuba player in the Boston Symphony,
was meticulously obeyed by a well-disciplined and all-power-
ful union. Beginning on August 1, the recording studios of
Columbia, Decca, and RCA Victor were effectively and de-
cisively silenced.

Some time elapsed before the effects of the ban were noticed. Since record companies had always made a practice of
planning their releases months in advance, sizable stockpiles
of unissued recordings reposed in the vaults; and these could
be drawn upon for many months (even years, if necessary)
to provide a monthly increment of new discs. With them the
industry hoped to call Petrillo's bluff. But the stockpiles
were inadequate in one vital respect. With relentless regu-
larity new songs kept appearing and catching the public's
fancy. They were heard over the radio, in the movies, and
at the theater—everywhere, in fact, but on records. A new
musical called *Oklahoma!*, which had recently opened in
New York, was captivating the country with its sunlit tunes.
But if you asked for them at a record store, you were out of
luck. *Oklahoma!* was not in the stockpiles.

Among the three leading companies, Decca was most af-
fected by Petrillo's interdiction; its revenue came almost
entirely from popular music. After thirteen months of
drought, Decca's parched coffers could stand it no longer;

and in September 1943 this company bowed to Petrillo's terms and signed a contract with the AFM. The terms specified royalties of from a quarter of a cent to five cents on every record sold, payable to the AFM, for the succor of unemployed musicians. This did not obliterate the menace of mechanical music, but it soothed its injury with the balm of money. One of Decca's first issues subsequent to its pact with the AFM was an album of songs from *Oklahoma!* performed by members of the New York cast. Decca's Jack Kapp soon learned what Columbia's Louis Sterling had discovered in England during World War I: that wartime musicals in original-cast recordings sell incredibly well. Americans were to buy 1,300,000 copies of the *Oklahoma!* album—at $5.00 apiece.

Columbia and RCA Victor continued to hold out. They questioned Petrillo's right to levy a private tax on employers and objected to the lack of any public control over the disposition of royalties. Since wartime demand for records so much exceeded the supply, Columbia and Victor hoped to subsist indefinitely—if need be—without new tunes. For the same reason, they decided to get along also without the marginal items in their catalogues. In Victor's case especially this led to a dolorous excision of prized Red Seal listings in favor of a few well-tried sellers. Although the Toscanini-Horowitz recording of Tchaikovsky's B-flat Piano Concerto could be readily obtained, its proven marketability having earned it a niche in the catalogue, Schnabel's recording of the Mozart F major Piano Concerto was summarily deleted; a work of no mass appeal, it had fallen a casualty of the war.

In the summer of 1944, after sustaining the ban for two years, Columbia and Victor scraped the bottom of the barrel. Their stockpiles, which once had seemed inexhaustible, were dwindling to the vanishing point. As if to worsen their plight, the War Production Board had relaxed its restrictions somewhat on the use of shellac. Supply could begin to meet demand. But it was to Decca, with its monopoly of current dance music, that the demand was channeled. Decca had even made an inroad into Red Seal territory by enticing Jascha Heifetz into a short-term recording contract. Heifetz had been a Victor artist since 1918; if he could be spirited away, further defections would surely ensue. At this juncture Edward Wallerstein—speaking for Victor as well as Columbia —had to admit that "the economic pressures on us are such that we can wait no longer and must now either sign or go out of business." On Armistice Day 1944 both companies concluded agreements with the AFM on terms similar to the Decca contract of September 1943. Their antipathy to a union-controlled royalty fund, however, had not gone unnoticed. The Taft-Hartley Act of 1947 made it illegal for the AFM to collect royalties in this fashion. This brought on another, and less effective, recording ban in 1948—which lasted until a trustee acceptable to both labor and management was found to administer the fund.

Within a few hours of its 1944 capitulation, Victor's studios resounded to the harmonies of Vaughn Monroe's orchestra as it recorded two songs from *Meet Me in St. Louis*. By dint of overtime work in Camden, these first post-ban recordings went on sale two days later. Columbia worked almost as fast with the Schubert and Bach-Gounod *Ave Maria*s interpreted by Andre Kostelanetz. A more noteworthy Columbia session came a few weeks later, when its first recording date was held with the newly won Philadelphia Orchestra. During the twenty-seven-month silence, Victor's contract with this orchestra had expired and Columbia had tempted it away. The domination of classical repertoire by Red Seal Records, uncontested for so long, was now definitely ended.

While the Petrillo ban was stifling the phonograph's voice in America, studios in Europe continued to turn out some new recordings despite the bombs, the dislocations, and the shortages. In France, under the cloud of German occupation, *Pelléas* and *The Damnation of Faust* were captured *in toto* on discs; in Holland the Telefunken engineers recorded Willem Mengelberg and the Amsterdam Concertgebouw Orchestra in brilliant, if erratic, performances of Beethoven; in Italy several unrecorded operas were added to the catalogues; in Germany an historically valuable series of Richard Strauss works conducted by the septuagenarian composer were issued by Deutsche Grammophon; and in England the semiofficial British Council, in conjunction with HMV, sponsored an extensive collection of orchestral and choral recordings of music by contemporary Englishmen. It would be misleading to suggest that wartime record making in Europe continued at the pre-1939 tempo; but the studios did at least remain open, and from one of them emerged a new concept of recorded sound.

Early in the war the RAF Coastal Command had approached the English-owned Decca Record Company with a secret and difficult assignment. Coastal Command wanted a training record to illustrate differences between the sounds of German and British submarines. Such aural distinctions were extremely delicate, and to reproduce them adequately on a record called for a decided enlargement of the phonograph's capabilities. Intensive work under the supervision of Decca's chief engineer, Arthur Haddy, led to new recording techniques and the kind of record that Coastal Command desired. Thereafter, these same techniques were adapted to musical reproduction. Unobtrusively, in December 1944, the first examples of "ffrr" sound reached English record buyers. The initials stood for "full frequency range reproduction." They were adopted as a Decca trademark in 1945 and quickly entered the phonographic vocabulary as descriptive of a new standard of reproduced music—brilliant and incisive in the treble, full and resonant in the bass, with a heightened sense of presence and room tone never before encountered on a phonograph record to such stunning effect. English Decca's early "ffrr" issues were more commendable for quality of sound than quality of music; but with the release in June 1946 of Stravinsky's *Petrouchka* conducted by Ernest Ansermet, this company was ready to combat all criticism. The Stravinsky score was replete with orchestral effects—growling noises *sul ponticello* from the double basses, shrill cornet roulades against drum accompaniment, bizarre diversions by piano and celesta, luminous climaxes from the full complement of strings, winds, brass, and percussion—and they were exploited by Ansermet and Decca's engineers to create a recording of dazzling impact. *The Gramophone* pronounced it "a new and very exciting page of gramophone history."

Late in 1946 imports of Decca's "ffrr" records reached the United States in substantial quantities. Their appearance was termed by one influential critic (Irving Kolodin) "the single most memorable event of the year," and even at $2.00 a record (twice the cost of domestic merchandise) they found a ready market. As a matter of fact, almost anything with grooves sold well in 1946. It was a year the like of which the record industry had never experienced before. Unrestricted shellac shipments from India had been resumed, skilled labor had returned to the record factories, and the combination of pent-up demand and swollen bank accounts boosted total sales for the year to 275,000,000 discs—more than double the prewar high. But this was only a prelude to 1947, during which 400,000,000 records were sold, as well as 3,415,000 radio-phonograph combinations. Those who had lived through the phonograph's dog days, fifteen years earlier, could hardly believe the evidence of the ledger books. A staple RCA Victor recording of a popular piano concerto, originally issued in 1929, sold 62,756 copies in 1946; in 1935 its total sale had been 102 copies. Even more spectacular was the reception accorded a new version of Bach's *Goldberg*

Variations interpreted by the harpsichordist Wanda Landowska. This was recondite music, for the connoisseur; when
RCA Victor issued it in January 1946 (just at the start of
the postwar boom), sales in the neighborhood of two or three
thousand albums were envisioned. Instead, 30,000 sets were
sold within three months and sales subsequently went well
over 40,000. Phenomena of this order showed that a great
new audience for recorded music existed. If the phonograph
record could only retain its hold on this largely untapped
market, its future seemed serene.

But there were already distant rumblings to give cause for
some misgivings. The phonograph record of 1947 was actually far more old-fashioned than its advocates cared to admit.
Its size and speed and grooving were no different from what
they had been in 1903, when a four-minute operatic aria was
considered the be-all and end-all of the phonograph's musical responsibilities; even the material of which records were
made was basically the same, though refinements in its tex-
ture had been evolved over the years. Within these limitations, records had improved constantly. But the limitations
still existed. All the tonal realism being captured by English
Decca and its competitors could not hide the fact that shellac
discs were scratchy and had to be changed—either manually
or automatically—every four minutes, nor did it prevent
many people from wondering whether Emile Berliner's
gramophone disc was not really *passé*, a hardy survivor from
another era enjoying one last fling.

The proponents of magnetic tape believed this to be so.
Tape did not pose a particularly new threat. Magnetic recording had been around for a long time; in fact, it was first
accomplished in 1899 by a Danish engineer named Vladimir
Poulsen, who based his invention, the Telegraphone, on the
ability of an electromagnet to create varying magnetic pat-
terns in a piece of steel relative to the varying electrical impulses actuating it. Poulsen used an ordinary carbon

telephone transmitter to convert sound into electrical impulses, and these in turn were made to actuate an electromagnetic recording head. Directly beneath this recording head passed demagnetized steel wire or ribbon traveling at a steady speed, which as it sped past the head was then magnetized according to the electrical impulses generated by the transmitter. To reproduce sound magnetized on wire or ribbon, the process merely had to be reversed: the magnetized steel passed under the electromagnet, producing varying electrical impulses that were then converted into audible sound by a telephone receiver. At the Paris Exposition of 1900 the Telegraphone won a Grand Prix and occasioned much favorable comment. As the first all-electrical recording and reproducing device, there was much to be said for it. Unlike the phonograph, with its hard metal stylus plowing abrasively through jagged grooves, the Telegraphone did not have to rely on mechanical energy for storing and producing sound. With friction at a minimum, Telegraphone recordings had a permanency that discs or cylinders sadly lacked; there was little to wear out, and experiments had shown that wire or ribbon recordings retained their magnetic properties intact after more than 2,200 playings. Most important of all, perhaps, was the continuity that Poulsen's invention made possible. The wire Telegraphone could operate continuously for thirty minutes, while the bulkier and less practical ribbon Telegraphone could be recorded upon continuously for an hour or more. But with these advantages went a substantial drawback: the Poulsen Telegraphone could speak no louder or more distinctly than an ordinary Bell telephone of 1900 vintage. This limitation seriously impeded its commercial development. The fairly crude telephone transmitters and receivers of that era were utterly incapable of reproducing music with any fidelity at all; and even if they could have given a reasonable semblance of musical sound, it would have been heard only at a whisper, owing to the lack of amplification in Poulsen's instrument. Had the condenser microphone and vacuum-tube amplifier been invented in 1900, the Telegraphone might well have superseded the phonograph—or at least given it some healthy competition. As things were, the commercial use of Poulsen's device was restricted to office dictation. A few Telegraphones were sold for this purpose (the DuPont Company bought twenty for its Wilmington office); but they caused more trouble than they were worth, and by 1910 magnetic recording had been relegated to the limbo of theoretical discussion.

Interest revived with the production of efficient microphones and amplifiers in the 1920s, at which time Germany took the lead in magnetic recording research and held it for two decades. A scientist named Pfleumer made great headway in developing a paper tape coated with an iron oxide sensitive enough for recording purposes. This tape was taken over by one of the large German cartels, which marketed it commercially in 1935 together with a compact recording-playback instrument called the Magnetophone. Even then, however, magnetic recording could not cope successfully with music. The 1935 Magnetophones were perfectly adequate as dictating machines, which is how they were sold, but they could not rival the phonograph when it came to reproducing the full spectrum of orchestral sound. By the early 1940s, German technicians had made some startling advances. Radio monitors who listened to the German broadcasting stations day after day for British and United States Intelligence soon realized that many of the programs they were hearing could not possibly derive from live studio broadcasts. Yet there were a fidelity and a continuity of sound, plus an absence of surface scratch, in the German transmissions that ordinary transcription records could never have yielded. The mystery was solved on September 11, 1944, when the Allies captured Radio Luxembourg, which had been under German control for four years, and discovered among the station's equipment a new Magnetophone of extraordinary capabilities.

It was a bulky instrument that used fourteen-inch reels of plastic tape coated with iron oxide; one reel played continuously for half an hour. What astounded American electrical engineers was the frequency response of this wartime Magnetophone. It could record sounds up to 10,000 cycles with superb realism, and thus had attained a fidelity equal to, if not surpassing, the finest phonograph records in existence. As an instrument for home reproduction of music, the German Magnetophone was hopelessly impractical. The low output of Magnetophone tape required elaborate and expensive amplifiers for satisfactory performance; the large reels and high speed at which the tape ran (30 inches per second) made for a cumbersome and noisy piece of equipment. But the Germans, at least, had demonstrated the potentialities of magnetic recording, and their work served as an incentive for further refinements.

In America several manufacturers tackled the problem of transforming magnetic tape into a readily salable commodity, most notably the Minnesota Mining and Manufacturing Company, whose "Scotch" brand of gummed cellophane tape had become a practically essential accoutrement of modern living. In this company's laboratories in St. Paul a staff of researchers under the direction of Wilfred W. Wetzel spent three years and $700,000 creating an improved magnetic tape with a new type of iron oxide coating that embodied magnetic properties far superior to anything devised by the Germans. As a result of their work, "Scotch" brand magnetic tape could record sounds up to 15,000 cycles at a speed of 7.5 inches per second, as compared to the Magnetophone's maximum of 10,000 cycles at 30 inches per second. In 1947 the Minnesota Mining and Manufacturing Company began full-scale production and almost immediately found an important and influential customer in the person of Bing Crosby, who was intent on recording his radio shows in advance but was dissatisfied with the quality of sound obtainable from discs. Crosby's espousal of the new medium started a landslide toward tape in the radio industry, where magnetic recording soon became standard for transcribing original broadcasts and for delayed airing of programs. The old disc recording instruments previously used for broadcast transcriptions were unsentimentally abandoned. In a short and significant contest, tape had prevailed decisively.

Was it now to win another contest in the home and displace the phonograph for good? As 1947 drew to a close there was reason to believe that it would. The superiorities of tape recordings to disc recordings seemed unanswerable. A compact, lightweight reel of tape would play uninterruptedly for half an hour; a bulky and heavy record for four minutes. Tape did not wear out; records showed evidence of real deterioration after thirty or so playings. A broken tape could be spliced quickly and easily by anyone; a broken record could be tossed into the trash basket. To those who reverenced good sound, tape at its best reproduced music more faithfully than records at their best. Admittedly, some difficulties remained to be circumvented. Both magnetic tape itself and the equipment on which to play it were still discouragingly expensive; moreover, no efficient method of manufacturing prerecorded tapes in quantity had yet been devised. But these were merely problems of production and technique that would surely disappear as a mass market developed for the new product. The certainty of that mass market was never doubted by the well-wishers of tape. To them, its inherent qualities seemed obvious and invincible. Sooner or later, they declared, the firmly entrenched phono-

This scene, from a 1915 Victor advertisement, was captioned:
"Dancing to the music of the Victrola is the favorite pastime."
The dancers at far left are Vernon and Irene Castle, who
then supervised Victor dance recordings.

A flat-top phonograph
manufactured by Aeolian-
Vocalion during World
War I. Phonographs were
made to look as little like
phonographs as possible.

Henry C. Harrison and Joseph P. Maxfield, developers of the electrical recording process, at the Bell Laboratories, 1925.

A tweedy Leopold Stokowski listens, score in hand, to the Orthophonic Victrola.

Mary Garden at an early Victor electrical recording session. The conductor is Rosario Bourdon, Victor's musical director at that time.

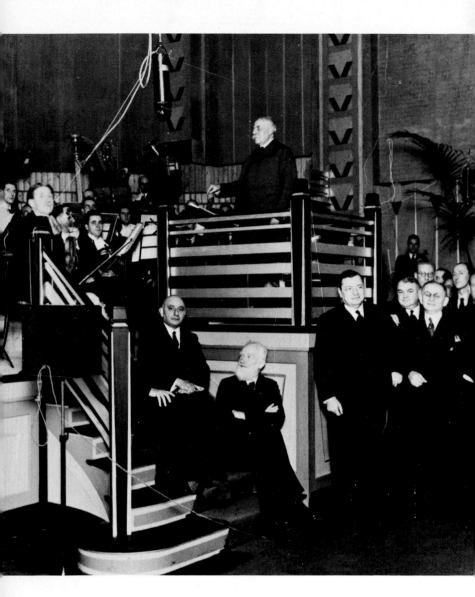

In November 1931, Sir Edward Elgar opened the
Gramophone Company's new Abbey Road studios in
London by recording his *Falstaff*. Seated on the steps
are Sir Landon Ronald, the company's musical adviser,
and Bernard Shaw. Standing to their left are Alfred
Clark and Sir Louis Sterling, chairman and managing
director of the newly formed Electric and Musical
Industries Ltd.

Generation gap in the recording studio. Here is Noel Coward, immaculately debonair, in the mid-1930s.

And here is Paul Simon in the early 1970s, recording a vocal track to mesh with a previously recorded accompaniment, which he hears via the headphones.

Peter Goldmark and William S.
Bachman, who together developed
Columbia's long-playing record.

At the recording session of *My F*
Lady, March 1956. Frederick Loev
Alan Jay Lerner, and Godda
Lieberson confer w
Stanley Hollowa

Elvis Presley has made more million-selling records (counting both singles and albums) than any other artist in phonographic history. This photo shows him in an RCA Victor studio at the beginning of his career, 1956.

Many black artists achieved worldwide celebrity as rhythm and blues records gained in popularity. A notable example was the blind musician Ray Charles.

Van Cliburn became a national hero upon his return to the United States from Moscow, after winning the Tchaikovsky Piano Competition in 1958. His best-selling recording of the Tchaikovsky Piano Concerto was made at this time.

Another best-selling classical record was *Switched-On Bach,* created on the Moog Synthesizer by composer-physicist Walter Carlos.

In Vienna's Sofiensaal, conductor Georg Solti leads the Vienna Philharmonic and singers in a scene from Wagner's *Ring*. The marked squares on the recording "stage" show the vocalists where to stand in relation to the stereo microphones.

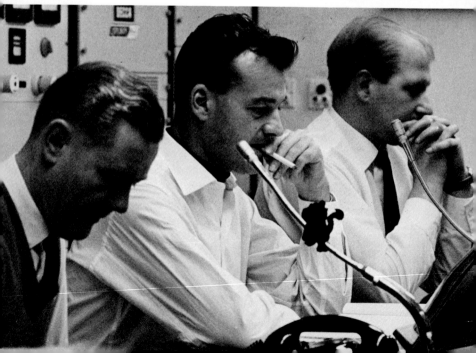

ewhere in the Sofiensaal, producer John shaw (flanked by two recording ineers) monitors the session over stereo akers. The microphones are for municating with the conductor in the e recording hall.

The Beatles changed the world's ideas about the very nature of pop music. This photo shows them in one of their earliest recording sessions for EMI, in 1962.

A more traditional kind of fare was served up by Mitch Miller and The Gang in the perennial *Sing Along with Mitch* albums.

Record retailing has come a long way since Bloomingdale's proudly opened its Graphophone department (*above*) in the early 1900s. Today the emphasis is on self-service, as at the Harvard Co-op (*below*).

graph record would have to defer to the call of progress. As of 1947 they were probably right. But history is a fluid thing, and just at that juncture the phonograph was about to embark on a new venture that would meet tape on its own terms and upset all the prognostications made on its behalf.

22 *RENAISSANCE AT A NEW SPEED*

ON AN UNSEASONABLY SULTRY FRIDAY AFTERNOON IN JUNE 1948 members of the press were summoned to a suite in the Waldorf-Astoria Hotel to hear about "a revolutionary new product" from Columbia Records. It turned out to be a nonbreakable microgroove disc with a playing time of twenty-three minutes per side; Columbia had named it the LP (Long-Playing) Record. Among the journalists present were several whose memories of the record business went back many, many years. They had heard all this before. From the ill-fated attempt of Neophone in 1904 to the ill-fated attempt of Victor in 1931, record companies had periodically dangled the promise of long-playing discs before an avid public. They had never worked, and the veterans who gathered for Columbia's press meeting were skeptical with good reason. But as the demonstration proceeded, their doubts became less insistent. Edward Wallerstein, who spoke on behalf of the new product, was flanked on one side by a stack of conventional records in albums, on the other by 101 LPs. Each represented an identical amount of music—in all, 325 different selections. The conventional records towered nearly eight feet high, the pile of LPs stood a fraction over fifteen inches. After dilating on this disparity, Mr. Wallerstein removed a symphonic recording from the eight-foot pile and played it for four minutes, until the usual break—right in the middle of a movement; then he took a microgroove version of the very same recording and played it on an

LP attachment that the Philco Corporation was manufacturing to sell for $29.95. Not only was there no trace of a break in the middle of the movement, but the quality of sound had suffered not at all. Indeed, some listeners believed that the recording sounded more lifelike on LP than it had on the standard record. A few questions were asked by reporters, and the meeting then broke up for the cocktails that invariably reward guests at a press demonstration. In such wise did a new chapter open in the history of the phonograph.

A flat disc can be made to play longer in only two ways: one is to slow down its rate of revolution on the turntable; the other is to diminish the width of the grooves and increase their number. Every attempt at a long-playing record had relied on one or both of these expedients. Columbia's LP Microgroove Record was no exception; its sole originality lay in the fact that it worked. Slow speeds and narrow grooves pose some vexing technical difficulties; for over three decades they combined to upset all efforts toward a practical long-playing record.

In 1944 a fresh start was made to surmount them. The Columbia Broadcasting System had set up a new laboratory for various lines of experimentation under the direction of Peter Goldmark, a Hungarian-born electrical engineer in his late thirties. As a CBS subsidiary, Columbia Records participated in its program; to Goldmark and his co-workers was delegated the task of developing a practical slow-speed microgroove record. Prior claims of television and war work served to postpone this research; but in 1946 it was given full attention, and in September 1947 Goldmark could report that his job was accomplished: he had devised a recording head capable of cutting hair-width grooves consistently, a pickup that would track them easily, and an electronic equalization system able to compensate for an otherwise disturbing loss of fidelity in the inside grooves. His prototype LP Microgroove Record played for twenty-three minutes per side, held 224 to 300 grooves per inch (compared to approximately 85 grooves per inch on the ordinary disc), and was pressed in vinylite, a nonbreakable plastic; the reproducer was provided with a turntable that revolved steadily at $33\frac{1}{3}$ rpm and a specially designed pickup of extremely light weight (six to seven grams of pressure) that afforded full-range reproduction free from rumble, hum, and distortion.

While Columbia's factory in Bridgeport prepared a separate division for pressing the new records and Philco's factory in Philadelphia tooled up for the manufacturing of new players, the secret of LP was well kept. Finally, in April 1948, with production already under way, the time was considered apposite for demonstrating LP to Columbia's great competitor at a meeting between high executives of both companies. In the hope of accomplishing a quick and painless change-over to the new record speed, Columbia offered to share its system of LP recording with RCA Victor. The most influential spectator at this demonstration, the Radio Corporation's president (David Sarnoff), is said to have spoken flatteringly of Columbia's development. He seemed to imply that RCA would willingly adopt the $33\frac{1}{3}$-rpm speed. But thereafter RCA maintained an equivocal silence, and in June the Columbia bigwigs determined to go ahead and launch the LP Microgroove Record by themselves.

Victor, seventeen years before, had unwittingly provided an object lesson in how not to merchandise a long-playing record. Columbia was now to profit from its rival's debacle of 1931. In 1948 a prospective LP customer had to invest only $29.95 to convert his phonograph or radio to the new records (later the price dropped to $9.95). Moreover, unlike the early Victor $33\frac{1}{3}$-rpm records, Columbia's LPs were not obvious patch-ups from noisy four-minute shellac pressings. Many years before, in anticipation of LP, the Columbia engineers had started recording a duplicate set of masters at each session on large acetate transcription blanks; by 1948 there existed a valuable backlog of high-quality, noise-free recordings readily transferable to LP.

Under these favorable circumstances the Columbia Microgroove Record made its debut, but it did not—in the summer of 1948—effect an abrupt mutation in record-buying habits. The first issues were by no means of uniform excellence: many early LPs tended to be hard, dull, and wiry in sound; sustained notes were wont to waver ever so slightly (producing an unpleasant effect called "wow"); and loud passages sometimes made a faint and untimely appearance ahead of the beat—through an annoying phenomenon known as "pre-echo." In view of such drawbacks, the majority of America's fifteen-million record buyers continued to look fondly at their prized collections of standard-speed discs. But to an enthusiastic minority the immediate advantages and future promise of LP were such as to make the microgroove records seem instantly desirable. Those advantages were fourfold: LP records offered listeners the cherishable satisfaction of hearing recorded performances without breaks in continuity; they minimized the twin woes of surface scratch and record wear; they alleviated the problem of storage; they provided more music per dollar than had ever been offered before. The Ormandy-Philadelphia Orchestra recording of Tchaikovsky's Fourth Symphony, for instance, sold for $7.25 on 78 rpm (five records in an album) but could be had on one twelve-inch LP for $4.85.* Even this comparison was not entirely fair to LP, since the 78-rpm records were pressed in shellac; had they been pressed in vinylite (a few postwar issues were published in both shellac and vinyl editions), the 78-rpm price would have reached $11. These considerations, together with a continuing improvement in LP sound quality, gave Columbia's new product substantial support from those dedicated collectors of classical music who spent

---

* Since then the average list price of LP records has fluctuated from a low of $3.98 (1955) to a high of $6.98 (1976).

$100 or more per year enlarging their record libraries. At the end of 1948, when LPs had been in the stores for six months, Columbia added up its sales figures and noted with satisfaction that 1,250,000 copies of the new records were already in use.

But suddenly the fortunes of LP faltered and threatened to decline. The strange silence from RCA Victor subsequent to Columbia's private demonstration of LP in April was now explained. Victor was replying with a microgroove record of its own, one that played at 45 rpm and required yet another special reproducing attachment, thus initiating the unhappy and ill-advised Battle of the Speeds. Victor's weapons were seven-inch vinylite records packed in albums that "fit on your bookcase shelf" and a compact player unit (originally priced at $24.95, later at $12.95) embodying the "world's fastest changer." There was the rub: RCA Victor's 45-rpm record played no longer than a conventional 78-rpm record; no matter how fast the changer worked, it still could not obviate the same upsetting breaks in continuity that had been plaguing the discriminating listener for decades. But was RCA Victor at all concerned with the discriminating listener? Its sponsorship of a short-playing 45-rpm record left one inclined to doubt it. As the *Saturday Review* editorialized at the time, all the evidence led one to suspect that RCA Victor had "limited itself to the convenience of one segment of the record public (the large mass market) and left the smaller, if more discriminating, public to take . . . consolation . . . from the improved quality of the new disc."

The spectacle of America's two largest companies struggling over competing speeds and types of records utterly bewildered most onlookers. Columbia and Victor had apparently signed the death warrant of 78-rpm discs; that much seemed clear. But what would take their place: Columbia's 33⅓-rpm LPs or Victor's 45-rpm short-plays? No one could tell, least of all the uninformed record buyer. Taking the path of prudence, he stopped purchasing records altogether until the smoke should clear and the battle be decided. The effect on record sales of his understandable wariness was emphatic. From an all-time peak of $204,000,000 in 1947, the value of retail record business slipped to $157,875,000 in 1949. The postwar record boom had been turned into a bust. Fortunately, the slump did not get out of hand. By the summer of 1949 public favor was plainly inclining toward Columbia's LP; and in recognition of this trend, several competing companies adopted the 33⅓-rpm record.* The first of these were three small firms, postwar additions to the record industry, catering to collectors of specialized musical tastes: Cetra-Soria, Vox, and Concert Hall. They were followed almost immediately by Mercury, a rather bigger power in the record orbit, and in August by the export division of English Decca, which now sold its merchandise in the United States under the "London" label. Capitol Records—a young giant in the industry—began in September 1949 to issue classical repertoire on long-playing 33⅓ rpm as well as on short-playing 45 rpm and 78 rpm (thus taking no chances); two months later, the largest uncommitted company in America, Decca, declared itself in favor of LP. Within eighteen months of its introduction, LP had been espoused by every record company of consequence, save RCA Victor, while the 45-rpm record—with which RCA hoped to undermine Columbia's innovation—had managed to find only one outside ally, Capitol, and that a faltering one.

Was the battle lost? It seemed so on January 4, 1950, when RCA Victor—with all the dignity it could muster—announced its intention of making available its "great artists and unsurpassed classical library on new and improved Long Play (33⅓ rpm) records." Along with the announcement went wholesale dismissals of RCA Victor executives who had par-

* Columbia's offer of rights to the LP process had been extended to all companies.

ticipated in the anti-LP vendetta. But anyone who felt inclined to swathe the 45-rpm record in black crape and
pronounce appropriate obsequies over its demise had not
reckoned with the power of Victor advertising. Following
sound Johnsonian principles, RCA spent a fortune publicizing 45 rpm as the preferred speed for popular music. In this
area, small unbreakable records had undoubted appeal, and
short playing-time posed no particular disadvantage. The
45-rpm campaign cost RCA about $5,000,000. But it worked.
Buyers of nonclassical records turned increasingly to the
convenient and well-advertised 45s, and one by one the major
companies (including Columbia) took up the 45s for popular
repertoire. By 1954, when more than 200,000,000 of them
had been sold, the president of RCA could boast that "the
'45' records now represent more than 50 per cent of all single
records sold."

The standard 78-rpm shellac disc had meanwhile suffered
a swift decline. Indeed, by 1950 it was no longer standard in
America except for ephemeral dance records, and even in
this domain it was fast giving way to microgrooved vinylite
of either the $33\frac{1}{3}$-rpm or 45-rpm variety. The old speed,
however, was to make one last heroic stand. It took place in
England to the accompaniment of some curious editorials
by Compton Mackenzie, editor of *The Gramophone*. A quarter century earlier this writer had deprecated the worth of
electrical recording; he was now to belittle the advantages of
LP. He wrote in 1949:

> I ask readers if they want to feel that their collections of
> records are obsolete, if they really want to spend money on
> buying discs that will save them the trouble of getting up to
> change them, and if they really want to wait years for a
> repertory as good as what is now available to them? . . . The
> substitution of a long playing disc is not a sufficiently valua-
> ble improvement to justify the complete abandonment of
> present methods of reproduction.

Apparently his die-hard view was shared by the directors of Electric & Musical Industries Ltd., who shaped the policies of HMV and Columbia in Europe. For more than four years after the microgroove LP was introduced in America, records bearing the HMV and Columbia labels in England continued to be manufactured only at the 78-rpm speed. During this period, English Decca and several smaller companies furthered the cause of long-playing records in Europe and profited enormously from E.M.I.'s intransigeance. When the HMV-Columbia combine finally did bow to the inevitable, in October 1952, its prestige and its volume of business had suffered badly.

Along with the rise of LP in America went two related phenomena: high fidelity reproduction and tape recording. The slogan "high fidelity" had been bandied about since 1934. It usually meant nothing at all—except employment for copy writers. America's leading providers of radio and phonograph sets held strongly to the opinion that most listeners preferred music reproduced at low fidelity (soft, mellow, and flabby) to music reproduced at high fidelity (loud, brilliant, and full-bodied). In *concept*, high fidelity was supposed to be attractive: hence the advertisements. In *practice*, it was supposed to be anathema: hence the weak, inefficient amplifiers, the tiny loud-speakers, the soggy tone controls foisted on an unwitting public. A few stubborn souls refused to take what was offered in the name of "high fidelity." Their ears urged them on to investigate, and they found that the components for genuine high fidelity reproduction—powerful and flexible amplifiers, sensitive and carefully balanced pickups, large and heavy loud-speakers mounted in separate enclosures—could be obtained, expensively, at certain radio supply houses. An infatuation with high fidelity components began infiltrating the ranks of discerning record collectors in 1947 and 1948. LP records, with their heightened musical attractiveness and acoustical potentialities, turned the quest for high fidelity into something of a national mania. New and supposedly better amplifiers, turntables, pickups, loudspeakers, and enclosures were eagerly purchased by the latest high fidelity recruit, who thereafter cast scornful aspersions on his neighbor's outdated equipment (all of a year old). Beginning in 1949, strange annual sonic saturnalias called Audio Fairs were held in several large American cities, whither thousands of high fidelity addicts came to bask in the shattering cacophony produced by a hundred exhibitors demonstrating their wares in unnatural proximity. Much of this was ludicrous, and many were the excesses perpetrated in the name of high fidelity. Gadgeteers of dubious musical sensibility delighted in employing their expensive equipment to cleave the ear with piercing piccolos and growling double basses such as never were heard in a concert hall. Bizarre recordings of thunderstorms and screaming railroad trains were concocted for those to whom high fidelity reproduction was an end in itself and not a means to musical satisfaction. Fortunately, the fanatics were in a tiny, though vociferous, minority. The wide and lasting appeal of high fidelity reproduction went to non-gadgeteers who merely wished the music they heard at home to approximate as closely as possible the sound of live music in the concert hall or opera house.

High fidelity reproduction depended for its success on high fidelity records, and high fidelity records in turn depended on the existence of tape recording. Magnetic tape, instead of displacing the flat disc, had become its precious helpmeet.* Tape's invasion of the recording studio, begun early in 1949, proceeded so implacably that within a year the old method

---

* Later (see Chapter 24) tape was to become a widely accepted alternative source of recorded music, but only after successful methods of packaging it in cartridges and cassettes had been devised.

of direct recording on wax or acetate blanks was almost completely superseded. Improvements in tape equipment and in tape itself had expanded the potential frequency response of recording to a range of 20–20,000 cycles—exceeding anything previously possible. In addition, tape was flexible (figuratively as well as literally) to a degree that discs could never equal. It could be recorded on continuously for thirty minutes or more, thus letting performers maintain the impetus and vitality of their interpretations without frequent interruptions, and it could be played back for immediate audition with no detriment to the recording. Even more important, it lent itself to "editing"—since various segments of tape could be spliced together in perfect continuity—and hence permitted the best parts of three or four different "takes" to be amalgamated into one composite recording. Tape was also amenable to other tricks: if someone happened to cough at a recording session during a moment of silence, the offending noise could be erased; if the over-all sound quality seemed too dead, an "echo chamber" could be employed to give it additional resonance. Eventually, of course, the recording on tape had to be transferred to a microgroove master disc, but at that stage it would already have been meticulously edited and approved by the performer. One of the earliest converts to tape recording was Arturo Toscanini, a musician of impatient temperament who had never accustomed himself to the tense start-and-stop atmosphere of direct disc recording. The flexibility of tape made him a changed man at recording sessions; to it we owe, among many others, his treasurable recorded interpretations of the Beethoven Ninth Symphony and *Missa Solemnis.*

An economic attribute of tape recording transcended all others in its effect on phonographic history. Compared to the old method, tape was enticingly cheap. For an investment of a few thousand dollars one could buy a first-class tape recorder, take it to Europe (where musicians were plentiful and low-salaried), and record great amounts of music; one could then bring the tapes back to America and have the "custom record department" of either Columbia or RCA transfer them—at a reasonable fee—to microgroove records. One not only could, one did. Between August 1949 and August 1954 the number of companies in America publishing LP recordings increased from eleven to almost two hundred. Although the majority of these never progressed beyond the stage of issuing records at a fitful and unprofessional tempo, there were among the newcomers a number of vigorous and imaginative enterprises that secured a firm toehold in the record business and promptly began to give it an entirely new complexion.

One of them, perhaps the most successful, was the Westminster Recording Company, formed in 1949 by three phonograph enthusiasts with a capital of $23,000, which in five years had built up a catalogue of five hundred LP records and was nearing the $2,000,000 mark in annual sales, primarily of classical music.* At the start, Westminster and its rival contemporaries faced a delimiting reality: the large, well-established companies had cornered the supply of famous performers and mined the lode of standard repertoire with pre-emptive thoroughness. Because of this, the post-1949 debutants concentrated their efforts on nonstandard literature performed by nonfamous musicians. In so doing they were extraordinarily successful, artistically and commercially. During 1950, the first year of substantial LP sales, America's small independent companies set a pattern by adding to the repertoire such esoteric works as Arnold Schoenberg's *Serenade*, Mozart's *Coronation* Mass and *Idomeneo*, Haydn's *Creation* and *Nelson* Mass, Kodály's *Te Deum*, Richard Strauss's *Aus Italien*, and Bach's *St. John Passion*—none of them ever committed in their entirety to records before.

---

* Alas, it later went bankrupt, a victim of overexpansion and a changing market for classical music.

Musical taste veered to the prevailing currents of the LP flood; the growing vogue for Vivaldi and other Italian instrumental composers of the seventeenth and eighteenth centuries, for instance, was directly attributable to the missionary work of records. Not all of this rediscovered music was imaginatively, or even adequately, performed. The very ease and cheapness of tape recording had brought a certain lowering of standards. Sometimes performances were superficially prepared and hastily recorded. But such malefactions could not detract appreciably from the unparalleled musical riches being lavished on the mid-twentieth-century listener. Jacques Barzun expressed it with an apt regard for historical perspective when he observed, in *God's Country and Mine:*

> This mechanical civilization of ours has performed a miracle for which I cannot be too grateful: it has, by mechanical means, brought back to life the whole repertory of Western music—not to speak of acquainting us with the musics of the East. Formerly, a fashion would bury the whole musical past except a few dozen works arbitrarily selected. . . . [Today] neglected or lesser composers come into their own and keep their place. In short the whole literature of one of the arts has sprung into being—it is like the Renaissance rediscovering the ancient classics and holding them fast by means of the printing press. It marks an epoch in Western intellectual history.

23 *1955: ANNUS MIRABILIS*

THOUGH NEITHER AUTHOR NOR PUBLISHER COULD KNOW IT at the time, the first edition of this book appeared at a turning point in phonographic history. The year 1955 was to see the emergence of new directions in music and new methods of marketing that would transform the record business beyond all recognition.

The industry seemed healthy enough when the preceding chapters were being readied for publication in the autumn of 1954. The microgroove LP disc had been securely established, new and adventurous companies were rapidly expanding the classical repertoire on records, and converts to high fidelity were multiplying. But appearances were a bit deceiving. Total U.S. record sales in 1954 amounted to only $213 million—less than in the boom years of 1946–47. Despite the new technology and the growing catalogue, records were failing to keep pace with the ballooning postwar economy. Goddard Lieberson, then executive vice president of Columbia Records, confided his misgivings one day in the company's old offices at 799 Seventh Avenue. "It's still a tiny business," he complained, with the worried frown of someone who understands a problem but hasn't yet found a solution. "It's like the book trade—low volume and inefficient distribution." That indictment would not remain valid for long. Records, like books, were soon to find a mass audience.

The seeds of this transformation were to germinate in

1955. Some were deliberately planted. Others seemed to sprout spontaneously from the cultural soil of the mid-1950s. Elvis Presley, for example. A few years earlier, he might well have remained a minor figure in the confined world of country music, a performer of some limited celebrity, shuttling between Memphis and Shreveport, Nashville and Texarkana, doing an occasional local radio show, recording for obscure labels. By 1955, when RCA put Presley under contract, the time had come for teenagers all over America—and soon all over the world—to adopt his kind of music and respond to his kind of charismatic vitality. The consequences for the record business were unforeseen and overwhelming.

Archeologists of pop music point to 1954 as the natal year of rock and roll and to Bill Haley and his band, The Comets, as the new music's first certified exemplars. Haley, a pudgy vocalist-guitarist in his late twenties, had been influenced by rhythm and blues and country and western—categories previously known in the argot of the record trade as "race" and "hillbilly." Both kinds of music had been around for decades, but neither had penetrated beyond the South and the black ghettos of New York, Chicago, and Detroit. Haley and his Comets combined the two styles and desegregated them. The amalgam was called rock and roll. Two of their records, released by Decca in 1954, were seminal: "Shake, Rattle, and Roll" and "Rock Around the Clock." They launched what we now know as the rock revolution.

From the start it had extramusical reverberations. "Rock Around the Clock" was the theme song for *Blackboard Jungle,* a film that dealt disturbingly with racial conflict and the clash of generations inside a decaying urban high school. In his useful *A Social History of Rock Music,* Loyd Grossman writes:

> *Blackboard Jungle* refined, distilled, and stylized the teenager as a j.d. (juvenile delinquent)—tough-talking, violent, black-leather-jacketed, white-tee-shirted, greasy-haired, cruel

yet sensitive, misunderstood. In a key scene, a sympathetic, but quite pathetic, young teacher tries to win his students' friendship by bringing his collection of rare 78-rpm jazz records into class. Within minutes the records are lying on the floor, shattered, broken to bits by the students. "Sorry, teach," one of them mumbles. These hooligans don't want to know about 78s, daddy-o, they've got rock and roll.

Haley was innovative but not magnetic. Rock and roll needed a superstar, and in the gyrating, long-sideburned person of Elvis Presley it found its messiah. Presley made his first records at the age of nineteen for a small Memphis label called Sun Records. Like Haley's, they combined the sounds of white country with black blues; unlike Haley's, they also conveyed machismo and sex appeal. These early discs had an immediate impact on the local Memphis market. *Billboard,* the record industry's weekly trade paper, characterized Presley as "a sock new singer," and executives in New York began to keep an eye on his ascendant career. Soon Presley was making appearances throughout the South and inspiring near-hysteria from throngs of female teenagers. The kid smelled of success, and in 1955 RCA bought his contract from Sun Records for $35,000. It was one of the best investments ever made in the record business. Within a year RCA had sold ten million Presley singles.

Teenage idols were nothing new in the record field. Frank Sinatra, Perry Como, Eddie Fisher, and Frankie Lane had recently come along, each in turn the object of worshipful adolescent affection. They were nice kids who sang songs that everyone could like. Presley was different: an outsider from the wrong side of the tracks, whose throbbing, insolent music seemed almost like a deliberate affront to the adult world. He was a harbinger of teenage revolt, a showbiz hoodlum who seemed to be saying that kids deserved a bigger piece of the action. There was something different about his audience too. Elvis's idolaters had real money in their pockets. The wartime baby boom and postwar prosperity had coincided to produce a generation of ubiquitous and affluent teenagers. This was a new element in the nation's social makeup, and the *New York Times*'s Jack Gould took perceptive note of it in a column written after one of Presley's early television appearances:

> Quite possibly Presley just happened to move in where society has failed the teenager. Greater in their numbers than ever before, they may have found in Presley a rallying point, a nationally prominent figure who seems to be on their side. Family counselors have wisely noted that ours is still a culture in a stage of frantic and tense transition. With even sixteen-year-olds capable of commanding $20 or $30 a week in their spare time, with access to automobiles at an early age, with communications media of all kinds exposing them to new thoughts very early in life, theirs indeed is a high degree of independence.

In retrospect the pop heroes of the late 1950s—Presley, Pat Boone, Paul Anka, Bobby Darin—are seen to have been rather ineffectual disturbers of the status quo, their petty gripes about the adult establishment merely faint omens of what was to come. But however mild the message, teenagers lapped it up. Already a potent economic force, they would in time become the chief sustenance of a billion-dollar record industry.

As the rock revolution gained momentum, another revolution was transforming the airwaves. During the late 1940s and early 1950s network radio began to unravel at the seams. Sponsors shifted their budgets to the mushrooming medium of television, and one by one the big radio shows went off the air. Suddenly the networks' powerful AM outlets were without a ready-made source of programming. They filled the gap with records. Instead of live shows emanating from the studios of New York or Hollywood, listeners were offered the latest pop releases, presented by a jaunty, fast-talking impresario known as a disc jockey. This kind of show was, of course, not unknown to radio. Al Jarvis in Los Angeles and Martin Block in New York had pioneered the "Make-Believe Ballroom" in the late 1930s, using records to simulate the atmosphere of a dance hall and interpolating comments with a panache that made the announcer the star of the show. Now, with the demise of network radio, every station in the country was getting its own disc jockeys and dinning the new records remorselessly into the airwaves. Rock was inherently suited to the radio medium, and its energetic rhythms forged a new style of presentation, as driving in its delivery of news, weather, and sports as was the music itself.

In 1955 the Storz chain of radio stations, based in New Orleans, introduced a formula for record programming that was to sweep the nation. It was called Top 40 radio. Todd Storz had observed that jukebox patrons repeated certain selections over and over again, and he reasoned that his radio audience might respond to the same kind of repetition pattern. They did. Storz's stations consistently beat their competition in the ratings races, and soon his "50,000-watt jukebox of the air" was copied from coast to coast. Essentially, the Top 40 formula consisted of picking forty discs each week and presenting them in a consistent style throughout the broadcast day. In a twenty-four-hour period the big hits of the week might get as many as thirty or even forty air plays. The play lists were based solely on popularity, as reflected in local sales activity and in *Billboard*'s national Top 40 tabulations. By hammering away at the same few hits day in and day out in every major market of the country, Top 40 radio exerted a galvanic effect on record sales.

Other stimuli were revitalizing the market for LP albums. On January 3, 1955, RCA reduced the price of every LP record in its catalogue to $3.98. Overnight the cost of a Red

Seal record was cut by two dollars, that of a pop album by one dollar. This was the most dramatic realignment of record prices since Columbia's bold half-pricing of 78s in August 1940, and, as then, a good many customers were found for the suddenly devalued merchandise. Columbia, Capitol, and Decca had no choice but to follow RCA's lead without delay. Small companies like Westminster, however, held firm. Their economic existence was predicated on a generous per-unit profit on small total sales. Demand for Bach cantatas was limited; at a retail price of $5.95 you could afford to put out an edition of, say, two thousand copies and end up with a small profit; at $3.98 you couldn't. And so there developed a strange imbalance: a Beethoven symphony conducted by Toscanini carried a list price of $3.98, whereas a Mozart trio played by uncelebrated Central European instrumentalists was quoted at $5.95. The disparity didn't make any sense, and it was not destined to endure.

The price cuts of January 1955 represented a last major effort to expand the record business through the traditional channels of regional distributors and local dealers, a retailing network which for half a century had been the mainstay of the industry. By the early 1950s this network was faltering. The neighborhood record store was dying, a victim of un-aggressive merchandising and inadequate stocks. Much of the business was being siphoned off by a few cut-price retailers—most notably Sam Goody in New York City—who offered huge inventories and whopping discounts in barnlike emporiums lacking frills or service. For the committed record collector who knew what he wanted, Sam Goody was just the place to get the most for a dollar. But the discount houses in New York, Chicago, and Los Angeles did not reach the grass roots, did not appeal to millions of potential new record listeners on whom the industry was pinning its future expansion. Behind RCA's price cut lay the hope that discounters would be neutralized and neighborhood record stores restored to their former importance. The low prices were widely advertised, and as an additional lure RCA devised a series of sampler records which sold for 98 cents and contained excerpts from current pop and classical albums. Never had there been a more massive effort to entice old and new customers into the record dealer's door.

But by then there were other—and, for many, more convenient—ways of purchasing records. Mail-order record clubs had already secured a firm beachhead in the business. Back in 1950, Concert Hall Records, one of the early independents, had formed the Musical Masterpiece Society to purvey its wares on a regular mail-order basis. It was followed by a club known as Music Treasures of the World, and before long by the prestigious Book-of-the-Month Club, which had sponsored a subsidiary operation called Music-Appreciation Records. BOMC's ploy was to sell education along with entertainment, its advertisements being directed to those "who enjoy good music but who are aware, too often, that they do not listen to it with complete understanding and appreciation." A Music-Appreciation Record (they cost $3.60, "to subscribers only") devoted one side to a performance of a standard piece and the other side to its musical analysis. Among them, the three enterprises were striking pay dirt. By 1955 they were accounting for about thirty-five per cent of the total dollar volume of all classical LP records sold in the United States.

Not a penny of this money was going either to the regular dealers or to the major companies. The clubs made their own recordings (usually in Europe), developed their own customers, and pocketed the proceeds. This was bad enough, but the prospects for the future seemed even more alarming. Music-Appreciation Records no longer wanted to content itself with second-string orchestras, conductors, and soloists. The club was spending an enormous sum to advertise a recording of the Brahms Violin Concerto by Endre Wolf and the London Symphony under Walter Goehr. The returns were good, but they would be that much better, the club surmised, if the recording were by Isaac Stern and the Philadelphia Orchestra under Eugene Ormandy. In due course, Book-of-the-Month started negotiating with a few of Columbia's and RCA's most celebrated artists, and because of the club's prestige and resources it was able to make some tempting proposals. The New York Philharmonic, for example, was reportedly considering an offer that would guarantee minimum royalties of $500,000 a year. Taking a hard look at this situation, the major record companies could foresee a future in which they would have to share not only the distribution but also the production of records with interlopers from outside the industry. Indeed, it was not too difficult to conceive of a time when the whole record business in America might be controlled by the book clubs. There was only one way to forestall such an eventuality: the major record companies would have to get into the club business too.

Columbia was first. In August 1955 the company announced the formation of the Columbia Record Club. As was to be expected, its dealers cried foul. They complained of being cast off, swept into the dustbin, deserted in an hour of need, and many of them vowed to boycott Columbia forevermore. But the company stuck to its guns and began to recruit members. Free merchandise constituted the bait with which these mail-order customers were snared. Columbia splashed a covey of album jackets across the top of its ads and offered to mail any four of them to a new member without charge. One's only obligation was to purchase four additional records from the club during the next twelve months. Unlike its predecessor clubs, Columbia's offered popular music as well as classical. It also offered recordings by performers of widespread celebrity: André Kostelanetz and Louis Armstrong, Mary Martin and Alexander Brailowsky, the New York Philharmonic and the Philadelphia orchestras.

It proved to be the right idea with the right ingredients at the right time. The club caught on beyond Columbia's most optimistic projections. Within twelve months 409,000 members were on the books.

RCA waited for two years to follow suit, in the forlorn hope that the traditional independent retailer could still be weaned back to prosperity. But despite lower prices, sampler records, cooperative advertising, and a variety of other incentives, the local record shops continued to lose ground. Eventually RCA gave up the struggle, joined forces with Book-of-the-Month, and launched the RCA Victor Record Club in January 1958. New members were offered the nine Beethoven symphonies performed by Toscanini and the NBC Symphony, a seven-record set originally priced at $50. It was now to be had for $3.98, provided you agreed to purchase six additional records from the club during the course of a year. In three months some 340,000 members had signed up.

As if discounters and record clubs were not enough of a problem for the neighborhood "mom and pop" outlet, yet another competitor had begun to muscle in on the record trade. This was the rack jobber, so-called because of the 4½-foot metal racks on which he displayed budget-priced albums in supermarkets, drug stores, and what were still euphemistically termed five-and-tens. Initially the rack jobbers had to make do with fairly sleazy merchandise. Since these interlopers were clearly encroaching on the industry's franchised outlets, the major record manufacturers refused to deal with them. But as rack sales grew in volume, there loomed again the specter of appreciable profits accruing to outsiders, and before long the majors as well were offering their wares to the racks. Along with the groceries, you could now pick up the latest Sinatra. This further demoralized what was left of the small record dealers, but by then the rack jobbers were much too powerful to ignore. In time they would account for more than half of total U.S. record sales.

Rock and roll, teenage affluence, Top 40 radio, mail-order clubs, discount shops, rack jobbers—all combined to lift the record business out of its postwar doldrums. In 1955, when these various influences began to take effect, sales of records in the United States increased by thirty per cent to $277 million. A year later they reached $377 million, and in 1957, $460 million. Almost overnight, records had turned into a growth industry.

24 THE SOUND OF STEREO

RECORDS WERE NOT ONLY SELLING BETTER, THEY WERE SOUND-ing better. No longer were engineers content merely to string up microphones above the orchestra and eavesdrop on a performance. More and more, records were being "produced"—were being planned, that is, in terms of electronic potentialities and conceived as entities in themselves rather than as mere duplications of concert-hall performance. Nothing exemplified the new approach more strikingly than the recording of Tchaikovsky's *1812 Overture* put out by Mercury Records in March 1956.

The recording endeavored to re-create the performance conditions which Tchaikovsky had originally envisaged for this patriotic war-horse—a performance out-of-doors, with a military band abetting the orchestra, and with Kremlin bells and a salvo of cannon resounding in the finale. Mercury's producers began by recording the strictly musical parts of the score in Minneapolis's Northrup Auditorium, using the Minneapolis Symphony Orchestra and the University of Minnesota Brass Band under the direction of Antal Dorati. Then they moved their recording truck to New Haven to put the bells of Harkness Memorial Tower on tape. Finally, they moved on to West Point and prevailed on the authorities to fire off a 1761 brass cannon for the benefit of their microphones. Back in the New York studio, the engineers superimposed these various tapings onto a final master tape, employing whatever electronic trickery seemed in order (for example, overlaying the bell clamor with a double-speed re-recording of itself, to create the cascade of tintinnabulation that a Muscovite would have heard when his city's thousand bell towers rang out simultaneously). No dynamic compression was employed in transferring the tape to disc, and not every needle could track the final measures without sometimes popping out of the groove. But on good equipment the record made a tremendous, soul-satisfying noise. It quickly went to the top of the classical best-seller list and stayed there for years.

Just as sales of the *1812 Overture* were gaining momentum, a new method of recording began to make its presence felt. It went under the name of stereophonic sound, and it really wasn't all that new. The notion of "two-eared listening" had been around for many years. Bell Laboratories had put on effective binaural sound demonstrations at the Chicago World's Fair of 1933, and in 1940 the Disney-Stokowski film *Fantasia* had shown what could be accomplished with multi-source music reproduction in a movie theatre. Only with the advent of high-quality magnetic tape, however, was stereophonic sound able to enter the home. Essentially, stereo aimed at reproducing the spaciousness, clarity, and realism of two-eared listening. Of course, everyone with normal hearing had been listening to standard monophonic recordings with both ears, but the loudspeaker itself conveyed only a one-eared image. Even if it reproduced the sound of a symphony orchestra picked up from a dozen scattered microphones, one heard in the end only a single-source reproduction of that orchestra. All the sound was eventually funneled into a solitary channel. Hearing with one ear was like seeing with one eye: clear and detailed, but flat; sharply contoured, but without depth.

Stereo could help to liberate sound from these one-eared limitations. In its simplest form, a stereo recording derived from two microphones placed several feet apart in the studio.

The sounds from each microphone went separately and simultaneously onto two independent channels—that is, onto adjacent tracks of a magnetic tape. During playback these two channels would be routed through two independent amplifiers and loudspeakers, the latter also placed several feet apart. And because the sonic image emitted by each speaker differed in slight but vital degree, an effect was re-created akin to the minutely divergent "points of view" of our own two ears.

"The most exciting development yet in music listening," proclaimed an advertisement by Ampex, the country's leading manufacturer of tape equipment, in the fall of 1955—yet another first for that innovative year. But the excitements of stereo promised by Ampex were still of a very special and restricted nature. Only a handful of stereo tape recordings had yet been released, and these were the products of small companies whose engineering expertise and musical resources left much to be desired. A year later the stereo scene had brightened. For some time RCA had been making experimental stereo tapings of all its important orchestra sessions, and by mid-1956 the company was ready to test the market with a few of its more successful efforts. For the Christmas trade that year RCA could offer a small but imposing catalogue of stereo tapes featuring the Boston Symphony under Munch and Monteux, the Chicago Symphony under Reiner, and such prestigious soloists as Gilels, Heifetz, Oistrakh, and Rubinstein. RCA was offering, too, the Victrola Stereo Tape Player, which packaged tape deck, stereo amplifier, and speakers in a pair of table-top units selling for $350.

No one hearing the early stereo tape recordings could fail to be impressed by their sense of spaciousness, by the buoyant airiness and "lift" of the sound as it swirled freely around the listening room. Stereo seemed to dissolve the walls; and better than even the finest monophonic recordings, it could clarify a complex musical construction, enabling the listener to sort out simultaneous strands (particularly in a large-scale work for chorus and orchestra) that had previously been forced into a muddy sonic impasto. One began listening to sound in a new way, savoring its breadth and depth as well as its melodic outlines and harmonic textures.

Stereo gave a boost to the lagging fortunes of recorded tape. The introduction of long-playing discs in 1948 had pretty well disposed of tape's *raison d'être* as an alternative source of recorded sound in the home. Now tape had a new lease on life. A small but growing market for stereo tapes began to develop, and soon other major record companies joined RCA in making a portion of their current releases available in stereo tape as well as mono disc form. But at the prevailing price structure no dramatic expansion of the stereo business could be expected. RCA's stereo tape of the *Symphonie Fantastique,* a particularly effective display piece for the two-channel medium, sold for $18.95 (as opposed to $3.98 for the same Boston Symphony recording on a monophonic LP disc), and to play it one had to make an investment in costly stereo tape equipment. At these prices, stereo tape was strictly for the carriage trade. Stereo would find a mass market only when its cost had been brought down, and that awaited the perfection of a stereo disc. Meanwhile, the record industry was not disposed to rock the boat. Business was booming; the stereo disc could wait.

But it didn't. Circumstances and the workings of a free economy imposed the stereo disc on an unwilling record industry long before its anticipated debut.

The challenge of impressing two well-separated channels in a single record groove—at the same time maintaining the playing time and high-fidelity characteristics of a monophonic LP disc—posed engineering problems of substantial proportions. Researchers on both sides of the Atlantic were grappling with them. But though one heard occasional rumors about work in progress, nothing seemed to materialize;

when questioned, record executives indicated that a stereo disc could not be expected for years. In the summer of 1957, however, an RCA engineer unwittingly let it be known that the Westrex Company (part of AT&T) had devised a successful method of putting two stereo channels into a single groove. His revelation was immediately denied, but a cat had been let out of the bag, and rumors began to fly thick and fast. To set the record straight, Westrex decided to demonstrate its new stereo disc at the Audio Engineering Society's annual New York convention in October. At the same time, engineers from the Decca Record Company in London flew over to demonstrate another stereo disc. And a few weeks later, Columbia chimed in with a third. But nobody wanted a repetition of the War of the Speeds, and in due course technical representatives from the major American and European companies met in solemn conclave and agreed on the Westrex system as the preferred choice. There was agreement too that the raw Westrex prototype needed considerable refinement before anyone could think of putting stereo records on the market.

Now enters Audio Fidelity, Inc., a smallish company that specialized in producing wide-range records for the so-called "hifinatic" market. Shortly after the initial Westrex demonstration, Audio Fidelity dispatched some stereo tapes to Westrex and requested the company to cut a stereo master disc from them—merely, they explained, for experimental purposes. At the time there was no phonograph cartridge on the market capable of playing a stereo disc. But this did not deter Audio Fidelity from duplicating the Westrex stereo master and putting copies of the "unplayable" record on sale. Within weeks of its appearance, Fairchild Recording Equipment Company had started manufacturing a stereo cartridge with which to play it. And suddenly the fat was in the fire. Other small record companies got into the stereo act, other cartridge manufacturers went into production, and the leaders of the industry, rubbing their eyes at the unexpected *fait accompli,* abandoned their well-laid plans for a controlled changeover to stereo and quickly slipped into high gear themselves. By September 1958 every record company of any importance in the United States was offering stereo discs for sale.

Most were of rather indifferent quality. The industry had been pushed into stereo production too quickly. Neither disc-cutting techniques nor cartridge design were up to former monophonic standards, and the hapless customer in 1958 had to accustom himself to instruments that would wander from one speaker to the other across a yawning chasm in the middle, as well as to accept a degree of fuzzy distortion that would have seemed intolerable in a mono LP. It is no wonder that enthusiasm was moderate. In December 1958 stereo discs accounted for a mere six per cent of total sales in dollars. The ordinary record buyer had adopted a wait-and-see attitude. Something irresistibly attractive would have to come along before he converted.

For the classical customer, the persuasive "something" turned out to be a recording of *Das Rheingold,* the first opera in Wagner's *Ring* tetralogy, and a work never before committed to discs. It came from the Decca Record Company Ltd. (London Records in the U.S.A.) and boasted an all-star cast, including the legendary Kirsten Flagstad in the last important recording of her career. But it was the sound, even more than the singing, that made people sit up and take notice. *Rheingold*'s producer, John Culshaw, fully grasped the potentialities of stereo. His aim, as he put it, "was that of re-creating in the studio an environment as close as possible to the theatre, with singers acting their parts in a production almost as elaborate as the real thing." Within Vienna's Sofiensaal, Culshaw set up a huge stage, marked off into numbered squares that served as guidelines for the deployment of his forces. Long before the sessions began, his whole production had been plotted out, in strict accordance with the composer's stage directions. When Wagner wanted a character to move, he moved; and at home the listener could hear his progress across the imaginary sonic stage created by stereo.

On occasion the stereo medium could even attempt to improve on the original. "Thus," Culshaw noted, "in Scene Three, Alberich puts on the Tarnhelm, disappears, and then thrashes the unfortunate Mime. Most stage productions make Alberich sing through a megaphone at this point, the effect of which is often less dominating than that of Alberich in reality. Instead of this, we have tried to convey, for thirty-two bars, the terrifying, inescapable presence of Alberich: left, right, or center there is no escape for Mime." For the Nibelheim scene, eighteen anvils of the type and size specified by Wagner were obtained, and for the Rainbow Bridge section the composer's full complement of seven harps was on hand. Conductor Georg Solti led all these forces with taut incisiveness; Culshaw employed his "effects" with knowledge and taste; and the engineers succeeded in getting everything into easily tracked stereo grooves. The result was overpowering. When *Das Rheingold* appeared in August 1959, record reviewers went agog over its magical moments: the passage of Wotan and Loge through the anvil-hammering Nibelungs' caverns, the piling of the hoard, the heaven-splitting thunder and lightning that dissolve the mists around Valhalla, and at the very end the Rhinemaidens' seductive song off in the distant depths while the gods cross triumphantly over the Rainbow Bridge downstage. Hearing all this, even an imperfect Wagnerite could not help but succumb to stereo.

While *Rheingold* was doing its work in the classical market, a record aptly titled *Persuasive Percussion* was engaged in the same kind of proselytizing on a much larger scale in the popular field. The advertisements ("greatest advance in sound since hi-fi was invented") had a familiar ring, but everything else about the disc was new: the label (Command), the jacket (an abstract design of dots), and the stereo engineering.

Its producer, a veteran bandleader named Enoch Light, believed that the ordinary listener would take to stereo only if it were made to sound entirely different from anything he had encountered before. Thus, instead of the broad "curtain of sound" which had been the early stereo ideal, Light favored two distinctly separate sound sources, and for them devised some delightful arrangements in which the musical line shuttled back and forth from one speaker to the other, like the ball in a ping-pong game. The record was wildly successful. For more than two years, *Persuasive Percussion* and its sequel *Provocative Percussion* dominated the stereo album business. Naturally, other companies followed Command's lead, and in due course the market became glutted with every conceivable kind of stereo gimmickry. By the time the public had had its fill, however, stereo was established as the preferred choice for home listening.

In changing over to twin-channel sound, the record buyer was also changing over to new and greatly improved listening gear. Few people bothered to make the requisite conversions of their old mono sets; it was easier and sightlier to start from scratch. For stereo's acceptance in the home had been facilitated by a progressive miniaturization of high-fidelity apparatus. Small "bookshelf" speakers were now capable of reproducing the full gamut of sound, from the lowest organ-pedal throb to upper frequencies beyond audibility; compact automatic turntables were combining the convenience of the old changer mechanisms with the performance capabilities of studio transcription equipment; miniature tubes and, later, transistors were enabling manufacturers to offer superior electronics in minimal space. High-fidelity componentry was also reaching out for a mass market; and as it proliferated, listeners grew increasingly impatient with the ill-defined, tubby sound that had been characteristic of "console" phonographs.

The stereo disc dealt a staggering blow to the nascent market for recorded tape. Sales of open-reel tape plummeted from $2.4 million in 1957 to $100,000 in 1958. Business began to improve slightly a year later, when Ampex introduced the four-track configuration, which doubled playing time by squeezing two pairs of stereo tracks onto standard quarter-inch tape. In an effort to make open-reel tape more palatable, Ampex also introduced such refinements as automatic threading and automatic reversal in their new equipment. Even without these aids, operating a tape machine was hardly a Herculean labor. It certainly didn't faze the aficionado who wanted to record Renata Tebaldi off the air from the stage of the Metropolitan. But for the casual listener who merely wanted to press a button and hear some music, open-reel tape continued to seem like a lot of bother. Despite stalwart efforts to promote four-track tape as a superior medium of recorded sound, the market for it remained insignificant. To reach a wide public, tape needed to be fool-proofed.

Much trial and error preceded the achievement of that goal. RCA tried first in 1958 with a tape cartridge designed to work in an automatic changer mechanism. It employed a plastic cartridge about the size of a paperback book which contained four-track quarter-inch tape wound between two hubs. During playback the tape ran at a speed of 3¾ inches per second (ips), traveling from one hub to the other past a window in the cartridge. Playing time was equivalent to that of an LP record. Unfortunately, the changers jammed at the least provocation, and the device never really got off the ground. Another automatic cartridge system came from the 3M Company (formerly Minnesota Mining) and its Revere-Wollensak subsidiary. This one employed a single-reel cartridge about three inches square. The changer mechanism fished the tape from its cartridge, wound it onto a take-up reel within the changer, then rewound the tape back into the cartridge. Columbia Records provided the repertoire for the tape, which ran at 1⅞ ips. The sound was execrable and the mechanism much too complicated. This system, too, soon vanished from the scene.

While memories of these disasters were still fresh, the giant Philips company in Holland unveiled a minicartridge for use in portable recorders. They called it the cassette. Philips's cassette recorder was first shown at the 1963 Berlin Radio Show and arrived in the United States a year later as the Norelco Carry-Corder. The tiny plastic cassette looked like a greatly miniaturized version of RCA's ill-fated cartridge. It employed eighth-inch tape at a speed of 1⅞ ips and had a playing time of up to ninety minutes. Moreover, it worked. Admittedly, the quality of sound left much to be desired; tape hiss and a restricted frequency range combined to make the early cassettes non-competitive with discs. But where portability counted for more than fidelity, the cassette was without rival from the very beginning. Later on, its fidelity was appreciably improved. In 1970, quality cassette players were introduced that employed a sophisticated piece of electronics known as the Dolby Noise Reduction System. The difference in performance was astonishing. "Dolbyized" equipment made the cassette competitive with discs or even open-reel recorders.

Meanwhile, tape had made a major incursion under the dashboards of American automobiles. Back in the 1950s, a Cleveland inventor named George Eash had devised a single-reel cartridge player employing the principle of the endless loop. Lubricated tape unwound from the center of a tape pack, fed past a window in the cartridge, and then rewound onto the outside of the same pack. It was called the Fidelipac and ran for a maximum of thirty minutes at 3¾ ips. Radio stations adopted the endless-loop cartridge for playing spot commercials, but nothing much else was done with Eash's invention until a promoter named Earl Muntz recognized its automotive potential. In the early 1960s he modified the device for four-track stereo and began a brisk business selling cartridge players for installation under the dashboards of cars. Next, a manufacturer of private airplanes, William Lear, modified it still further by doubling the number of tracks to eight and developing a playback unit for cars that automatically switched from one pair of stereo tracks to the next. Because of the additional tracks, Lear's Stereo 8 cartridge had a total playing time of more than an hour (with slight interruptions in continuity while the player switched tracks).

Ford Motors offered Stereo 8 equipment as an optional built-in accessory in its 1966 models, and RCA provided the recorded repertoire. Soon other automakers and other record companies adopted the Stereo 8 cartridge, and sales began to skyrocket. Its success is hard to explain. The Stereo 8 cartridge works solely for playback (unlike the cassette, which can be used for recording as well). Since it turns in only one direction, a selection can't be repeated without having to run through the entire tape. And though a Stereo 8 cartridge takes up less space than an LP disc, it lacks the ultimate compactness of the cassette. Well, there is sometimes no accounting for taste. Stereo 8 was a hit from the start, first in cars, later in the home, and it finally established tape as a major competitor of the disc. In 1975, sales of Stereo 8 cartridges in the United States amounted to $583 million, or twenty-five per cent of all recorded music sales. It should be noted, however, that this has been a strictly American phenomenon. Elsewhere in the world, the Stereo 8 cartridge has run a poor second to the cassette.

The wide-scale acceptance of tape cartridges opened the door to wide-scale tape piracy. Illicit duplication of recordings had always been a minor annoyance. When Congress drafted a copyright act back in 1909, it neglected to cover phonograph records in the legislation, and records were thus fair game for bootleg operators. For years nothing much was done to stop them. Record companies hesitated to take pirates to court, fearing the precedent of a possible adverse decision. Until the late 1960s, the problem seemed relatively unimportant. Pirating discs wasn't easy: it involved the use of costly and cumbersome pressing equipment, and that effectively discouraged most potential bootleggers. Tape was something else altogether. Tape duplicators were both inexpensive and portable, and it became a simple matter to copy and sell Stereo 8 cartridges on the black market. Pirated cartridges began to proliferate, and by the early 1970s both record companies and their artists were being fearsomely bilked. In 1972 a Federal law extended copyright protection to recordings, and since then tape piracy has been on the decline. Even so, enforcement is difficult, and the Recording Industry Association of America (RIAA)—which successfully lobbied for the copyright legislation—estimates that one in every five tapes sold is still illegal merchandise.

At one point the RIAA estimated that some $250 million a year was being spent on pirated tapes. That was more than the total record business in 1954. Even if the RIAA's figure was somewhat exaggerated, it served to indicate how the overall market for recorded music had grown in the intervening years. To follow its fortunes during this astonishing period, we must now return to the time when RCA began to reap the fruits of its contract with rock's first great superstar.

25 *EN ROUTE TO A MASS MARKET*

Elvis presley's first record for rca, "heartbreak Hotel," appeared in February 1956 and found a million buyers within three months. For years thereafter practically every disc bearing Presley's name succeeded in passing the million mark. His dominion over the early years of rock was absolute. RCA had made a very lucky strike; through all the fads and fetishes of the era, Presley's popularity remained undimmed. Other companies were not so fortunate. Producers combed the boondocks for new rock artists and fresh material, and studios around the country worked overtime, churning out releases as if they were bottle caps—on the "buckshot" theory that one among them might just possibly hit the bull's eye. Occasionally it happened. A singer would emerge into sudden and intense popularity, sell a few million discs, then just as suddenly fall from favor. Finding hit singles had never been easy, but in the late Fifties and early Sixties the process seemed totally unpredictable.

A few small operators played these singles sweepstakes more shrewdly than the majors. The decade from 1954 to 1964 was a golden age for independent labels like Atlantic, Chess, Imperial, King, and Specialty. They pioneered an exciting new sound, compounded of urban blues, bop, and gospel, that went under the catchall rubric of rhythm and blues. The phrase was really a euphemism. It meant the music of black people. Both the music and the market had

324

been all but abandoned by the large companies after World War II, and the vacuum was filled by so-called "r & b" labels. To them went credit for recording and promoting some of the most accomplished and consistent talent around. King Records launched the careers of Otis Redding and Nina Simone; Atlantic discovered Ray Charles and LaVern Baker; Chess had Chuck Berry; Fats Domino was on Imperial; Little Richard on Specialty. Although records by these artists were intended primarily for black people, white teenagers began to ferret them out, and the major labels paid them the ultimate compliment of issuing pallid "covers" (that is, imitation versions) of their material in performances by white artists. Curiously, only one of these rhythm and blues companies maintained its momentum past the early rock era. This was Atlantic, founded in 1947 by Ahmet Ertegun and Herb Abramson, two jazz buffs who had met in Washington while Ahmet was still studying philosophy at Georgetown University. The firm leapt from success to success, and in 1967 it was bought by Warner Brothers for $17 million. With Ertegun still at the helm, it now forms part of WEA (for Warner-Elektra-Atlantic) International, reputedly the largest record company in America.

Given the high stakes and volatile nature of the pop singles market in the 1950s, it is not surprising that record companies went to extraordinary lengths to promote their new releases. The key to best-sellerdom lay in air play. If a new record wasn't heard on Top 40 radio, it had virtually no hope of taking off. But how was it to be singled out for attention? Something like 130 new releases were sent to the nation's major AM stations each week. "If a disc jockey had to listen to all these records," one of them told a *Life* interviewer, "he'd go to the kookie house." To ensure that prominent deejays listened to the right ones, record companies began to pay them consultant fees. The practice was known as payola. To a hardheaded record executive, paying a disc jockey was no different than paying for advertising: the expenditure in both cases resulted in exposure of product. And compared to the kind of international bribery that American corporations were to engage in a decade or so later, the modest emoluments meted out to the deejays seem almost beneath notice. But the 1950s were more innocent days, and when *Time* ran a lurid account of a disc jockey convention under the headline "Booze, Broads, and Payola," the fat was in the fire.

There ensued a thoroughgoing congressional investigation. "The impetus behind these hearings," writes rock historian Carl Belz, "was undeniably related to an assumption that rock was 'bad' music, that it encouraged juvenile delinquency, and that it could only have been forced on the public by illegal activities." In the end, Congress passed a law making payola a crime punishable by a fine of up to $10,000. It succeeded in driving payola underground. It did not make record companies any the less concerned about getting their releases played on the air.

The tempest over payola deflected attention from an important evolution in the record business. Pop singles, on which AM radio subsisted, were losing out to long-playing albums. By 1960, only about twenty per cent of the total dollars spent on records went for singles. To be sure, it was a juicy twenty per cent. The profit margins in 45 rpms were mouth watering. A release that might cost as little as two or three thousand dollars to record and promote could earn back a hundred thousand or more in profits. But with 7,000 new singles released each year, the odds against hitting the best-seller list were formidable. Playing the pop singles sweepstakes was not much different from playing roulette (in fact, a successful independent label of the period was called Roulette), and companies with large overheads concluded that they needed to build on steadier foundations than the quixotic favorites of Top 40 radio. In the growing market for albums they found a dependable base of operations.

Original-cast recordings of Broadway shows became for a while the crown jewels of the album trade. Decca's *Oklahoma!* (1943) and Columbia's *South Pacific* (1949), splendid sellers both, had already more than hinted at the potential public for this kind of fare, but they were only dress rehearsals for *My Fair Lady*. The Lerner-Loewe musical opened in New York on March 15, 1956. Within a month, Columbia's original-cast recording had reached the shops and was selling like a Presley single. Not everyone could get to the show, but anybody could enjoy it vicariously on the phonograph—and for less money than the price of a ticket. Eventually, sales of the *My Fair Lady* album passed the six million mark. The profits in this case derived from more than record sales. At the shrewd urging of Goddard Lieberson, by then Columbia's president (and also the album's producer), CBS Inc. (parent company of Columbia Records) had put up the entire financing for the show. CBS thus participated in all of *My Fair Lady*'s considerable dividends. Up to 1965, the show had taken in $66 million in boxoffice receipts throughout the world; another $5.5 million was received for the film rights; and the end of the payout is not yet in sight.

None of this was lost on the competition. Record companies bid feverishly for original-cast rights to just about every new musical that came down the pike. But though there were many successful Broadway albums in the years to come, including a few—*West Side Story, Fiddler on the Roof, The Sound of Music, Hair*—that sold in the millions, nothing ever quite matched *My Fair Lady*. And along with the hits went some disastrous flops, shows that died in New Haven or expired in New York after the first reviews. Every large record company in America suffered the ignominy of paying for rights to an original-cast recording that never, in the end, got made.

Closely related to Broadway show albums, and just as lucrative, were the soundtracks of Hollywood musicals. Here the pace was set originally by the film score of *South Pacific,* which appeared on the RCA label in 1958 and eventually sold eight million copies. Columbia did equally well three years later with the soundtrack album of *West Side Story.* But the bonanza of all time was *The Sound of Music,* released by RCA in March 1965. The film broke all boxoffice records, surpassing even *Gone With the Wind,* and its soundtrack album has had the largest sale of any LP in history—fifteen million copies to date.

It could be argued that albums like these were merely riding on the coattails of Broadway and Hollywood. But record companies had their own success stories to tell too. Columbia, for example, initiated a long series of best-sellers in 1958 with a medley called *Sing Along with Mitch*—Mitch being Mitch Miller, a former virtuoso oboist who had forsaken the classics to become a pop producer and TV personality. This first album ran the gamut from "Down by the Old Mill Stream" to "Till We Meet Again" and set the pattern for subsequent sing-alongs of old-time favorites. Some twenty million were sold before the series finally ran out of steam. Collections of lushly scored mood music, with titles and cover art to match the soothing sonorities of the contents, found avid customers no matter how often the formula was repeated. And out in California a new company called A & M Records struck pay dirt with catchy collections of instrumental standards rendered in the quasi-Mexican idiom of Herb Alpert's Tijuana Brass.

None of this fare was of the sort to appeal to rock-and-rollers. Had the rock revolution collapsed? Even Presley seemed to have defected since his tour of duty with the army. (Distraught fans had tried to get him exempted. Beethoven, they pointed out, was never conscripted. "That," the head of Elvis's draft board replied, "was because Beethoven wasn't an American.") On his return to civilian life in 1960, Presley began to merge into the mainstream of popular music. Among his 1961 hits were Presley-ized versions of *"Torna a Sorrento"* and *"Plaisir d'amour"*—perplexing departures from the raunchy, jiving material with which he had first captured the affections of America's teenagers. Despite his tamer persona, Presley's records continued to sell in vast quantities. He has, in fact, had more million-selling titles than any other performer in history.

All this substantiated a growing conviction among record moguls that rock was a passing aberration and that future prosperity lay in cultivating the so-called MOR (middle-of-the-road) repertoire. A noticeable slowdown was evident in the industry's growth pattern since the quantum jumps of the late 1950s. After leaping from $213 million in 1954 to $603 million in 1959, the business levelled off. In 1963, four years later, annual sales were still below $700 million. This seemed to give further evidence that the momentum of rock and roll had been spent. Then the Beatles appeared and all bets were off.

From an apprenticeship in grotty Liverpool nightclubs, the Beatles rocketed overnight to international notoriety, performing—in defiance of all probability—an inventive and insouciant version of American rock and roll. Their phonographic career began in 1961, while the group was playing in an obscure Hamburg night spot called the Top Ten Club. During the course of this engagement, the Beatles were hired as the backing group for pop singer Tony Sheridan on a recording for Polydor called "My Bonnie." Copies found their way back to Liverpool record counters and began to enjoy a modest success there. A local shopkeeper named Brian Epstein took note of it, introduced himself to the group, and became their manager. He tried first to interest the British Decca company in his new clients. Decca wasn't interested. Then he met George Martin, a producer for EMI. "When I listened to the tapes," Martin recalls, "I understood why everyone had turned them down—they were awful. But I asked Epstein to send the boys down for a test. When I met them, I thought they were great. I didn't think their songs were very good. But I offered them a contract."

The Beatles' first disc for EMI's Parlophone label—"Love Me Do" backed with "P.S. I Love You"—was released in October 1962. Soon the British Isles were awash in a flood of Beatlemania. Screaming fans mobbed the group's every appearance and turned each new release into an instantaneous best-seller. By the end of 1963, seven million Beatles singles had been sold in Britain alone. Across the ocean, at the headquarters of Capitol Records in Hollywood, this craze was viewed with some early skepticism. Capitol had been taken over by EMI in 1955 and enjoyed the right of first refusal on any material emanating from the parent company. Astonishingly, Capitol refused the Beatles. The collective wisdom in Hollywood decreed that they were a peculiarly British taste, not suitable for export. As a result, some of the Beatles' earliest singles appeared in the United States under the imprimatur of Swan, Vee Jay, and Tollie—small labels that didn't seem to share Capitol's reservations. It didn't take long for the West Coast colossus to experience a change of heart. Capitol exercised its option in time to release "I Want to Hold Your Hand" on December 30, 1963. Within three weeks it had sold a million copies. Hard on its heels came the Beatles' first LP on Capitol, *Meet the Beatles*. Issued early in 1964 to coincide with the group's arrival in America, the album had sold more than three million copies by the end of March.

The Beatles not only revitalized the dormant rock revolution, they altered its direction. This, even more than the prodigious sales of their records, accounts for the Beatles' enduring impact. They changed the world's ideas about the very nature of pop music. "After the Beatles," Loyd Grossman notes, "the rock performer began to be seen not just as an entertainer but as a social visionary, a cultural trendsetter, a questing, fashionable, archetypal citizen of a new society—Beau Brummell, William Blake, and Thomas Jefferson rolled into one and put on stage with an electric guitar. The Beatles expanded the conception and scope of operations of pop music and made rock and roll the centerpiece of an entire youthful culture."

They also pioneered the "concept album" and showed how recording studio techniques could become an integral and liberating part of the rock experience. This they accomplished in *Sgt. Pepper's Lonely Hearts Club Band,* released simultaneously in Britain and the United States in June 1967. Using sophisticated multi-track recording equipment, electronic sound generators, and some 700 hours of studio time, producer George Martin imposed a gorgeous overlay of noises and "psychedelic" effects onto the Beatles' own music-making. Never before had pop music so creatively exploited the resources of electronics. *Sgt. Pepper* was recognized at once as an esthetic breakthrough: not just a compilation of hit singles, like previous rock albums, but a musical statement to be savored as a totality. The album was the Beatles' biggest seller—seven million copies to date—and it hastened the decline of the 45-rpm single. After *Sgt. Pepper,* the pop record business was essentially an album business. Singles were important only for launching new artists or obtaining air play on AM radio. By 1975 their share of the total record market had dropped below eight per cent.

Sgt. Pepper appeared at a moment when the counterculture was emerging as an inescapable presence in American society. From its beginnings in San Francisco the hippie lifestyle had spread across the country, impinging on city, suburb, and town. Half the U.S. population was now under twenty-five years of age, and wherever you looked there were long-haired, blue-jeaned kids "doing their thing"—which could mean anything from playing guitars and smoking pot to disrupting college campuses and burning draft cards. For the Woodstock generation, rock was not only a favored form of entertainment but a vital conduit of communication, not only a listening experience but a psychic involvement. They consumed it voraciously: the Beatles first and foremost, then other groups from Britain, and finally a succession of new American groups and superstars—The Monkees; Simon and Garfunkel; The Lovin' Spoonful; Janis Joplin; The Mothers of Invention; Blood, Sweat, and Tears. Those false prophets in the record industry who had given rock a premature burial went off into early retirement and in their place came young executives with a keener appreciation of its potential. Mo Ostin, now president of Warner Bros. Records, recalls: "When we saw the numbers that those records could sell in, we said 'Wow, there's something here.' You'd struggle with a middle-of-the-road artist to sell maybe 300,000 albums when you could sell two million Jimi Hendrix albums. Frank Sinatra never sold two million albums. Dean Martin never sold two million albums. I don't think there were too many artists who ever sold two million albums until this wave of 'involving' records." His sentiments were echoed throughout the industry. All sights were now trained on the youth market, and when the returns for 1967 were in, the American record industry discovered it had passed the billion-dollar mark in annual sales.

The classics accounted for only a tiny slice of this billion-dollar pie. Beethoven had not kept pace with the Beatles. To be sure, dollar volume had not suffered—indeed, each year classical sales registered a modest increase—but progress was infinitesimal compared to the dynamic acceleration on the pop side of the ledger. In share of market the classics dropped from around twenty-five per cent of total sales in the 1950s to around five per cent in the 1970s. This still amounted to a lot of records, but in an industry where success was measured in terms of exponential growth, it seemed like pretty small potatoes. Rock had created mass-market expectations which the classics could not sustain.

Only twice during this period did a classical release attain the kind of success that had become routine in the pop category. The first occasion came in 1958, when a young Texan named Van Cliburn unexpectedly won first prize at the Tchaikovsky Piano Competition in Moscow. This victory took place at the height of the Cold War, and Cliburn returned home to find himself a national hero, anointed with an invitation to the White House and a ticker-tape reception in New York. RCA lost no time in recording him as soloist in the Tchaikovsky Piano Concerto — a repeat performance of his Moscow triumph. Rushed into immediate production, the record quickly sold a half million copies and in time passed the coveted million mark. Its fortuitous success encouraged hopes that a mass market for classical music was ready to be tapped. But subsequent recordings by Van Cliburn failed to match the sales of his Tchaikovsky Concerto. The demand for it had been a fluke, the result more of patriotic euphoria than appreciation of a talented young interpreter.

The other classical best-seller came exactly ten years later with a Columbia album entitled *Switched-On Bach*. This was a collection of short Bach pieces rendered electronically on the Moog Synthesizer. A young musician with a background in physics, Walter Carlos, had made the record on his own, purely as a demonstration of how effectively traditional music could be re-created by electronic means. It was a remarkable achievement. Bach's terraced polyphony emerged with stunning clarity, rhythms were razor sharp, and the other-worldly tones generated by the Moog's oscillators and modifiers put such familiar chestnuts as "Air on the G

String" and "Jesu Joy of Man's Desiring" in an intriguing new light. Columbia issued the disc as an offbeat novelty, little suspecting that *Switched-On Bach* was to become the most popular classical album of all time, achieving a sale of 1.2 million copies to date. But it too turned out to be a one-time phenomenon. Though subsequent collections of electronicized classics sold well, none met with anything like the same kind of success.

Far below these solitary peaks the classics continued to thrive, if not always to prosper. The market for classical music was large enough and affluent enough to sustain ambitious recording programs, but it was a market open only to those few firms with a truly global reach. International companies like Columbia and RCA, EMI and Decca-London, Deutsche Grammophon and Philips could offset the escalating costs of classical record production by sales through a worldwide network of branches and subsidiaries. Smaller companies, beset by shrinking profit margins and inadequate distribution facilities, found it increasingly difficult to compete. Some expired altogether, others survived by drastic retrenchments. Much of the initiative for classical production moved to Europe, just as it had in the 1930s. British, German, and Dutch crews even crossed the Atlantic with their own equipment to record the great orchestras of Boston, Chicago, Cleveland, Los Angeles, and Pittsburgh. Only the Philadelphia Orchestra and the New York Philharmonic remained the private preserve of American companies.

This shift in orchestral allegiances was symptomatic of an overall loosening of contractual ties. Fewer musicians now appeared exclusively on one label. These more fluid working arrangements were to benefit producers and artists alike. Singers especially relished the freedom to participate in opera recordings without contractual fetters. A versatile and sought-after artist like the soprano Montserrat Caballé would move from RCA to EMI to Decca-London to Philips according to the repertoire proposed to her. Producers no longer were obliged to work with a limited roster of company artists but instead could assemble casts as close to the ideal as possible. This development led to a proliferation of splendid opera recordings and to an unprecedented expansion of the repertoire. Given a sufficiently glamorous lineup of singers, even a rarity like Rossini's *Siege of Corinth* could sell enough copies to earn a modest profit. Indeed, musical rarities became the rule rather than the exception in classical record releases. Large-scale projects devoted to the complete works of one composer developed a public for music that had lain dormant for decades. Columbia's initiative in recording the nine symphonies of Gustav Mahler under the direction of Leonard Bernstein instigated a Mahler revival throughout the world. There were many such "integral" sets—of Mozart piano concertos, Schubert lieder, Haydn symphonies, the Wagner *Ring* —and to single out a few for attention does an injustice to the others. It lies beyond the province of this book to document in detail the prodigal expansion of the classical repertoire on records over the past quarter century. It is enough to point to the pages of the Schwann catalogue and to reaffirm Jacques Barzun's testimony that the existence of this vast musical universe on records "marks an epoch in Western intellectual history."

The universe was vast but the public was limited. Cliburn and Carlos had reached a mass market with their million-sellers, but these were oddities in a business that normally operated on a penny-ante scale. Demand for standard repertoire was feeble. There had been customers for Beethoven symphonies in the days when music lovers were changing over from 78s to LP, and again when they switched from mono to stereo, but by 1970 the market for this kind of meat-and-potatoes fare had begun to reach the saturation point. With twenty-six different stereo versions of the *Eroica* Symphony already available, there seemed little point in putting out yet another. Something special was needed to re-awaken interest in the standard classics. For a while there was hope that quadraphonic sound would provide the answer. Quadraphony was hailed as the next giant step in the perfection of reproduced sound—"as great an advance over stereo as stereo was over mono." Instead of two channels and two speakers, quad had four. As originally conceived, the two additional channels (issuing from speakers placed behind the listener) were meant to convey "ambient" sound—which is to say, the fractionally delayed impulses reflected from the rear of the recording hall. Later on, certain producers decided that the two rear channels could be more dramatically exploited: instead of merely carrying reflected sound, they would create a new omni-directional sonic experience called "music in the round" or "surround sound." A few recordings were actually made with orchestral musicians forming a circle around the quad microphones. But in neither guise, whether "ambient" or "surround," did quad succeed in revitalizing the classical record business. Few people seemed to want four speakers in their living rooms, and record manufacturers further solidified sales resistance by failing to agree on a standard method for engraving quad sound on a disc.

Despite the setback with quad, the breakup of the Beatles, television, inflation, recessions, devaluations, and other calamities, Edison's invention continued to prosper. According to *Billboard*'s latest count in 1975, there were seventy-three million phonographs in the United States alone, and heaven knows how many in the entire world. Records were sold like toothpaste. It took ninety years for U.S. record sales to reach an annual total of a billion dollars. It took only seven more years to reach the second billion. Some observers doubted whether progress like that could be sustained indefinitely. For twenty years the business had benefited from an unnatural bulge in the nation's demographics: a disproportionate percentage of the population had been of adolescent age.

Now that bulge of under-twenty-fives was beginning to flatten out. America was aging. By the year 2000 a majority of the population would be over thirty, and no one could know what effect this would have on an industry that had tied its fortunes so closely to an expanding society of adolescents.

Yet whatever was to come, the phonograph could approach its centennial with the sense of a mission fulfilled. The crude machine that talked talk had developed into an instrument of infinite resource. A partisan historian could perhaps be forgiven for claiming it as the chief marvel and solace of the century.

INDEX

of names, titles, and companies

NOTE: Musical compositions are to be found under their titles, not under composers.

339